The Magic of Beverly Sills

MUSIC IN AMERICAN LIFE

A list of books in the series appears at the end of this book.

The Magic of
Beverly Sills

NANCY GUY

UNIVERSITY OF ILLINOIS PRESS

Urbana, Chicago, and Springfield

Publication of this book was supported by a grant from the
Henry and Edna Binkele Classical Music Fund.

Library of Congress Cataloging-in-Publication Data
Guy, Nancy, 1960-
The magic of Beverly Sills / Nancy Guy.
    pages cm — (Music in American life)
Includes bibliographical references and index.
ISBN 978-0-252-03973-7 (hardcover : alk. paper)
ISBN 978-0-252-09783-6 (e-book)
1. Sills, Beverly. 2. Sills, Beverly—Performances. 3.
Operas—Performances. 4. Opera audiences. 5. Music fans.
6. Sopranos (Singers)—United States—Biography.
I. Title.
ML420.S562G89   2015
782.1092—dc23 [B]   2015014470

Beverly Sills, the acclaimed Brooklyn-born coloratura soprano who was more popular with the American public than any opera singer since Enrico Caruso, even among people who never set foot in an opera house, died on Monday at her home in Manhattan.

—Anthony Tommasini, *New York Times*, July 4, 2007

Contents

Acknowledgments

The years I spent researching and writing this book have been among the most joyful of my career due in no small part to the shared enthusiasm of many people for my subject, Beverly Sills. Roy C. Dicks has spent more than four decades meticulously documenting Sills's career, including collecting "private" recordings and programs. Throughout my research and writing process, Roy has shared these materials and his thoughts with profound generosity. Charles Freeman Stamper, who owns what surely must be the largest collection of items related to Sills on the planet, has also been enormously generous. Whenever I had trouble locating an obscure news article or performance program, if one of them had it in his possession, he would scan and e-mail me the materials, frequently within minutes of my sending a query. I often had the feeling that Roy and Freeman were just down the hall, and that we were all in this together. They were not alone in providing me with companionship on this journey. Pete Buchanan came into my life shortly after Sills's death. He has been a constant source of love, encouragement, and unbridled enthusiasm. Many other Sills fans, whom I now consider friends, also provided positive energy as they shared their personal experiences. Among those with whom I have had the pleasure of spending a good deal of time (either in person or through social media) are Pirooz Aghssa, Katrine "Cage" Ames, Richard Anderson, Jim Barnett, Thom Billadeau, Bill Bond, Taylor Cornish, Joe Malloy, Brian Morgan, Antonio Martinazzo, A. Robert Nelson, Dan Patterson, David Ponder, Ron Runyon, Kathyrn Ryder, David Tidyman, and David Wylie.

It is not uncommon for ethnomusicologists to study traditions that they themselves do not practice. In focusing on the art of an operatic singer, there were questions of vocal production and performance practice that I simply could not have engaged with were it not for the assistance of masters of this tradition. I was very fortunate to have met the New York–based voice teacher Gerald Martin Moore, who has been incredibly generous in sharing his expertise. Moore took the time on numerous occasions to educate me on matters of vocal health, technique, and style. George Shirley, professor emeritus at the University of Michigan, also opened my eyes to issues related to vocal production and performance, as did my colleague professor emerita Carol Plantamura.

Many of Beverly Sills's former colleagues were enormously generous in sharing their time and thoughts. Susanne Marsee was the first of these artists with whom I met. I was alerted to Ms. Marsee's presence in Pittsburgh when I read her touching memorial to Sills published in the *Pittsburgh Post-Gazette.* When I was invited to give two research talks on Taiwanese music at the University of Pittsburgh, I contacted her, even though I still had not seriously considered writing a book about Sills. Many of the insights Susanne shared during our first meeting in January 2008 profoundly impacted my understanding of Sills the woman and Sills the performing artist. Throughout the years of conducting my research, whenever I hit a roadblock in making a contact, or when I needed assistance in understanding some aspect of the creative process, I would write or call Susanne, who never failed to help. Susanne's kindness and generosity of spirit buoyed me from the start of this process to the end. I am also deeply grateful to Charles Wendelken-Wilson, who was the second of Sills's colleagues to meet with me. He had been my orchestra director when I played French horn in the Ohio All-State Youth Orchestra in the late 1970s. Despite his failing health, we met in Dayton, Ohio, in August 2008, less than a year before his death. His candid recollections of working with Sills fundamentally shaped my understanding of Sills's artistry. I can barely express the intensity of the day I spent with Tito and Gigi Capobianco—who probably spent more time creating with Sills than any of her other collaborators. I feel love for the two of them and am extremely grateful to have had the chance to meet Gigi before her passing in April 2011. Thanks are due to their son Dan Capobianco for making my contact with his parents possible. I must also extend special thanks to Robert Hale and Dominic Cossa for their significant contributions to this project. Finally, I thank Charles Wadsworth for two wonderful afternoons in New York City in which he recalled his years of collaboration with Sills. Other artists with whom I had the pleasure of discussing their experiences with Sills include Richard Beeson, Joseph Citarella, Frank Corsaro, Cynthia Aaronson Davis, Anthea de Forest, Joseph Evans, Rhoda Levine, Marlena Kleinman Malas, Spiro Malas, Lotfi Mansouri, Samuel

Ramey, Gianna Rolandi, Julius Rudel, and Daniel Shigo. I am also grateful to Susan Woelzl, the New York City Opera's press and public relations director for thirty years, for sharing her memories of Sills, for allowing me access to materials that are now dispersed or destroyed following the dissolution of Sills's beloved opera company, and for introducing me to several of Sills's former colleagues. I am indebted to Beth Bergman, who has been a leading photographer of opera in New York for more than four decades. It was through her photographs that I was able to gain a sense of Sills in roles for which we have no video documentation. Beth is a consummate professional and has been very kind in sharing her materials and insights over the years of our contact.

My home institution, the University of California, San Diego (UCSD), offered various forms of support. I am grateful for two consecutive quarters of sabbatical leave during which I wrote the bulk of the first draft. Four separate grants from the UCSD Committee on Research supported my travel to research collections in the Library of Congress, the New York Public Library for the Performing Arts, and the John L. Price Jr. Musicarnival Archives at the Cleveland Public Library. Generous support from Dean Seth Lerer and the Arts and Humanities Fund for Innovation made it possible for me to travel to sites in Florida, New York, and Arizona, where I met with Sills's former collaborators. Sound engineer Tom Erbe, on the faculty in my department, was of terrific assistance in helping me work with bootleg recordings of live performances whose pitch and tempi had been distorted over decades of dubbing. I am especially grateful to department chair Rand Steiger, who allowed me to adapt my course load to suit my evolving research interests. In my graduate seminar "Theorizing the Performative Moment," participants Joe Bigham, Jeff Kaiser, Jonathan Piper, and Ben Power were a quartet of well-read and inquisitive intellectual companions (as well as accomplished musicians) as we tackled the question of how best to write about and theorize the act of musical performance.

This is my second book with the University of Illinois Press, and it has been a gratifying experience both times. My first book on Peking opera in Taiwan was contracted by the late Judy McCulloh, founder of the Music in American Life series, the series to which this book belongs. Judy was a wise, kind, and efficient editor. Her successor Laurie Matheson has carried on Judy's noble tradition by being supportive and humane, while gently shaping the project. I am grateful to have had the opportunity to work with both Laurie and Judy. I also had the luxury of working with two other fine professionals who helped transform my manuscript draft into this book. Carol Terry, in her role as a thoughtful and efficient developmental editor, shaped the document into a more evenly proportioned work. Copyeditor Anne Rogers went beyond the call of duty in rooting out the many insidious typos that found their way into the manuscript.

From 2010 through 2015 I presented parts of this work in various venues. I am thankful to all the audiences who engaged with the material and helped me to develop my arguments through their critiques. I am especially grateful to those who organized my speaking opportunities: L. K. Kam, who invited me to be a keynote speaker for the Taiwan Musicology Forum Annual Conference held at National Chiao-tung University; Helen Rees at the University of California, Los Angeles; Ying-fen Wang at National Taiwan University's Graduate Institute of Musicology; Larry Witzleben at the University of Maryland, College Park; Mina Yang at the University of Southern California; and Bell Yung at the University of Pittsburgh.

I have received help from librarians and archivists at numerous institutions. I am especially grateful to Bob Kosovsky at the New York Public Library for the Performing Arts, Dorothy and Lewis B. Cullman Center, Music Division. Bob was responsible for seeing that the NYPL acquired Beverly Sills's personal scores when they were put up for auction in 2009. During numerous trips to New York City to work with these scores, Bob was always helpful in seeing that I gained smooth access. I also acknowledge assistance from the following individuals and institutions: the Library of Congress, Music Division; the Duke University Rare Book, Manuscript, and Special Collections Library; San Diego State University Special Collections and University Archives; the Richard M. Nixon Presidential Library and Museum; the interlibrary loan department at UCSD; Jean Collins and Amy Dawson at the Cleveland Public Library, and *Los Angeles Magazine*'s archivist Eric Mercado.

Various individuals have been of terrific help along the way, including Peter Salk, who graciously permitted me to quote in full one of his father's letters to Sills. Diana Price was of kind assistance at two different stages in this project. She introduced me to Charles Freeman Stamper in July 2008, and she helped me gain easy access to her father's Musicarnival materials, which are now held at the Cleveland Public Library. Thanks are due to Dick Cavett, who gave permission for me to see recordings of Sills's appearances on his talk show, and to Tony Converse, the producer of Mr. Cavett's show, who made my contact with Mr. Cavett possible. I am also grateful for Paul Batsel's assistance in contacting the reigning "People's Diva," Renée Fleming, on my behalf.

I am fortunate to have a group of friends and colleagues who read portions of the book manuscript, including Cynthia Aaronson Davis, Catherine Diamond, Tracy McMullen, Carol Plantamura, Jane Potter, Miller Puckette, Helen Rees, Amy K. Stillman, Garry Wills, Mina Yang, and Bell Yung. Other friends and colleagues provided much-needed moral support and encouragement as I made the rather risky decision to shift my research focus from Taiwanese and Chinese musics to Western opera, including Anthony Davis, Patricia Hall, Nadine Hubbs, Joseph S. C. Lam, Susan Narucki, and Gillian Rodger.

It is hard to imagine how I would have started—or completed—this project were it not for the support of my friend Deborah Barber. When I called Deborah to see if I could crash with her so that I could attend Sills's memorial at the Metropolitan Opera, she not only offered me her sofa bed, but she lined up with me at six o'clock in the morning to get tickets for the memorial as well. Deborah opened her home numerous times when I traveled to New York and always provided a much-needed sounding board as I wove my way through Sills's New York.

One of the greatest joys afforded by this project was getting to know Meredith Holden Greenough, who is a warm and loving person. Our afternoons together were among the high points of this journey. I have also had the pleasure of having frequent and candid contact with Sills's cousin Kenny Morse. Lastly, I offer my sincere thanks to Beverly Sills for enriching my life in ways that I continue to discover.

The Magic of Beverly Sills

INTRODUCTION

Writing about Beverly Sills

The evening of July 2, 2007, while packing for a music conference and listening to the radio, I heard news that stunned me: Beverly Sills had died. I still cannot account for the force of the effect this news had on me. It affected me in profound and completely unexpected ways. I had not thought much about Sills over the previous twenty-five years; however, I never ceased remembering, and marking as a major event in my life, the day in 1977 when, as a teenager, I heard her in recital in my small hometown in the midwestern Rust Belt. This book grew out of a desire to grasp the connection I felt to Beverly Sills, a performer I did not personally know. This study explores the many facets of Sills's appeal as an opera singer, a performing artist, and a public figure of extraordinary strength, grace, and good humor.

The research for this book represents a radical break from all of my previously published work, most significantly in terms of focus and theoretical orientation. As a graduate student, I was very much interested in the details of music making and the functioning of musical systems; however, almost all of my publications focus on music and the political environment, or other entanglements involving music and power contestations. I went to Taipei, Taiwan, in 1992 to conduct research on creative processes in Peking opera for my PhD dissertation. Recent and radical changes to China-Taiwan relations were allowing for direct contact after forty years of enforced separation. I found that, rather than creating new operas, Taiwan's Peking opera troupes were mostly either commissioning entire works from mainland Chinese artists or copying mainland-created works from videotapes imported from China. In reaction to this new, dynamic environment, I shifted the focus of my research from the creative process to the political environment and the ways in which cross-strait policy dictated the artistic practices of Taiwan's Peking opera performers (see Guy 2005). My engagement with context, rather than the specifics of music and performance, was influenced by changes in Taiwan's political environment. After this work, I continued to be fascinated with the relationship between music and Taiwan's spectacularly dynamic political environment, and turned my attention to music's role in campaigning, state celebration, protest, and other such musical expressions of political orientation and ethnic identity (Guy 2000, 2002, 2007, 2008). While the research was fascinating, I grew weary observing endlessly volatile, often hate-filled, conflict. The height of mean-spirited protest came in 2006 during the round-the-clock, several-months-long "Anti-Corruption" protest against the democratically elected president Chen Shui-bian. The protesters' use of music, mostly well-known popular songs and a few newly composed songs, was fascinating. However, what the protest meant for Taiwan's future, as well as for the meaning of the nation's recent past, was deeply disturbing.

The morning after hearing of Sills's death, I still felt affected by the news. I traveled to Vienna, where I would deliver a paper on the "Anti-Corruption" protest at the International Council for Traditional Music conference, and collected Sills's obituaries published in local newspapers as I traveled from airport to airport. The academic paper I presented was especially well received by Taiwanese attendees who had supported the protest against President Chen (Guy 2007), however, its positive reception brought me to a peculiarly joyless moment in my research career.

In studying music, one deals directly with emotion and viscerally experienced meaning. This work is exhilarating when developments are positive, but a steady diet of negativity can be difficult to bear. Having observed that scholars who write about happiness often get very hopeful and cheery while those writing on negative subjects such as child abuse and torture can become depressed, Sissela Bok, moral philosopher and author of *Exploring Happiness,* suggests that it is important for scholars to observe how their research influences their own happiness (Bok 2010, 153).

Once I started listening to Sills again after a break of more than two decades, I rediscovered pleasure in music—pleasure that had sadly escaped me for more years than I care to admit. This compelled me to turn my attention away from my context-rich, but musically impoverished, work on music and politics. I needed to bring musical performance back to the center of my interests. Rather than documenting political struggle, which often brings out the worst in people, I needed to explore the best that human beings can produce: magnificent, detailed, and transcendent art. Beverly Sills's passing forced me to recall a time when music, both playing it and listening to it, brought me intense emotional and intellectual pleasure. The more I listened to Sills (and then to other music that I had not listened to for many years), the more invigorated I became. Sissela Bok could not be more correct in observing that the subjects of our scholarly inquiry can directly influence our happiness and well-being.

My intense revisiting of Sills's artistic output, coupled with a new appreciation for her strength of character in the face of numerous personal tragedies, kindled in me a feeling nothing short of love. The fans with whom I have collaborated while researching this project share this feeling, as do most of Sills's former colleagues whom I have had the honor of interviewing. I used to enjoy a sense of elation and hopefulness when attending victory rallies after important elections and inaugural performances in Taiwan. However, little in my research life has compared to the intense and intimate feeling generated during the hours spent with people, now in their sixties, seventies, and eighties, as they recalled the years that they spent creating art with Sills as being the happiest of their professional lives.

Academics are typically discouraged from admitting to our passions in prose. The fear of having the objectivity and, therefore, the veracity of our work questioned has resulted in a lack of scholarly attention being paid to the celebrities and performers whom we most admire. Not only are we afraid of being seen as irrationally exuberant, but also of being labeled as a *fan*, a notion that carries its own negative cultural baggage. Joli Jensen's survey of popular and scholarly literature finds that the concept of *fan* often involves images of social and psychological pathology. Fans are frequently characterized as excessive and emotionally unbalanced. In other words, they are portrayed as deviant "fanatics" (Jensen 1992, 9).

Kirsten MacLeod homes in on the pathologizing of fandom by academics as a tactic to "uphold an élitist 'us/them' dichotomy between forms of engagement with cultural life" (2004, 119). In the introduction to her essay "In Praise of Brigitte Fassbaender," Terry Castle demonstrates the serious anxiety that surrounds being cast as a fan: "To 'come out' as the fan of a great diva is always an embarrassing proposition—as difficult in its own ways, perhaps, as coming out as a homosexual" (1995, 20). By openly declaring the "peculiar power" that diva Fassbaender has over her, she launches a preemptive strike aiming to deflect critical attack (ibid., 21).[1]

The musicological literature on opera abounds with belittling jabs at fans. It is no secret that some of opera's most fervent fans are gay men. Therefore, Carolyn Abbate's dismissive description of the "cults" surrounding famous singers as being made up of "fans who may worship wardrobes as passionately as they do musical virtuosity" (2001, 50) seems not only dismissive, but also homophobic. Abbate's self-conscious distancing from fandom fundamentally influences her work. In her book *In Search of Opera,* she almost completely avoids discussion of specific singers or performances even while admitting that their absence "may well seem a great irony, even a fatal defect" (ibid., xii).[2]

In his passionate article "The Diva's Fans: Opera and Bodily Participation," Clemens Risi calls for scholars to be as brave in admitting their susceptibility to "the allures of opera and voice" as the singers who expose "their vulnerability on the stage, walking on the very cutting edge of the humanly possible, at the constant risk of failure." To do so is, as he admits, "bound with serious dangers." Scholars writing on voice, therefore, typically focus their energies on the abstract, concentrating on technical details of vocal production rather than "writing on the experience of voice" (2011a, 53). Theater scholar David Román has wisely observed that for intellectuals to "indulge in our feelings of pleasure and, more to the point, to write about them, is viewed as unprofessional, a form of fandom that should be relegated to the publicists or left to our private theatre journals. Our knowledge of the history and performances of stars is information that is presumed to have no real cultural value, the frivolous theatre gossip of overly enthusiastic fans. *We are bullied into keeping our love of theatre outside our scholarship*" (Román 2002, vix; emphasis added). The consequences of succumbing to these pressures are grave. Illustrating this point, Román notes that there would be little documentation of dancer Chita Rivera's distinguished career in the theater, if it were not for popular press coverage and the occasional mention in her collaborators' memoirs.

Excepting her autobiographies, nearly the same can be said of Beverly Sills. Just two academic articles place her at their centers (Hart 2004; Siefert 2004). This is the first scholarly book. Sills is not exceptional in being excluded from the focus of academic writers. One is hard-pressed to name a single book written by a musicologist or theater scholar on the work of a contemporary opera singer (here defined as one whose career flourished after 1950). Philip Gossett's invaluable tome *Divas and Scholars*—based on years of direct and dedicated engagement with some of the world's finest performers of Italian opera—offers priceless vignettes of various artists at work. Gossett's aim, however, is not to take any one singer as his scholarly focus. Of particular interest to my study is that Gossett, whose knowledge of the repertoire under his study is unsurpassed, boldly identifies himself as "a fan, a musician, and a scholar" in his book's opening pages (2006, ix).

In her powerful article "For a Politics of Love and Rescue," anthropologist Virginia Domínguez makes an impassioned plea for intellectuals to be open about the feelings their work engenders toward their subjects, especially feelings of love: "It is about time that we recognize [love] when it is there, value it rather than denigrate it, and flaunt it because we are proud (for good reasons, i.e., not blindly) of the persons we love and of the quality of the work that love (and those people) enables us to produce" (Domínguez 2000, 388). As Domínguez notes, loving does not mean that we present only positive characteristics of the people about whom we write, nor does it mean that we avoid conflict or debate in accessing our subject's contributions (ibid., 366). In this book, I am open about my Sills fandom. There have been times in my life when I have loved her passionately, and I believe that my experience as a teenager of hearing her in recital has remained an influence to this day. Returning after decades of little or no engagement with her singing, I now bring a critical eye (and ear) developed over years as an academic to both my own engagement with Sills and to Sills's artistry.

Structuring the Story

Chapter 1, "The Beverly Sills Phenomenon," identifies Beverly Sills in the American imagination at the time of her debut at the Metropolitan Opera in April 1975. She was a widely recognized figure in American popular culture in the mid-twentieth century. As amazing as Sills was, it is hard to imagine that she would have the same degree of media presence if she were at the height of her powers today. Examination of the "Sills phenomenon" casts light on the roads that American popular and performing arts cultures have traveled during these few decades. Her career unfolded at a time when opera still had a footing in the mainstream media. Her fame also corresponded with a period when performing arts institutions in the United States were experiencing significant growth. This expansion was part of an overall bolstering of the infrastructure as the nation reached the zenith of its jubilant post–World War II development. Sills's surge into the American popular consciousness took place within the context of this forward momentum and patriotic optimism. The January 17, 1969, issue of *Life* captured the zeitgeist with its cover story, "Our Journey to the Moon," and a profile article on Beverly Sills.

As America planned lunar missions, it also built cultural institutions, and Sills performed at the opening of many of them. Her meteoric rise to fame came in the fall of 1966 only after her home company, the New York City Opera (NYCO), moved to the New York State Theater in the newly constructed Lincoln Center for the Performing Arts. She was a featured artist when the NYCO performed Handel's *Ariodante* during the opening weeks of the Kennedy Center in Washington, DC, in 1971. She also performed at the Wolf Trap National Park for the Performing Arts during its opening season in 1971, even before construction of the dressing rooms was complete.

It is essential to remember that neither Sills's prominence in the opera world nor her broad popular appeal would have been possible without her artistry as a singer. Therefore, her singing artistry, particularly in live performance, is at the center of this study. This work explores what was at play as she joined her performing colleagues and audience to her and joined her audience members to one another in moments of palpable *communitas*. I interviewed many artists with whom she worked closely and from them have endeavored to reconstruct a sense of what it was to be in the moment with this consummate performer.

Chapter 2, "From Early Life to Breakthrough"; chapter 3, "From Breakthrough to Stardom"; and chapter 4, "From Stardom to Retirement," cover Beverly Sills's life and career. Although this book is not a biography, these chapters consider aspects of Sills's personal life insofar as they fundamentally influenced her development as a singer and performer. Because the focus of this book is her artistry, the discussion ends with her retirement from singing in 1980.

The purpose of these biographical chapters is to sketch an outline of Sills's artistic development, to consider her most significant artistic collaborations, and to identify the most important roles and performances of her singing career. Key life events are included insofar as they shaped her personal and artistic growth.[3] The aim in covering this biographical territory is not to report on unknown or salacious aspects of Sills's personal life, but to set the foundation for more topical discussions in other chapters. The core sources for the biographical data are largely those published in the mainstream media during Sills's life. I complement this well-worn narrative with insights gained through conversations with Sills's friends, former colleagues, family members, and various primary sources such as her personal correspondence. I also seek to correct inconsistencies in chronology and other such errors that were perpetuated across the body of writings on and by Sills.[4]

These three chapters draw on critics' reviews and other printed and Internet sources to outline the debate that surrounded and continues to surround Sills's performance. Clearly, not everyone was enamored with Sills's voice, acting skills, or persona. However, certain patterns emerge from the corpus of critical reviews that are useful in framing controversies surrounding not only Sills, but the artistic output of other opera singers as well. On the surface, much of this seems to fall into the catchall category of aesthetic preference, but broader themes emerge out of this opaque realm. Some of these grow directly from engagement with artistic output—for example, the deeply personal preference for certain types of vocal timbres. Some critics prefer creamy, rich voices while others prefer light, silvery ones. The "size" of a singer's voice is also a recurring theme and represents, in my opinion, an issue that must be viewed with some degree of historical depth. The question of balance between dramatic expression versus beauty of vocal tone also ignited much heated prose across the body of Sills's reviews.

Chapters 5 and 6 discuss Beverly Sills's fans—those who found themselves loving her. The phenomenon of fandom is of vital interest to my inquiry. Simply put, I aim to explore what it was that attracted people, including myself, to Sills.

What do they remember of her on stage, in recordings, and on television? How did Sills interweave with their understandings of themselves? What has Sills meant within their individual lives? I have also sought, within the vast reservoirs of fan memories, details of specific performances, especially those for which we have no video record.

Chapter 5, "Loving Sills," explores themes that recur across the large body of materials related to Sills fandom. Within a few weeks of Sills's passing, I began to correspond with a number of Sills's ever-loyal fans. Locating her now disparate admirers three decades after she last sang in public was made possible only through the social networking aspects of Internet sites, including blogs, Facebook, and even eBay back in the days (c. 2007) when one could contact bidding competitors directly through the auction site. I found several of my closest collaborators in YouTube comment sections, which are highly contested zones where alliances are formed and bolstered as the traits of operatic divas are vehemently attacked and defended. Over the years, the relationships I formed with some of these fans have continued to grow. What began as "virtual ethnography" has blossomed into group pilgrimages to New York City, Hollywood, Houston, and Hayward, California, as well as individual visits to one another's homes. The cyber element of our social networking continues to thrive as many of us converge regularly on Facebook and in group e-mail messages. I have continued to gather details of their memories of being in Sills's presence, and I continue to be struck by the ways in which she remains part of their daily lives.

My explicitly ethnographic research method is unusual for a scholarly investigation of Western opera, as is my attention to the personal reception of the operatic experience. A notable exception is *The Opera Fanatic: Ethnography of an Obsession* (2011), in which sociologist Claudio Benzecry uses theories and methods from cultural sociology in his work with opera fans from nonelite socioeconomic classes in Buenos Aires. He shows that engagement with this high art form is not a matter of forming distinctions as a means of domination as Pierre Bourdieu famously asserted, but that the opera fans with whom he worked engage with the art because they love it; it provides them a means for self-transcendence and belonging. There are a few studies that focus specifically on the subjective, personal engagement with opera, such as Wayne Koestenbaum's groundbreaking *The Queen's Throat* (1993), Sam Abel's lesser-known but brilliant *Opera in the Flesh* (1996), and Terry Castle's important essay on diva worship, "In Praise of Brigitte Fassbaender" (1995). These three works deal with sexuality and explicitly with gay and lesbian attraction to opera and its singers. This theme also has a place in my own ethnographic work with Sills's admirers.

In addition to those lucky enough to have spent their evenings in the theater as Sills transformed herself into Queen Elizabeth I, Anne Boleyn, and other tragic or comic heroines were millions of Americans who came to know Sills through her frequent appearances on popular television programs in 1960s, '70s, and '80s. From the perspective of the contemporary United States, where access to opera is extremely limited in the mainstream media, this phenomenon raises the question of how Sills managed to appeal to such a broad and diverse viewing audience.

Evidence from the lives of Sills fans dispels the misguided assumption, and often hostile charge, that opera appeals only to urban elite audiences. Sills's fan base reached across socioeconomic borders. Her mass popularity occasionally met with hostility from those who assumed the role of gatekeepers of high culture. I analyze how her public persona and media presence became a site for the contestation of public culture as she challenged distinctions between elite and mass culture. My main sources for documenting this aspect of her career are obituaries and online epitaphs, interviews with fans, and the published writings of critics. From these varied voices emerges evidence that Sills was highly successful in transcending class-bound definitions of culture. As one fan wrote, Sills "elevated opera from elitist to a shared experience, where one got to experience the possibility of the human voice as Olympian."[5]

Chapter 6, "Sills in the Lives of Her Fans," details ways in which Sills and her artistry brought meaning to and shaped the lives of seven individual admirers.

Chapters 7 and 8 explore Sills's artistry by first taking up the theoretical notion of magic in performance, and then focusing on its manifestation in a Sills's performance of Donizetti's *Anna Bolena*.

Chapter 7, "Experiencing Magic," considers the notion of magic as it pertains to Sills's artistry in performance. Reflecting on her singing career, Sills wrote: "I can't finally analyze what I did or why people liked what I did. All that fits into the category of unnameable magic" (1987, 347). The presence of an elevating quality in performance, which goes beyond supremacy in skill, is often simply glossed over as "magic" or a number of other words—such as "presence," "charisma," "magnetism," "radiance," "mesmerism," and "It" (as in the *It factor*)—that point to facets of this quality. In-depth analysis of this "unnameable" phenomenon is almost by definition forbidden territory for an academic. We are, after all, supposed to be objective. However, several recent books by performance-study scholars have brushed aside these concerns and made terrific strides in theorizing the seemingly ineffable (e.g., Dolan 2005, Fischer-Lichte 2008, and Goodall 2008). In *Stage Presence*, Jane Goodall takes as her umbrella concept *presence*, which, following Sills's usage, I term *magic*. Goodall's aim is not to demystify presence, but to examine how this quality has been articulated throughout the history of writings on Western theater and several other forms, including opera and ballet. She rejects the idea that presence is inexplicable or unnameable, particularly since "the notion of presence has inspired some of the most memorable passages in the literature on performance" (2008, 7). I, too, have found that many of the most breathtaking descriptions of Sills in performance have been those in which people have sought to communicate the experience of being in the moment when Sills was radiating this quality. Impervious to academic taboo, magic has been mentioned frequently and unself-consciously in my discussions with Sills's colleagues and fans, although I have been careful not to be the first to reference the subject in these conversations. Nevertheless, the word, and hence the concept, almost inevitably finds its way into conversations on various aspects of Sills's artistry.

Taking Sills's artistry as a case study of magic in performance, I turn to the thoughts of her former colleagues and continuing fans in seeking memoric residue of this aspect of her performance. I also watch and listen for evidence of magic in the audio, video, and photographic records of her time on stage. I am aware of the risks of pursuing such an aim within the context of academic study, particularly within opera studies, in which attention is only slowly being turned to performance as opposed to works, composers, and, more recently, stage directors. For encouragement and inspiration, I keep in mind stage director Tito Capobianco's casual pronouncement as he drove Gigi, his wife and artistic collaborator, and me to lunch during our nine-hour visit discussing Sills: "Be courageous and accept the fact—magic exists" (interview, July 28, 2010).

Chapter 8, "Listening for After-Vibrations," focuses on the manifestation of magic in Sills's performance of Donizetti's *Anna Bolena*. This chapter seeks to recover something of how her art was experienced in the hot moment of performance by those in the house. There is no known video recording of Sills as Anna Bolena. I employ a variety of sources that until recently have rarely been utilized by opera scholars. Central to my work is a copy of Sills's heavily annotated personal score and numerous bootleg recordings. These illicit recordings not only preserve the performers' audible actions, but sometimes those of audience members as well. Thus they communicate sounding residue of experiential moments that are typically surrendered as lost ephemera. Other vital sources are written and verbal accounts of the production in preparation and performance, as well as still photos from live performance. This constellation of sources allows us to know in specific instances what Sills intended, to hear what she did in performance, and to hear her audience's reactions.

Chapter 9, "Engaging with Sills's Artistry," considers the powerful communication expressed through the artistry of Sills as a singing actress. She chose her repertoire for intense roles that communicated emotion to her listeners, sometimes to the detriment of the maintenance of her voice.

An afterword, "Discovering Sills's Influence," considers my journey on this project and brings me back to my original question: Why was I so affected by

Beverly Sills's death? Along the way, this quest reconfirmed the magic I perceived as a teenager seeing her in recital many years ago.

Opera has the power to "decommission rationality," finds Carolyn Abbate; certain aspects of its performance are simply "inscrutable to the mind" (2001, 36, 29). By employing a fundamentally ethnographic research method in approaching the seemingly inscrutable, I look to the feelings and experiences of those who fell under Sills's spell. I seek not only to memorialize this artist's work, but also to get at the heart of opera's ability to move its listeners to a transcendent realm where they experience magic. The personal stories of Sills's fans gathered here bear testament to the power of magic to influence, deeply and positively, those who encounter it. For some, the world is never quite the same after being moved by an extraordinary performance.

CHAPTER 1

The Beverly Sills Phenomenon

The morning of April 8, 1975, newspapers around the United States as well as overseas announced that Beverly Sills had finally made her debut the night before at the Metropolitan Opera, the nation's most prestigious opera house. The *Cleveland Plain Dealer* headline nicely summed up the milieu: "Pandemonium Greets Beverly Sills in Overdue Met Debut." Sills took the stage as Pamira in Rossini's rarely performed tragic opera *The Siege of Corinth* (L'assedio di Corinto). Reporting from New York, the music editor of the *Dallas Times Herald* wrote that it was "far and away the hottest ticket in this town."

Most people in the audience that evening had purchased their tickets as soon as the season was announced the previous fall. Recognizing the enormous demand her debut would create, the Met seized the opportunity to replenish its coffers and made the event a gala, charging its highest prices. Boxes went for $500 (about $2,260 in 2015 dollars), while individual seats were priced as high as $60. Scalpers demanded upward of $100. According to the *Philadelphia Inquirer,* "more than 200 persons thronged the lobby and front doors in hopes of buying returned tickets. Some even wore signs around their necks pleading for tickets." A rumor circulated that one man paid $1,000 for his seat. Those seeking a place in the standing-room section lined up Friday afternoon for tickets going on sale Saturday morning at ten o'clock. The Met Guild announced that demand for the run of five performances was so great that it had to turn down seven thousand ticket requests.

During the previous days, media outlets big and small reported on Sills's upcoming performance. *Los Angeles Times* music critic Martin Bernheimer remarked: "It was impossible . . . to pick up any publication other than the telephone book and not read about Beverly Sills."[1] In fact, Sills's image even graced the cover of the San Diego phonebook. *Newsweek* magazine wrote: "As the countdown for Beverly Sills' historic debut at the Metropolitan Opera began last week, the commotion approached hysteria. Television, the daily press, the news and fashion magazines all devoured her as if she were America's antidote to Southeast Asia" (Saal 1975, 86). The day after the debut, the front page of the *New York Daily News* was evenly divided between a bold-type headline announcing that the South Vietnamese presidential palace had been bombed and a large photo of a beaming Sills as she exited the Met stage with the simple headline: "Beverly Bows—Brava!" Charles Wendelken-Wilson, the principal conductor for Sills's performances of *Lucia di Lammermoor, Maria Stuarda,* and *La Fille du Régiment* during the 1970s at the New York City Opera, placed her popularity partly within the turbulent context of the Vietnam War era. He reminisced about the warm reception she always received when she made her first stage entrances: "She was the New York girl up there—the hometown lady. There we were still wondering what we were doing over in Vietnam and here she was, the symbol of America at its best" (Wendelken-Wilson interview, August 1, 2008).

On the evening of Sills's debut, the Metropolitan Opera House buzzed with "sheer excitement and electricity" the likes of which had not been seen since the company moved to Lincoln Center in the fall of 1966 (*Cincinnati Enquirer,* April 9, 1975). Critics came out in droves. Television cameramen prowled the lobbies hoping to capture glimpses of luminaries. These included Hollywood stars Danny Kaye and Kirk Douglas; great singers such as Jessye Norman, Licia Albanese, Rose Bampton, Risë Stevens, Robert Merrill, Bidu Sayou, and Maria Jeritza; and other eminent personalities. Of the general feeling, Pulitzer Prize–winning historian Garry Wills reported hearing someone say: "I've been here often when the house was full, but it never seemed so full as tonight." Wills concluded that the "4,000 people seemed to swell or pulse with extra life" (*Memphis Commercial Appeal,* April 16, 1975).

From the moment Sills made what was meant to be an inconspicuous stage entrance—dressed in a silver-trimmed gown in "Beverly blue" as the press termed it—the audience went wild, shouting, "Brava Beverly." They rose to their feet for an ovation that lasted about two minutes. *Newsweek's* Hubert Saal observed that it was as if the audience roared with one giant voice, "At last" (1975, 86). The crowd cheered after each of her arias. Applause stopped the performance for about five minutes at the conclusion of her fiendishly difficult act 2 aria. With tears in her eyes, Sills remained in character, silently facing forward as she waited for the cheering to subside. At the opera's end, flowers and confetti rained down on the stage during her eighteen-minute solo ovation. Chapter 3 includes a more detailed analysis of her performance that evening. For now, an excerpt from Harold C. Schonberg's extensive *New York Times* article "The Total Theater of Beverly Sills" reported: "Throughout the opera she gave—well, a Beverly Sills performance. The singing was warm, eloquent and moving. There were some remarkable leggiero passages. There was radiant Sills femininity, and there was the haunting color she was able to impart to lyric passages. There also were the well-known troubles above the staff. As if anybody cared about that. Beverly was on the stage of the Met, giving all she had. That was the only thing that mattered" (April 13, 1975).

Sills's Met debut marked a crucial milestone. She had been singing to sold-out houses regularly for nearly a decade with her home company, the New York City Opera in the New York State Theater only a hundred feet across Lincoln Center Plaza from the Met. Sills had already performed in almost every important opera house in the world. Her exclusion from the Met stemmed from what Sills termed a "clash of personalities" between her and Met general manager Rudolf Bing (Moore 1975, 15). No doubt he resented her and her New York City Opera colleagues for inadvertently stealing his thunder in 1966 soon after the Metropolitan Opera opened its new theater at Lincoln Center with a resounding flop. For the grand opening, Bing had commissioned a new opera, *Antony and Cleopatra*, from American composer Samuel Barber in an elaborate production by Franco Zeffirelli, who had also written the libretto. Schonberg of the *New York Times* wrote: "Almost everything about the evening, artistically speaking, failed in total impact." It was "artifice masquerading with a great flourish as art" (September 17, 1966). Writing in more colorful terms, Shana Alexander of *Life* magazine reported: "Much of what went on was a truly operatic disaster. Being there was a lot like having a front-row seat at an earthquake" (September 30, 1966, 30B).

Eleven days following the Met's fantastic flop, Norman Treigle, Maureen Forrester, and Beverly Sills opened the New York City Opera season with Handel's *Giulio Cesare* in an elegant Tito Capobianco production. Audience members and the press alike were stunned by Sills's performance. As Winthrop Sargeant observed, with the *Julius Caesar* performance, there "was an ebullient realization on everybody's part that New York's own opera company and New York's own singers had reached a peak of success that—for the time being, at least—left the big, international Metropolitan Opera behind. And the largest factor in the triumph was Miss Sills—charmingly seducing the Roman Emperor, singing like a nightingale, projecting across the footlights the most attractive of operatic personalities" (1973, 81). She shot to stardom instantly. Suddenly, Sills was invited to perform at major venues around the world. Her success, at what seemed to have been his expense, initiated the feud that smoldered between Sills and Bing until after he retired in 1972. His snubbing of her became a cause célèbre, which ultimately formed a key cornerstone of her public image as an all-American success story.

Rudolf Bing was born into a well-to-do Viennese family, became a naturalized British citizen, and was rumored to prefer European over American singers. At the very least, American singers were expected to build their careers in Europe before starring at the Met. Sills, whose strong will and forthright personality were apparent to all who saw her on television or read her interviews, aired her feelings on this apparent anti-American bias in the press early on. In a December 1968 *Cleveland Plain Dealer* article titled "Met Waits While Beverly Sills Says: 'I Don't Need Europe,'" Sills was quoted as saying, "Frankly, I resent Mr. Bing's attitude that American singers first must go to Europe to gain experience. Frankly I am trying to destroy this attitude at the Metropolitan. I'll match my experience with anyone's." On the eve of her Met debut, Sills was cited in the *New York Times Magazine* saying: "In a sense, I revolutionized the operatic scene, because I proved you can make a great international career without the Metropolitan. I'm the only singer who's done that, and I'm proud of that, so it's all worked out for the best. It's all right. It really is" (Barthel 1975, 16). Sills's staunch belief in American talent, operatic training, and performing institutions only strengthened over time. Her national pride was not lost on the American public, whose patriotism was on the rise as the nation's bicentennial celebrations approached.

There was more to Bing's disdain for Sills than the fact that she did not work her way up through the European ranks: she did not put on airs. Sills never lost her Brooklyn accent, which she often peppered with Yiddish expressions. And, rather than hiding that she came from a modest background, she spoke freely of her times of financial struggle. Writing the day after her Met debut for the *Herald* of Melbourne, Australia, Peter Michelmore explained that Bing simply did not care for Sills: "For an opera star she seemed too happy-go-lucky, too unaware of her stature, and sometimes, when she described an opera plot in Brooklyn street slang, his hair would stand on end."

Bing hurled a classist insult at Sills in his only direct mention of her in his 345-page memoir, which he published the year of his retirement. In discussing his opposition to the New York City Opera taking up residence in Lincoln Center, Bing explained that he initially worried that the two companies might stage similar repertoire. However, over the years, there was only one "fight" related to programming. Naturally, the unpleasantness centered on Beverly Sills. She wanted to perform Donizetti's three Tudor queen operas: *Anna Bolena, Maria Stuarda,* and *Roberto Devereux.* However, Spanish soprano Montserrat Caballé hoped to undertake the trilogy at the Met. Bing cattily commented, "[W]e finally accepted the fact that Beverly Sills of the City Opera, having been born in Brooklyn, was entitled to priority in the portrayal of British royalty" (1972, 290). This slur was reported in *Time* magazine in an article reporting on the publication of Bing's book, which only bolstered the perception of Sills's as an all-American diva (October 23, 1972). Throughout her singing career (and even now as her artistic legacy continues to be debated), Sills was targeted by gatekeeping elitists, such as Bing, in retribution for her down-to-earth, often cheery, sometimes imposing, and always Brooklynese manner. Of course, it was precisely these qualities that drew a broad range of people to her and her artistry, many of whom might otherwise never have known opera.

As part of her meteoric rise to fame following her brilliant performance as Cleopatra in fall 1966, Sills gained significant, mainstream media attention. A vital facet of her image known to the American public by the time of her Met debut was that she had overcome crushing setbacks and personal tragedies. Foremost among these were her two children's disabilities. Her eldest, Meredith, known affectionately as Muffy, is profoundly deaf. As the extensive November 22, 1971, *Time* cover story on Sills put it: "In a piece of Sophoclean irony, Muffy would never hear the sound of her mother's singing" (81). Sills's second born, Peter, called Bucky, was diagnosed as severely developmentally disabled, autistic, and epileptic. The family was forced to institutionalize him when his care became more than they could manage at home.

The *New York Times Magazine*'s lengthy feature article, "The True Story of Beverly Sills: Who Leads a Kind of Soap Opera Life on the Grand Opera Stage," was one of the first detailed depictions of her personal sorrows (September 17, 1967). Sills's story reached a much broader audience with *Life* magazine's two-page "close-up" photo essay, "Unpretentious Prima Donna," published January 17, 1969. *Life* was one of the most important general weekly magazines in the United States from the late 1930s through the early 1970s (Doss 2001, xiii). Just a year after the Sills profile appeared, each issue of *Life* was estimated to reach as many as forty million people. Divided almost equally between text and photos, the Sills piece covered many biographical themes that were repeated over and over in the popular press for the next decade and a half, including her steel-willed determination and down-to-earth manner, her children's disabilities, and her long road to operatic stardom. The article's three photos depicted Sills as a performer and as a wife and mother. There was a large color image of her as the spectacular and exotic Queen Shemaka in Rimsky-Korsakov's *Coq d'Or*; an adorable shot of her bending down to kiss her nine-year old daughter, who was in her school uniform and, as the caption relays, had just returned home from her school for the deaf; and a rather zany photo of Sills and her husband enjoying drinks sitting outside on lawn chairs. The article begins with a quote from Sills: "Opera is a wonderful opportunity to be someone else for three hours a night; it's good to take on someone else's *tsuris*." The author explains that *tsuris* is Yiddish for troubles and concludes that Sills's use of the word "tells a lot about this lady whom critics consider one of the world's few great coloratura sopranos. She is unaffected and unsinkable—she has a son who is mentally retarded and a daughter born deaf" (Dunn 1969, 37). Her absence from the rosters of the Metropolitan Opera comes up briefly as Sills says dismissively, "Sure, I'd like to sing there . . . but they'll have to offer me a role that will make me happy" (ibid.).

The April 21, 1969, *Newsweek* cover story, which followed her debut at Milan's famed La Scala opera house, told of how doctors diagnosed her daughter's profound hearing loss just two months prior to their discovery of her son's devastating maladies. Highlighting her indomitable spirit, writer Hubert Saal noted that her initial reaction was to give up her singing career; however, "instead of disabling her," these tragedies "propelled her to the pinnacle of her art" (1969, 69). Saal's article also appeared in a condensed version in the *Reader's Digest*, a magazine with an enormous circulation that frequently celebrated "the possibilities of the American Dream and extolling the optimism of that view of life" (Sharp 2000, xiv). Sills's life story certainly contained many of the themes central to the American dream with its ideology that an individual can attain success through strenuous effort and perseverance.

Sills was a self-admitted workaholic. This topic was illustrated many times over in the five-page *Time* magazine cover story. As she crisscrossed the globe in 1971, the year of the article's publication, her itinerary included more than one hundred operatic, concert, and recital appearances. When asked why she kept up such a grueling schedule, Sills quipped, "I'm already 42: what am I saving it for?" (*Time*, November 22, 1971, 74). Her compulsion for hard work stemmed in no small part from her need for escape from her personal woes. Performance was a perfect vehicle as she could take on Violetta's or Lucia's or someone else's troubles for three hours a night while forgetting her own. *Time* touched upon this subject briefly as it reported on moments of "piercing sadness"—as when Muffy puts her fingertips on the speaker to "feel" the sound of her mother's voice, or when Beverly "grows uncharacteristically abstracted, her voice trailing off, the brightness fading from her face" (82). As those close to her knew, in these moments, she was probably thinking of one of her regular visits to see Bucky. "But such moments are over quickly, because Beverly shakes them off firmly: there is work to be done" (ibid.).

Within two months of the 1969 *Newsweek* cover story, Sills made her first appearance on a nationally syndicated talk show. Her initial invitation came from Dick Cavett in June 1969. When Cavett moved his show from the afternoon to late night six months later, his opening lineup included Beverly Sills, Woody Allen, and Robert Shaw. *Variety* magazine observed that the "opera star, perhaps Cavett's best 'discovery' as a talk show participant, brings great warmth, color, humor and sparkle to a show—along with her spectacular voice" (December 31, 1969, 30). Johnny Carson followed Cavett's lead and invited Sills to appear on *The Tonight Show* fifteen times beginning in 1971. According to Sills, Carson suggested that if she came on his show, she would humanize opera. He encouraged her to "*Show 'em you look like everybody else, that you have kids, a life, that you have to diet*" (Sills 1987, 197). In addition to being interviewed by Carson and interacting with the evening's other guests, Sills would typically perform two numbers: an abbreviated opera aria or art song, and a more popular piece such as a Jerome Kern or Victor Herbert number. Sills even guest-hosted *The Tonight Show* twice, although not until 1978 and 1979. She ended up appearing on every major talk show of her day. She was a guest on *The Mike Douglas Show* at least five times and a cohost once in 1971. Merv Griffin invited her seven times, three prior to her Met debut. Other nationally broadcast talk show appearances included several episodes of Dinah Shore's show and at least one episode of *The David Frost Show.* She even appeared on game shows such as *What's My Line?*

By the time of her Met debut in 1975, Beverly Sills was a familiar face with a compelling story and a brilliant artistry. Her performances on prime-time and late-night television programs and feature articles in leading magazines, as well as extensive touring, gained her a large following of admirers and fans. Beverly Sills was a household name and something of an American cultural hero. As music critic John Ardoin, writing for the *Dallas Morning News,* put it: "There she stood on the stage of the Metropolitan Opera, the darling of the U.S. opera-going public, a heroine who was climaxing an all-American success story." In his syndicated newspaper commentary, "Bravos for Sills," and in the context of a nation recently rocked by leadership failures, most notably the Watergate scandal that ended with the resignation of President Nixon in August 1974, Garry Wills analyzed the outpouring of affection for Sills.

> We all need heroes and legends, and fairy tales that come true. But this appetite, one of the best things in us, has not been fed much recently. The act of admiring is becoming atrophied. Our leadership brings us ogres and nightmares instead of heroes and myths. That may be why New York went a bit sappy over Beverly Sills. Ten years too late, she finally sang at the Met—a dream come true. Not so much her dream, but that of opera lovers. And everyone in town was an honorary opera lover on April 7. (*Chicago Sun-Times,* April 14, 1975)

Referencing the eighteen-minute standing ovation at the performance's end, Wills surmised that the audience "did not want the evening to be concluded—heroes are rare these days and hero worship never so starved as now. And Beverly is the authentic article" (ibid.).

CHAPTER 2

From Early Life to Breakthrough

Beverly Sills published three autobiographies—*Bubbles: A Self Portrait* (1976), *Bubbles: An Encore* (1981), and *Beverly: An Autobiography* (1987).[1] In the ten years following her breakthrough performance as Cleopatra in Handel's *Giulio Cesare* in 1966, Sills was approached by more than thirty authors who each hoped to pen her biography. Finally, when one letter of intent posed a veiled threat, Sills's brother Stanley, who worked in publishing, suggested that Sills write her own book as a way of thwarting an unauthorized biography. Once Stanley announced in the *Publishers Weekly* that Sills's autobiography was forthcoming, Sills quickly got to work. Stanley, whose publishing company produced the book, suggested she begin by choosing two to three hundred photos that best documented her life and career. He envisioned a book comprised mainly of photos with captions providing the bulk of the text. As a means of composing this text, Stanley advised Sills to speak her photo captions into a tape recorder. Filling in spare moments in hotels and airplanes, Sills filled eighteen ninety-minute tapes during her concert travels; her editors shaped these into the 240-page book.[2] *Bubbles* boasts sixteen pages of color images and two hundred black-and-white photographs.

Bubbles was rushed to bookstores in mid-December, perhaps a bit late for the 1976 holiday season. The first printing contained a magnificent typo in the first sentence of the first chapter: "When I was only three, and still named Belle Miriam Silverman, I sang my first aria in *pubic*" (Sills 1976, 12; emphasis added).

Once the error was discovered, the publisher recalled all unsold copies and sent out a second printing. *Bubbles* landed on the *New York Times* "Best Seller List" in late February 1977 and alternated between the ninth and tenth positions for five nonconsecutive weeks. In December, the *New York Times* named *Bubbles* one of the "Best Sellers of the Year." The book is full of good humor and is wonderfully positive. The overriding theme is that Sills met challenges and overcame them. The 1981 volume is a reprint of *Bubbles* with the inclusion of an epilogue by writer Harvey E. Phillips that covers the highlights of her final years performing and the first two years of her term as the general director of the New York City Opera (NYCO).

Beverly: An Autobiography came out seven years after her retirement from singing and near the end of her term as the general director. *Beverly* is strikingly different from *Bubbles* in tone and appearance. The focus shifted significantly from photos to text. Instead of the rather lighthearted, positive nature of *Bubbles,* in *Beverly,* Sills tells her story with candor. *Beverly* fills in many details, but neither book deals in any depth with her thoughts on musical performance, nor is much said about her everyday creative practice or activities as a singer. Although she shares colorful glimpses into a few moments in specific performances, these precious insights are rare in both books.

In the many interviews that Sills gave during the course of her singing career, and across all of the profiles of her published in the popular press, there is rarely a deviation from a standardized account of her life story, which Sills seemed to have developed in the mid-1960s. It was likely under the influence of her publicist, Edgar Vincent (whom she retained in 1966 just prior to her performances as Cleopatra) that this narrative congealed. Edgar Vincent was one of the most highly regarded classical music publicists in New York. His other clients included Lily Pons, Anna Moffo, Eileen Farrell, Shirley Verrett, Plácido Domingo, Samuel Ramey, André Kostelanetz, Erich Leinsdorf, and Georg Solti. Vincent became Sills's professional mentor and a staunch guardian of her personal privacy and public image. During my interview with director Tito Capobianco and his wife and artistic collaborator Gigi, who was one of Sills's closest friends for many years, Gigi confided that Sills was a very private person (Capobianco interview, July 28, 2010). As close as Sills and Gigi were, Sills kept many details of her private life to herself. Over the years, Edgar Vincent and Sills's relationship transcended the professional; they became close friends. Critic John Rockwell, who occasionally lunched with both Sills and Vincent, told me that the last time he saw ninety-year-old Vincent following Sills's death, the light had gone from his eyes (phone conversation with author, July 20, 2008).[3]

The Child Star

Belle Miriam Silverman was born May 25, 1929, in Brooklyn, New York, to first-generation immigrants from eastern Europe.[4] She was the youngest of her parents' three children and the only girl. As she described it, her family was a very traditional, European Jewish family. Her father, Morris Silverman, who worked as an assistant manager for an insurance company, was a strong, handsome, and domineering figure. Her mother, Shirley, was by all accounts a radiantly beautiful and charismatic woman. Shortly after Morris's untimely death in 1949, Shirley became a Christian Scientist, a practice and belief system that takes the power of positive thinking as a central tenet (Sills 1987, 49). Sills credited her mother with instilling in her the ability to not dwell on the negative, to not lament her problems, but to seek ways to make things better, to always move forward (Jackson 2007). Shirley was an opera lover. Her kitchen housed the family's Victrola on which she played her extensive collection of opera recordings, including 78s of Lily Pons and Amelita Galli-Curci. Sills seems to have been particularly attracted to Galli-Curci's voice. As a small child, she memorized and was able to sing—with only approximate Italian pronunciation, of course—the twenty or so Galli-Curci arias in her mother's record collection. Given Sills's love for singing, her mother sought opportunities for her child to showcase her talent and to gain instruction. The children's radio program Big Brother Bob Emery's *Rainbow House* represented the first of such opportunities. Every Saturday morning, for only fifty cents, children who arrived in the WOR studio in Manhattan would be given instruction in tap dance, elocution, and singing. After an hour of lessons, the best students were selected to perform on that day's broadcast. Sills, then known as Bubbles Silverman, became a regular on the show at the age of four.

Her career as a child star continued, now under her stage name Beverly Sills, in *Uncle Sol Solves It*. Filmed in August 1937, just a few months after her eighth birthday, this short movie represents our earliest documentation of Sills in performance. She plays the part of a child who is destined to become a great opera singer. Ironically foreshadowing the trajectory of her own career, her character wants to study in the United States, although she is under pressure to pursue operatic training in Europe. Uncle Sol solves it by agreeing that she should stay home because, as he says: "there are plenty of good teachers in the USA." Sills's performance of Arditi's "Il Bacio" is flabbergasting as it reveals that prototypes of some of the physical mannerisms characteristic of Sills's mature performance style and stage presence were already in place. Most obviously, these include the use of her hands in a palms-out, fingers-slightly-spread position as they sometimes shadow the rising and falling of the melodic line with her forefingers occasionally mimicking in perfect time runs and leaps. Furthermore, already in evidence is the rather uncanny way in which Sills organically integrated the music into her physical movements; she seemed to embody the musical line. A simple example exhibited in this case, as in upbeat arias in operatic dramas, is the way in which she bobs gently in time with the music. A clip of this performance, under the title "Beverly Sills at 8 Years Old!," is posted on YouTube; it is also included in the *Great Performances* documentary "Beverly Sills Made in America," first broadcast in 2006 and published in DVD format by Deutsche Grammophon.

Sills's mother decided that her daughter's musical gifts deserved to be fostered. One day in October 1936, while walking down the street near Carnegie Hall, she saw a copy of the trade magazine *Musical Courier: The Weekly Magazine of the World's Music.* Estelle Liebling's photo graced the black-and-white cover with the caption: "Teacher of Operatic, Stage, Screen and Radio Artists." Mrs. Silverman phoned Liebling and arranged for an audition. After some confusion about who had come to audition, the child or her mother, Sills sang her "Il Bacio." Although she found her phonetically learned rendition amusing, Liebling agreed to teach Sills for fifteen minutes once a week (Sills 1987, 20). Thus began their student-teacher relationship that lasted until Miss Liebling passed away thirty-four years later. Liebling was one of the most highly regarded voice teachers in the United States during her era. She produced more than seventy-five Metropolitan opera singers over the course of her five decades of teaching (Fowler 1994, 5). Sills would become one of her most famous students, in addition to Amelita Galli-Curci and actresses Kitty Carlisle and Meryl Streep. Miss Liebling insisted that Sills take piano as well as voice lessons. She became quite an accomplished pianist, no doubt contributing to her extraordinary musical literacy, which surpassed that of many singers.[5]

With Liebling's encouragement, Sills, at age ten, applied to audition for the *Major Bowes' Amateur Hour,* the nation's highest-rated radio program.[6] Following in the tradition of the amateur hours of late nineteenth-century music halls, Bowes's program was part of a craze for amateur entertainment in Depression-era America (Melnick 2011, 331). One source estimated that against the backdrop of economic desperation, the odds for an auditioner to make it through the hoards of applicants and onto the show were approximately seventy thousand to one (Dunning 1998, 426). Modeled after the vaudeville hook, the Major would strike a gong when performers failed to make the grade as weekly contestants vied for the top prize. Similar to today's *American Idol* and *America's Got Talent,* audience members called in to support their favorite acts. Sills won the weekly contest with her first appearance on October 26, 1939, singing "Caro Nome" from Giuseppe Verdi's *Rigoletto.*[7] Bowes then invited her to appear on his weekly hour-long program of concert music and variety acts, the *Capitol Family Hour.* She made her first appearance a month later on the seventeenth anniversary of the program and was a regular guest until the program ended in May 1941 (Dunning 1998, 424).

A number of employment opportunities came Sills's way as a result of her exposure on television. She played the role of an abused, but musically talented, child on thirty-six episodes of the radio soap opera *Our Gal Sunday* from January to September 1940. Her voice was probably heard in every American home with a radio after she recorded the "Rinso White" jingle as part of Lever Brothers's laundry-detergent campaign. With the $1,000 she earned for the commercial, she bought herself a good piano and withdrew from public performance for two years. During this time, she continued her voice and piano lessons.

Training and Touring

Sills's hiatus ended at the age of fifteen when, with Miss Liebling's encouragement, she auditioned for Jacob J. Shubert of Broadway's most powerful theatrical family.[8] "J. J." was organizing a Gilbert and Sullivan tour with stops in his family's theaters in the East and Midwest. The two-month tour was grueling, with six performances a week and only three or four nights in each of the twelve cities they visited. Sills played seven roles in seven operettas including the title role in *Patience*. The first night that she played Patience, she made a self-realization that rang true for the rest of her singing career: she did not suffer stage fright. As she recalled in *Beverly*: "[O]pening night came and I walked out onstage for the first time, I was almost high with excitement, and I didn't blow a single line. I was probably too young even to *think* about doing that. Whatever the reason, that performance set a pattern for me: I never developed stage fright" (Sills 1987, 35). Years later, stage director Tito Capobianco shared that this was especially true of Sills on opening nights (Capobianco interview, July 28, 2010). He said she often gave her best performances the first time she brought a role before a live audience; she thrived on the challenge of pulling it all together under the pressures of opening night.

Eight months after her first Shubert tour concluded, she joined a second one with her salary increased by 30 percent. This time, at age seventeen, she played the lead roles in a "modernized version" of Lehar's *The Merry Widow* and *Play Gypsy Play*, which was a retreaded version of the Shubert's hit *Countess Maritza* from the 1920s (McNamara 1990, viii). Shubert billed her as "The Youngest Primadonna in Captivity" (Sills 1976, 32). Not only did she gain invaluable practical knowledge on the Shubert tours, such as learning how to project her speaking voice and other aspects of stagecraft, but perhaps, most important, she realized that her "desire to perform in front of an audience had become insatiable" (Sills 1976, 29).

When Sills returned home from her second three-month tour, her parents informed her that her days of touring as an operetta singer were finished. They reasoned that if she wanted to be a serious opera singer, she needed to stay home and study full time. It was just as well. The entertainment climate changed and operettas rather suddenly lost the favor of the American public. There never was another Shubert tour, nor did the theater magnate produce another operetta in any of his many Broadway theaters.

Sills took the next several years as a period of intensive study. As she mentioned in her autobiographies, and as many of those interviewed for this book have elaborated, Sills was an extremely disciplined and hardworking musician. In one of the rare glimpses into the nitty-gritty of her creative practice, she shared something of her experience with pedagogue Liebling:

> Miss Liebling was very strict and formal with me. When she was at the piano, she never let me read music over her shoulder, and she got *very* annoyed the few times I showed up unprepared. One of Miss Liebling's favorite admonitions to me was "Text! Text! Text!" which she said whenever she felt I was merely singing notes and not paying attention to the meaning of the lyrics. Miss Liebling wanted me to sing the way Olivier acts, to deliver what I was singing in such a way that my audience would respond emotionally. (Sills 1987, 41)

Sills's emphasis on textual meaning and her emotional coloring of each utterance or phrase become one of the defining characteristics of her performance as a mature artist. In fact, her acute attention to text, and especially its pathos, is one of the aspects of her artistry her aficionados cherish most.

With Liebling's blessing, Sills sought additional instruction from a number of artists during these years of intensive study. One of the first was Italian-born Giuseppe Bamboschek, a conductor on the musical staff of the Metropolitan Opera for many years and eventual artistic director and principal conductor of the Philadelphia Civic Grand Opera Company.[9] Liebling felt that Sills would benefit from studying the Italianate singing style with this master who had worked with Galli-Curci and other eminent singers. She also gained an opportunity to be coached by Mary Garden when the retired diva visited New York in 1949. Garden, a Scottish-born American soprano, spent many of her most productive creative years in Paris. Due in no small part to her close working relationships with composers Debussy and Massenet, Garden became a vital force in French opera in the early twentieth century. Garden was largely responsible for introducing New York audiences to contemporary French opera beginning with her *Thaïs* in 1907. She coached Sills on both *Thaïs* and *Manon*. Although Sills reports that their relationship during their six weeks of coaching was far from harmonious, it is important to note that this experience linked Sills directly to the French performance style as it had evolved in the creative cauldron of Paris at the turn of the century. Another way in which Garden, who was renowned for her "subtly evocative acting" (Tolansky 2012), may have influenced the young Sills was in her insistence on giving a total performance. In fact, Sills recalled that Garden worked with her primarily on acting; she gave scant attention to musical details in their coaching sessions (Sills 1987, 68). Garden was an uncommon, early example of a "singing actress" in the same sense that Sills later adamantly defined herself. The reception to Garden's 1907 New York *Thaïs* reveals a common theme that ran through the critical reaction to both women's artistry. Garden's critics praised her acting, but they were not entirely receptive to the quality of her voice. In reply to the reviews of her *Thaïs*, Garden was cited in the *New York Herald* as saying:

> I know full well that I have not a great voice, and I do not make any claim to such heights. I am not a Melba or a Calvé and do not expect to be compared with such singers.
>
> My art, on the other hand, is one quite separate from that of other operatic singers, and the success I have won and hope to win is not the success of vocal cords; it is by an art quite different from that of other opera singers. . . . I want to be judged not alone by my singing or my acting or my stage appearance, but by these combined into one art that is entirely different from all the rest. (quoted in Pennino 1989, 63)

Garden's response resonates strongly with Sills's own defense of her approach to opera as drama many years later. Her internship with Garden led Sills to travel to Paris, where Garden suggested she continue her study of contemporary French repertoire with Max de Rieux, artistic director of the Paris Opéra (Sills 1987, 55). In a class with seven other students, Sills furthered her study of *Manon* and *Louise* during the eight-week-long workshop in Paris. She would have at least one more period of intensive study of *Manon* as an apprentice when she spent several weeks under the tutelage of Rosa Ponselle, who hired Sills to perform the role with her Baltimore Civic Opera Company production in April 1953.

Once she returned from France, Sills was eager to take the stage as an opera singer. However, there were no significant opportunities on the immediate horizon. Miss Liebling suggested that she audition for a Charles L. Wagner tour. Wagner tours typically were composed of about seventy performers (including two leading casts and a thirty-piece orchestra) who traveled to as many as sixty cities during nine weeks. In announcing the tour's stop at the nation's capital on an earlier tour, the *Washington Post* reported that under Wagner's system, the group only had one opera in its repertoire. Therefore, the "performance achieves a polish and smoothness not possible in small companies when the repertoire is larger" (December 14, 1949). Wagner contracted Sills for his twelfth-annual tour that took to the road on October 1, 1951. Wagner signed Sills to sing the demanding leading role of Violetta in Verdi's *La Traviata*. Tenor John Alexander, who would become her longtime friend and colleague, played Alfredo.[10] The tour traveled across great swaths of the country from eastern cities and towns such as Syracuse, New York, and Pawtucket, Rhode Island, through the Midwest, and as far west as Denton, Texas. They even wove their way through the Deep South with stops in several Florida cities and small towns in Alabama, Louisiana, and Mississippi.

Désiré Defrère, a stage director for the Metropolitan Opera, acted as the production's artistic director. He coached Sills over the course of the nine weeks in an experience that she found transformative. Defrère taught her acting skills and techniques of stagecraft that she employed for the rest of her career (Sills 1987, 58). These included the power of standing "absolutely still" when she needed to draw the audience's attention to her. He also instilled in her the importance of character analysis and development. From Defrère, she learned that in assuming her character, she must be clear in her own mind about what the character looked like and how old she was. When playing characters based on historical or literary figures, Defrère urged her to research their backgrounds. Sills took this to heart. In her biography of famed bass Samuel Ramey, author Jane Scovell (Sills's acquaintance and neighbor for many years) wrote that in preparing her roles, Sills

> virtually stalked her characters and wound up knowing them perhaps better than they knew themselves. When she was researching Elizabeth I [for Donizetti's *Roberto Devereux*], she read dozens of books on the subject, not just about the Queen, but also about the entire era of English history. She went to London for recording sessions and stepped up her research. She visited museums and galleries and stood for long periods of time in front of paintings and portraits of Elizabeth. She went to the Victoria and Albert Museum to see Elizabeth's death mask, and she visited actual historical sites the Queen was known to have frequented in her lifetime. Sills wanted to form a complete picture in her own mind before she presented her Elizabeth to the public. The result was impressive. She looked and acted just like the Queen. Beverly Sills brought the same intensity of preparation to all her roles . . . that was her way of doing things. (Scovell 2009, 150)

The tour also taught her that she could perform even when physically ill. The original plan for the Wagner tour was for Sills to alternate her performance of Violetta with another soprano. Unfortunately, the other singer became seriously ill and Sills ended up singing fifty-four of the tour's sixty-three shows, even though she herself caught a cold. This was her first experience of performing under less than ideal physical circumstances. During the course of her career there were numerous occasions in which she sang with a cold or laryngitis or even a serious flu, and sometimes worse. Regardless of her circumstance, Sills rarely canceled performances. All in all, Sills surmised that she "learned more about opera during that tour than in any other nine weeks" of her life (1987, 59).

Sills spent the first half of 1952 with sporadic engagements. In September, she went on another Wagner bus and truck tour. This time she was cast as the "docile and passive" Micaëla in Bizet's *Carmen* (McClary 2002, 114). Sills recalled that she was bored to death with the role and learned very little on her second tour (1987, 62).

The New York City Opera Debut and Singing the Spectrum

Sills's first major professional break came when, with Miss Liebling's help, she arranged to audition for the founder and head of the San Francisco Opera, Gaetano Merola, while he was visiting New York. Merola hired her on the spot to perform in the fall 1953 season. At the time, the San Francisco Opera was second in prestige in the United States only to the Met. Sills made her debut as Elena (Helen of Troy) in Boito's *Mefistofele*. Although the role of Elena was not particularly taxing, this was her first experience sharing the stage of a major opera house with several of the world's greatest singers, including Jan Peerce, Licia Albanese, and Nicola Rossi-Lemeni. Merola, who unfortunately passed away before Sills arrived in San Francisco, also signed her to play the fifth maidservant in three performances of Strauss's *Elektra* and two performances as Donna Elvira in Mozart's *Don Giovanni*. The legendary Tulio Serafin was on the conductor's podium as Sills took to the stage as the hot-blooded Elvira, a role that gave Sills far greater opportunity for dramatic involvement than did the rather one-dimensional Helen of Troy. In a turn of bad luck, when the young woman playing the Valkyrie Gerhilde in Wagner's *Die Walküre* canceled, Sills was asked to fill in. In the rush to the stage, no one checked to see if Sills's winged brass helmet fit properly. Near the performance's end, the helmet tumbled off her head; worse yet, she rushed downstage to pick it up. After the performance, Kurt Adler, who was serving as the interim artistic director in the wake of Merola's passing, angrily asked her if she was drunk. Still the headstrong young woman from Brooklyn, she responded by telling Adler to drop dead (Sills 1987, 72). Within three months, the board of the San Francisco Opera named Adler to the post of general director, and Sills was not invited to perform with the company again for eighteen years.

Back in New York, Sills was hired to perform in the new television series *Opera Cameos* on the now long-forgotten DuMont television network.[11] The series of half-hour programs, which ran from November 1953 to January 1955, featured each opera's most famous arias with the show's host filling in the dramatic narrative.

Sills starred in *La Traviata, Tosca, Thaïs,* and *The Pearl Fishers.* So far, only clips from her *Traviata* have surfaced. These provide a rare opportunity to listen to the pristine voice of the young and strikingly beautiful Beverly Sills.

Having garnered fine reviews in the roles of Donna Elvira and Elena in San Francisco, and with the significant exposure that the *Opera Cameos* appearances afforded her (at least in New York and Washington, DC, where DuMont broadcast), Sills and Liebling agreed that it was time for her to audition for the New York City Opera. How could she fail given her recent success at the far more prestigious San Francisco company? But, fail she did—seven times. As Sills tells the story, she did not do well during her first audition in December 1953. She attributed her lack of success with the other six auditions to her comportment. She believed that she should present herself as a serious artist, so for her first seven auditions, she wore subdued clothing and her hair in a bun. Prior to her eighth try in early 1955, she asked the secretary to general director Joseph Rosenstock, the man who had auditioned her, to help her gain insight into why she kept meeting with rejection. Rosenstock's secretary reported that he felt Sills had a "phenomenal voice but no personality" (Sills 1987, 77). Armed with this information, she wore a jumper with no blouse beneath, black mesh stockings, and the highest-heeled shoes she could find. Finally, Sills caught his attention. He signed her to make her company debut as Rosalinde in *Die Fledermaus* in October 1955.

In the period between her first and final New York City Opera auditions, Sills sang four performances of *Aida* in Salt Lake City in July 1954 at the football stadium of Brigham Young University. She would sing the role two more times: once in a concert version in Patterson, New Jersey, in October 1955, and again in a run of performances with the Central City Opera in Colorado in July 1960. After her career took off, she would not have considered singing Aida, which is typically performed by sopranos with much heavier and more forceful voices than hers. In his book *Opera in Central City,* Allen Young commented that this type of miscasting, such as Sills singing Aida, sometimes happens before artists mature as stage performers (1993, 47). She performed several other roles, including Carmen, Mimi, and Tosca, which were certainly not in her *Fach* (voice and role category), in the days before her stardom afforded her the luxury of picking and choosing her repertoire.[12]

Her performances at the Musicarnival in Warrensville Heights outside of Cleveland, Ohio, were among her last appearances as a struggling, but ambitious, young artist. The Musicarnival was the brainchild of John L. Price, who ran the successful tent-theater operation for twenty-two summers beginning in 1954. According to a program from the 1956 season, Price's "gigantic blue big-top theatre" seated up to two thousand audience members in fourteen circular rows of canvas yacht chairs that surrounded the round stage. Broadway musicals such as *Oklahoma* made up the lion's share of Musicarnival's repertoire, although Price experimented for several seasons with introducing his public to opera, always with English-language text. In his second season, he programmed a production of *Rosalinde*, which was a Broadway version of Strauss's *Die Fledermaus.* Price traveled to New York in search of opera singers; Sills answered the audition call. She sang Rosalinde's "Csárdás" as her audition piece. Price remembered: "After three notes we didn't have to hear any more, but we let her sing the whole goddam [*sic*] thing" (Vacha 2004, 46).

From various sources, we know that many essential elements of Sills's artistry were already in place, though not yet fully developed, during her first season with the Musicarnival. Hinting at her seemingly innate ability to integrate physical movement with the musical line, the *Erie Dispatch* reported that as Rosalinde, Sills "reaches for a high D as gracefully as she flicks her fan or raises her champagne glass" (quoted in Vacha 2004, 47). Musicarnival stage director Bill Boehm remarked on Sills's charismatic pull as she instantaneously assumed her character in performance. He mused: "She would come to rehearsals looking like the cleaning lady—very down-to-earth. . . . When she stepped on that stage, she was no cleaning lady—she was radiant, in her beautiful red hair. She was the epitome of elegance" (ibid.).

Following her success as Rosalinde, Price invited Sills back to play the title roles in the next season's productions of Lehár's *The Merry Widow* and Bizet's *Carmen.* During the summer of 1956, Sills gave twenty-eight consecutive performances in leading roles, first in *The Merry Widow* and then as *Carmen.* Of her *Merry Widow,* William F. McDermott of the *Cleveland Plain Dealer* wrote:

> In the course of a long apprenticeship in play reviewing, I have seen many performances of "The Merry Widow," both here and abroad, and I have never encountered a better player in the name part than Beverly Sills in the current Musicarnival production. She has a regal presence, a striking, comely appearance and an easy sureness of technique. . . . But Miss Sills' greatest contribution to the play is her singing voice. It is well-trained, true, supple and filled with a natural melodiousness. You have the impression that she would be equal to more difficult and exacting music. (July 31, 1956)

Carmen, a role typically sung by a mezzo-soprano, was most definitely not in Sills's *Fach.* Nevertheless, hers was a dynamic Carmen. Jack Warfel of the *Cleveland News* remarked on Sills's strong stage presence: "Early in the performance she establishes her importance to the action. When she's not on the stage the audience can feel the letdown" (August 14, 1956). McDermott, writing for the *Cleveland Plain Dealer,* found Sills's acting fell short of other more "impassioned and tumultuous" portrayals of Carmen that he had previously witnessed. What he felt she lacked in acting, she made up for in singing: "Miss Sills has a wonderfully flexible voice, pure, true and warmly musical. . . . She has in her the substance of a great operatic career" (August 14, 1956). The Musicarnival *Carmen* marked a notable moment in Sills's development as an artist because it brought Sills together for the first time with bass-baritone Norman Treigle in the role of Escamillo; Treigle would become one of her most scintillating and important artistic collaborators.

Her next season at the Musicarnival as the lead in Puccini's *Tosca* was not quite as taxing, with only a weeklong performance run. Competing to be heard over the large orchestra is one of the challenges facing singers of Puccini operas. However, the ensemble accompanying Musicarnival performances was a vastly reduced orchestra of rarely more than twenty musicians. This no doubt assisted Sills in reaching beyond the natural limitations of her light, silvery voice. In fairness, it must be noted, though, that a little over a decade later when Sills performed all three roles in Puccini's *Il Trittico,* the in-house recording, which is still in circulation among opera lovers, evidences that she had no trouble being heard over a full orchestra.

In his *Cleveland Plain Dealer* review, Herbert Elwell praises Sills's Tosca on all fronts: the musical, vocal, and dramatic. Importantly, he directly addresses her ability to meet the difficult vocal demands of Puccini's work.

> Special honors rightly went to Beverly Sills, whose portrayal of Floria Tosca had the vitality and artistic stature that one associates only with the finest operatic talent. This stunning auburn-haired young woman has a magnificent soprano of golden texture and rich variety of color.
>
> Ringing out with natural splendor, it was equal in every way to the heavy demands made upon it in this opera, and it was employed not only with fine musical intelligence but with an intense sense of the dramatic.
>
> Her trueness of pitch, her rhythmic awareness, her refinements of shading and general flexibility were as admirable as her projection was authoritative and emotionally moving. Real pathos as well as vocal skill made her "Visse d'arte" [*sic*] an achievement of rare distinction. (June 25, 1957)

In the context of a stage mishap during one of the *Tosca* performances, Sills demonstrated her commitment to sustaining dramatic tension, along with her ability to command the audience's attention, even as things threatened to fall apart. One evening at the climax of Tosca and Scarpia's riveting act 2 scene, disaster struck. As Sills's Tosca sank her knife into the corrupt and lecherous Scarpia, the capsule that was meant to cover his chest in blood misfired, spraying Sills instead. William Chapman, who was playing Scarpia, "collapsed on the stage more in suppressed laughter than in simulated pain" (Vacha 2004, 51). Fissures in the dramatic tension threatened to open as the audience teetered on the verge of laughter. As historian John Vacha reports: "The only one not about to laugh was Sills, who was determined to avoid the disintegration of her carefully sustained characterization" (ibid.). Covered in fake blood and wearing a strapless green evening gown and high heels, Sills recovered the moment by delivering Chapman a swift and solid kick. "Miraculously, that also seemed to quiet the audience, perhaps fearful themselves of the wrath of Tosca's fury" (ibid.).[13]

Sills's last role with the Musicarnival was the lead in Douglas Moore's *The Ballad of Baby Doe* in September 1958. She had already performed this work to critical acclaim in New York with what was by this time her home company, the New York City Opera. The Cleveland-area press raved over not only Sills's performance, but also the opera and production generally; however, the audience dwindled after the opening night. Unfortunately, Price's efforts to bring opera to the masses failed at the box office; he finished out his next eighteen years of Musicarnival seasons offering more popular fare. Price expressed his disappointment over *The Ballad of Baby Doe*'s dismal ticket sales: "It is real Americana, a part of our history, and I presented the finest production of it that has ever been done anywhere. Nobody came. So to hell with the damned peasants! Let them come to see the warmed-over-Broadway slop they seem to like so much!" (Vacha 2004, 54).

With her New York City Opera debut on October 29, 1955, as Rosalinde in Strauss's *Die Fledermaus,* Sills was finally in the company of many of the artists who would be by her side when she reached stardom. Stardom, however, was still eleven years away. The *New York Times* piece "City Opera Signs 10 New Singers, Including Chinese Bass-Baritone" in no way anticipated Sills's future as the company's prima donna (September 20, 1955). Photos of two of the debutants, soprano Jacquelynne Moody and bass-baritone Yi-Kwei Sze, appeared at the top of the article. Only Mr. Sze's background was discussed in any detail. All the other singers garnered no more than a sentence or two. Following her debut performance two days later, the *Times* favorably reported: "Miss Sills acted with complete assurance and with a wicked glint in her eye. She looked the part, and sang it with an attractive voice of good size and supple technique. She even held on to the high D at the end of the 'Czardas,' a note that most sopranos are anxious to embrace as little as possible" (October 31, 1955). Between her debut and her skyrocketing to fame in fall 1966, Sills sang Rosalinde at least nineteen more times with the New York City Opera. More than half of these were on company tours to locations mostly in the Midwest. She also sang three performances of the role with the Cincinnati Opera in the summer of 1967. This work, especially when sung in English as it was in the New York City Opera production, is light for operatic fare and was predictably well received in the hinterlands between major cities. Sills would return to Rosalinde at the very end of her singing career when she no longer had the vocal or physical stamina to perform more dramatically taxing roles to her satisfaction. The less challenging, late-in-the-career, "cream puff" roles, as she termed them, included Rosalinde, Norina in *Don Pasquale,* Rosina in the *Barber of Seville,* and Anna in *The Merry Widow.*

Other roles in her first decade with the New York City Opera included Philine in Thomas's *Mignon,* "Coloratura" in Weisgall's new opera *Six Characters in Search of an Author,* Donna Anna in Mozart's *Don Giovanni,* Marguerite in Gounod's *Faust,* and Violetta in Verdi's *La Traviata.* Philine, though only a secondary character, was very well suited to her vocal talents. Philine's main aria, "Je suis Titania," is a coloratura showpiece. Sills reports that it "lived up to its reputation as a showstopper" when on opening night, she received the first standing ovation of her career (1987, 97). Although the audience was enthralled with her performance, the *New York Times* gave her a rather unremarkable mention: "Beverly Sills was an attractive Philine, turning out a sprightly and secure 'Je suis Titania' with all its florid difficulties" (September 26, 1956). Though she had sung Violetta many times during the Charles Wagner tour and for the *Opera Cameos* program, these were her first Violettas on a New York stage. She only garnered a lukewarm reception from critics. The *New York Times* reported, "Miss Sills did not have nearly enough brilliant assurance for the 'Sempre libre' [*sic*] of the first act" (October 12, 1957). The stars had not yet aligned in a way that allowed Sills to deliver a breakthrough performance. It would take a decade of life-changing events and maturation as a performer before she would develop into the phenomenon that took the opera world and the American public by storm.

Marriage, Children, and Artistic Growth

Part of Sills's maturation process began with her betrothal to Peter B. Greenough. They met in late November 1955 at a party sponsored by the Cleveland Press Club to promote ticket sales for the NYCO tour on which Sills would perform her Rosalinde. According to Sills, she and Peter were struck by love at first sight. They were married a year later, on November 17, 1956, before a small gathering in Miss Liebling's studio in New York. Peter was twelve years her senior. He hailed from a wealthy Boston family, although he had been based in Cleveland since 1940 when he was hired at the *Cleveland Plain Dealer,* which was owned by members of his family. Greenough was an associate editor for the paper at the time of their marriage. Before they met, and throughout their courtship, he was engaged in a bitter divorce and custody battle. The Cleveland press had a heyday reporting on the salacious details of the broken couple's bad history as well as their settlement negotiations. Upon their marriage, Sills became the stepmother to three daughters, the youngest of whom was developmentally disabled and institutionalized. The older girls (aged ten and seven when the divorce was finalized) were traumatized by their parents' split, particularly by their mother's antics surrounding their custody, which included kidnapping them when they were in their father's temporary custody (Sills 1987, 107).[14] Sills's relationship with the two elder girls was fraught from the beginning, a situation that reportedly persisted beyond their father's death nearly fifty years later in 2006.

Following their honeymoon, they moved to Peter's mansion on the outskirts of Cleveland, where Sills met with deep-rooted anti-Semitism, the likes of which she had never experienced. She also faced serious disapproval from members of her own extended family, particularly on her father's side, for having married outside of their faith. Although she had concert engagements in various locations around the country, as well as her *Tosca* performances at the Musicarnival in the summer of 1957, Sills wrote of being very lonely in her midwestern home. As a result of the company's fiscal crisis, the New York City Opera canceled its spring 1957 season, only lengthening the time of her isolation from her New York–based friends, family, and artistic colleagues.

Faced with a serious budget deficit, the NYCO administration found a creative path forward that ended up placing Sills in one of her signature roles. The Ford Foundation granted the company $105,000 in support of a season devoted to American opera. The arrangement was for the NYCO not to commission or debut new works, but to perform operas that had been previously presented either by the NYCO or elsewhere. The goal was to facilitate these works' entry into the standard repertoire. The opera to open the spring 1958 all-American season was *The Ballad of Baby Doe* composed by Douglas Moore with a libretto by John Latouche based on the true story of late nineteenth-century Colorado silver king Horace Tabor and his loyal second wife. Moore was not satisfied with either of the sopranos who performed the title role in the opera's original cast in 1956 at the Central City Opera Festival. He arranged to hold auditions for a new Baby Doe. Moore and Emerson Buckley, who had conducted the premiere in Colorado and would conduct the New York performances, auditioned numerous sopranos before the NYCO's general director Julius Rudel and others coaxed Sills to fly in from Cleveland and give it a try. She was resistant because she had heard that Moore envisioned Baby Doe as a petite, kittenish character. At nearly five feet nine, Sills was certainly not diminutive. As is clear in *Beverly,* she was self-conscious of her size. However, after singing her opening number, the opera's most famous aria "The Willow Song," Moore declared: "Miss Sills, you *are* Baby Doe" (Sills 1987, 122). More than fifty years later when I flipped through her *Baby Doe* score, which had been purchased at auction with her personal scores by the New York Public Library for the Performing Arts, I found a card taped inside from Moore to Sills: "to Beverly whose voice and heart will always remain part of Baby Doe."

The NYCO gave four performances of the work in the spring of 1958.[15] Writing of the April 3 premiere, Howard Taubman gave Sills only a tepid review: "As the loving and loyal Baby Doe, Beverly Sills was attractive; her performance should take on flexibility with further experience in the part" (*New York Times,* April 4, 1958). When they performed the opera again in the fall 1958 season, Taubman assessed Sills more favorably: "Beverly Sills is thoroughly credible as the delicate and faithful Baby Doe, and her singing has refinement and vocal velvet" (*New York Times,* October 10, 1958). In fact, he had high praise for the entire endeavor: "The City Center performance has been shaken down into a most attractive affair. The company is young, spirited and capable of convincing acting and singing. After attending performances in some of the famous theatres in Europe's capitals, one comes back to the City Center with renewed appreciation of all it accomplishes with modest means. This is a more versatile and more satisfying opera house than far more illustrious ones in Europe" (ibid.).

At the close of the spring 1959 NYCO season, the production's primary cast recorded the opera with funding from the Koussevitzky Music Foundation. Because of their limited budget, they recorded the entire opera in only one or two takes. Originally released on the MGM Classics label in 1959, it received a second, far inferior pressing on the ancillary Heliodor label in 1966.[16] Nevertheless, this is the earliest commercial recording of Sills and the last one until the 1967 release of the NYCO's production of Handel's *Giulio Cesare* on the RCA Victor label.[17]

In an introductory essay to the liner notes that accompanied the 1999 Deutsche Grammophon compact-disc release, Sills offered insight into her experiences as Baby Doe. Following the modus operandi that she developed under Désiré Defrère's tutelage, Sills learned everything that she could about the real Elizabeth "Baby Doe" McCourt (1854–1935). She even copied McCourt's hairstyle from photos. Sills gave twenty-eight performances as Baby Doe during the course of her career; Walter Cassel was her Horace Tabor all but three times. She took the stage as Baby Doe for the last time in late December 1969. Thinking back on her experiences, Sills recalled:

> At every performance Walter Cassel, as Horace, made me cry. When Horace was dying he would look up at me and sing "You were always the real thing, Baby" and I would sing, in reply, "Hush, close your eyes. Rest." Then I would take him in my arms and bawl like a baby. It was difficult to do the final aria after that scene. Walter and I lived those roles when we were on stage; there was never a moment during the performances when I didn't believe he was Horace Tabor. And even offstage he never called me Beverly or anything else, just "Baby."
>
> Baby became an integral part of my operatic experience; it was difficult to shake her off even after I left the opera house. (Sills 1999, 9)

Her deep investment in a character, and in the performative moment, became a signature feature of Sills's involvement as a singing actress. The magic that her depth of commitment created is the primary focus of chapter 7.

Sills was seven months pregnant with her first child when she made the Baby Doe recording. Her daughter, Meredith Holden Greenough, known throughout her life affectionately as "Muffy," was born August 4, 1959. She suffered from hyaline membrane disease and yellow jaundice at birth and spent the first several days of her life in an incubator. When Muffy finally came home, she was a happy and apparently resilient baby. A contented Sills commented: "We were now a family in every way" (Sills 1987, 130). Even her rather dismal social life in Cleveland could not dampen Sills's spirits now that she had Muffy. She did not perform for almost six months following Muffy's birth. When she returned for the NYCO's spring 1960 season, she only sang five performances (four of these were as Baby Doe; one was as the character "Coloratura" in Weisgall's new opera *Six Characters in Search of an Author*). She performed her last *Aida* in July at the Central City Opera Festival in Colorado and did her final stint as Tosca in November.

In October 1960, Sills was pregnant for a second time, and the NYCO was in financial trouble again, forcing it to cancel the spring 1961 season. She was on track to stay home with her toddler while awaiting the arrival of her son when, in a family power struggle, Peter was edged out in a competition for the chief editorship of the *Plain Dealer*. The upshot was that he chose to take a position as a financial columnist for the *Boston Globe*. Sills was quite happy to leave Cleveland for their new home in Milton, Massachusetts, on the outskirts of Boston. Between November 1960 and February 1961, she made three concert appearances. The most notable of these was as a soloist with the New York Philharmonic at Carnegie Hall with André Kostelanetz conducting; they would work together numerous times throughout her career.

Sills gave birth to her son Peter Bulkeley Jr., or "Bucky" as the family lovingly called him, on June 29, 1961. Her husband's namesake, the child was the first male born to the Greenough family in nearly five decades. Now the mother of two beautiful children, Sills was on cloud nine (Sills 1976, 91). However, her joy would soon be shattered. As Muffy was approaching her second birthday, she was still not speaking. A hearing test showed that she had profound hearing loss. Sills recalled saying to her husband as they left the doctor's office that the only good news was that this was the worst day of her life. Things could only get better. Sadly, they got worse. Around the same time, they began to worry that something might be wrong with Bucky. The photographer Sills hired to take Bucky's baby pictures found he could not get Bucky to look in the direction of the birdie that he dangled before the child. When Bucky was six months old, their worst suspicions were confirmed; a doctor's examination revealed that Bucky was severely mentally disabled. Two decades later, they learned that Bucky, like his sister, was deaf.

In her two autobiographies, and in countless interviews and articles, Sills points to the pain she felt for her children's disabilities as fundamentally transforming her attitude toward performance. From the time Muffy was born in August 1959 through her second birthday, Sills rarely performed; she was content to stay home with her family. Several years later, she admitted that her divided attention during those years threatened to derail her career (Saal 1967a, 58). From July 1959 through February 1962, she worked with the New York City Opera just five times. She only returned to performing regularly after discovering her children's disabilities. Her first engagement was with Sarah Caldwell who invited her to perform *Manon* with her recently founded Boston Opera Group in late winter 1962 along with John Alexander and Norman Treigle. In *Beverly*, Sills recalled how performance became a haven from her new, painful reality:

> I had a curious reaction to my return to opera. I loved to sing, and the best part of opera for me had always been the learning and rehearsing. Performing had been a sheer pleasure for me, as well, but it didn't feel that way when I sang *Manon*. In fact, after I learned about the kids' problems, I never felt such a pure excitement again. I enjoyed *Manon* for a different reason: For three hours a night I forgot about my own troubles and concentrated on hers. It was a great source of escape—that's what opera became for me. I couldn't wait to get to the theater and become somebody else. (1987, 144)

Using the stage as a retreat had a freeing and intensifying effect on Sills's performance. *Opera News* reported that many "believed that the tragedies of her children had tempered both voice and person in the forge of life, freeing her as an interpreter. She was revealed more sharply than ever as an actress as well as a singer" (Bowers 1970, 20). As Sills recalled in her interview with *Newsweek* critic Hubert Saal: "I was always a good singer . . . but I was a combination of everyone else's ideas, the director, the conductor, the tenor. After I came back, I talked back. I stopped caring what anybody else thought. At first it was a destructive attitude. I was so full of self-pity that I used to walk down the street and ask myself who in those crowds had suffered as much as I?" (1969, 75). Saal conjectured: "Once she rid herself of the bitterness, she was freed." Sills continued: "I felt if I could survive my grief, I could survive anything. Onstage I was uninhibited and I began to have a good time. Once my voice was free, I was free to use my hands and my body" (ibid.).

Furthermore, the nature of her interaction with her fellow performers changed. Sills believed that her experiences with her children turned her into a more compassionate person. She began to listen to people who were performing with her in a way that she had not previously (Barthel 1975, 64). In his extended profile essay on Sills published in the *New Yorker* in 1971, Winthrop Sargeant articulated best how this transformation brought a deeper poignancy to Sills's performance and cleared the way for her to communicate emotion with uncommon intensity and directness to her listeners:

> The tragedy had given her a new self-assurance. Having tasted the worst, she no longer had the slightest doubt of her ability to weather the ups and downs of her career. Not only was there an added degree of self-assurance; there was a new emotional depth to her operatic characterizations—a new tenderness, a new willingness to communicate her personal sorrows to audiences, even though she was doing it indirectly, by way of a tragic character. It was at this time, in fact, that the mature diva Beverly Sills began to make a profound impression on critics and on the public. (1971, 56)

A number of key moments and experiences central to her continuing development as a singing actress occurred in the period between her return to the stage in the winter of 1962 and her breakthrough performance of Cleopatra in Handel's *Giulio Cesare* in the fall of 1966. Perhaps one of the most unexpected came in a single performance as Charpentier's *Louise* with the NYCO in October 1962. The basic story of *Louise* is simple, although the opera was somewhat revolutionary at the time of its premiere in 1900 partly due to its portrayal of working-class life. As Tim Ashley writes, *Louise* is a "proletarian, anarchic hymn to erotic fulfillment" (1999, 73). In short, Louise is a seamstress from a working-class family who is courted by a romantic poet. Over her parents' strong objections, she runs off to Paris to be with him. Meanwhile, her father falls ill. She returns to her parents' home, but is drawn back to her lover once her father regains his health. In an emotional conclusion to the opera, her distraught father curses Paris as she makes her escape. Norman Treigle, who was one of the finest thespians of his generation of operatic singers, played the father to Sills's Louise. Tenor John Alexander played her lover and Jean Morel, whom she adored, conducted. According to Sills, the chemistry between this quartet of players was remarkable: "We all performed at the very peak of our abilities, and meshed so well that the audience probably thought we'd been singing *Louise* together for years" (1987, 145).

Of particular importance, this would be the first of many times when Sills and Treigle would enter deeply together into the drama; for them, the performance became their only reality. Sills recalled that in the final act, when Louise decides to forsake her father,

> Treigle, caught up in the father's role, got so furious with me that he picked up a chair and threw it at me. I ducked (the chair hit the scenery) and then ran off the stage with Treigle sobbing out after me at the top of his voice: "Louise,

Louise." When it was over, we were both crying. Jean Morel, the conductor, put his arms around us both, kissed us, and we three walked out on stage to take our bows, bawling our heads off. . . .

That night, in his hotel room, Norman wrote me a "Dear Bev" love letter: ". . . Watching you and hearing you just now in the aria and duet filled me with such beauty, admiration and emotion that I could hardly stand it. There are only a few people who have ever made me feel this way on stage and you are one who is on top of them all." (Sills 1976, 94)

In both Sills's and Treigle's reflection on their performance, we see several of the telltale signs of "flow" as it has been described and theorized by psychologist Mihaly Csikszentmihalyi. Persons in flow become one with the activity; their actions flow as if they are automatic (Csikszentmihalyi 1990; Jackson 1992). With this single performance of *Louise,* Sills and Treigle entered together deeply into the flow state for the first of many times. A further exploration of flow as it pertains to Sills in performance is central to the discussion in chapter 7.

Although Miss Liebling is credited with training Sills's voice impeccably and imparting to her an uncommonly solid musicianship, Sills made her most profound growth as an actress when working with gifted directors and partnering with outstanding singing actors. In interviews for this book with Sills's former colleagues, three roles are frequently cited as being vehicles through which she took her greatest strides as a singing actress in the years between her return to the stage and her breakthrough Cleopatra. These are as Donna Anna in Mozart's *Don Giovanni,* Marguerite in Gounod's *Faust,* and all three heroines in Offenbach's *The Tales of Hoffmann.* Notably, Norman Treigle, who was by this time Sills's dear friend, played a vital role in the key productions of these works.

Throughout the 1960s and '70s, the NYCO employed some of the most innovative stage directors working in opera. Their productions were regularly more dramatically daring than those of the Metropolitan Opera, and the NYCO singers were typically more invested in acting than many of those on the stage across the Lincoln Center plaza. Thinking back on Sills's development as an actress, Julius Rudel recalled: "When she first came to us, her voice was crystal, crystalline, and beautiful and true, and she had incredible technique in terms of flexibility and so on. Dramatically, she was a little bit removed. I describe it as [though] she almost stood beside herself and watched herself perform. [She] was amused at it in a way; bemused at it, perhaps, is more accurate. And it was only when she expanded her repertory that she became dramatically more involved" (Rudel interview, October 6, 2009).

In Rudel's estimation, her first major expansion as an actress came in the role of Donna Anna in a production of *Don Giovanni* in fall 1963. Rudel hired William Ball, a stage director best known for having founded the American Conservatory

Theater, to devise and direct the production. Rudel opined that Ball "had a lot to do with opening up the dramatic door for her" (ibid.). Her first performances in the production took place outside of New York City when the company toured to Ann Arbor, Michigan, and upstate New York. When she finally performed Donna Anna in New York in the fall of 1964 it was with Norman Treigle in the title role. Rudel recalled that when they toured in August 1965 to Palo Alto, California, their performance became "a little legend." When Rudel returned to the Bay Area in 1980, people still came up to him and remarked about their Palo Alto *Don Giovanni*. Writing for the *San Francisco Examiner,* Charles Boone's review of the storied performance opened: "Fabulous is the only word which can describe the production of 'Don Giovanni' given at Stanford Saturday afternoon by the New York City Opera. . . . [T]he company again proved that it knows how to achieve an extremely high standard of excellence in all aspects of opera production" (August 10, 1965). Of Sills, Boone wrote, "Beverly Sills, as Donna Anna, made a beautiful contribution through her warm, supple, velvety voice. She and John McCollum, in his role as Don Ottavio, brought the house down with their arias in front of the statue of the Commandant. Her showing as Constanza in Wednesday's 'Abduction from the Seraglio' was a big success, but this rendition of Donna Anna was a real triumph" (ibid.).

Marguerite in Gounod's *Faust* was another role that became an important vehicle for Sills's growth as a thespian. In each of these three examples, Norman Treigle was an important collaborator as she explored the possibilities presented by her character. Her first performance as Marguerite took place in February 1963 with the Boston Opera Group under the artistic direction of Sarah Caldwell. The *Boston Traveler* piece, headlined "Sarah Scores, Sills Thrills," notes that not only was Sills's voice a "lovely one, rich with emotion, but she is an appealing actress" as well (February 16, 1963).

Paul St. George, writing for the *Boston Pilot,* captures the sense that Sills is already in the space where she takes the stage as an escape from her own personal reality: "In her every gesture, attitude and expression she loses herself in the part and plays not a simpering-ingenue-Marguerite but a very real and womanly woman who is nonetheless all young innocence" (February 18, 1963).

Interestingly, Frederick H. Guidry of the *Boston Monitor* also commented on Sills's physical gestures and her ability to capture the audience's attention with subtleties and near silences: "Miss Sills has a pleasant facility with French and an actress's instinctive knowledge of the dramatic power of economical and smooth movement and gesture. Although her 'Jewel Song' won expected enthusiastic applause, the higher audience tribute came in moments of intensely respectful silence during her softest passages. Her command of the stage—as in prayerful murmurings in prison—exceeded what the music itself arranges" (February 17, 1963).

Sills did one performance of *Faust* with the NYCO in November 1964 before the production went on a brief midwestern tour later in the month. When the show opened again in New York in fall 1965, Winthrop Sargeant remarked on Sills's artistic growth during the previous five years:

> I was astonished at the progress she has made since the first time she appeared, as the heroine of "The Ballad of Baby Doe." Miss Sills is now a *spinto* soprano of quite respectable accomplishments. She has always been very pretty to look at, but the other night she was much more than that. Her intonation was impeccable, her French diction excellent, she succeeded in starting her "Jewel Song" with a closer than commonly heard approximation of a real trill, and the role's coloratura passages held no terrors for her. Beyond all of this, she acted the part with the assurance and the feminine warmth that only first-rank divas bring to it. (Sargeant 1965a, 199)

Sargeant also commented that the NYCO production was "far preferable to the pretentious hodgepodge at the Metropolitan" (ibid.) and that Norman Treigle was "one of the greatest of Mephistos" (ibid., 200). Sills and Treigle performed *Faust* together in several other productions over the next few years with the most significant being Frank Corsaro's major rethinking of the work for the NYCO in 1968.

Partnering with the Capobiancos

Sills worked in more productions devised and directed by Tito Capobianco than any other director. Their first meeting took place in Cincinnati while working on Capobianco's new *The Tales of Hoffmann* production. Prior to Cincinnati, Sills first performed the opera with Treigle in New Orleans in February 1964. As she always did, even in her first engagement in the opera, she played all three heroines (Olympia, Giulietta, and Antonia). She performed *Hoffmann* again in a concert version at the Grant Park Band Shell in Chicago in August 1964 with Julius Rudel conducting, John Alexander as Hoffmann, and once again with Norman Treigle in all four manifestations of evil (Lindorf, Coppélius, Dapertutto, and Dr. Miracle). She had one more *Hoffmann* experience in Boston in March 1965 with Sarah Caldwell directing before she went to Cincinnati to work with Tito Capobianco.

Norman Treigle was responsible for Sills being part of the July 1965 Cincinnati Opera production of *Hoffmann*.[18] When Capobianco invited Treigle to perform the four demonic roles, Treigle urged him to hire Sills to sing the three lead soprano roles. Capobianco agreed sight unseen. Sills's first meeting with Tito and his wife Elena Denda "Gigi" was disastrous; from there, things only got worse. Apparently, when Sills walked into the first rehearsal, "Tito's face fell" (Sills 1976, 102). He and Gigi began gesticulating wildly to one another; Gigi kept staring at Sills, who wondered how she could have offended them. After the rehearsal,

Gigi explained that, in forming his conception of the opera, Tito had imagined a petite coloratura playing the part of the mechanical doll Olympia.

As they developed her Olympia, things became so heated that Sills stormed out of a rehearsal. Gigi, always the diplomat, found her sitting beside their hotel pool holding Bucky. In a July 2007 interview with the Capobiancos in their Lutz, Florida, home, Gigi recalled their conversation regarding the dance movements she and Tito had devised for Sills to perform:

> "Miss Sills, if you cannot do that, we will change it. Nothing is written in blood."
>
> She said, "Well, I could do that."
>
> I said, "And then what's the problem? Why don't you try? If you don't want to do it with people in rehearsal, we do it with you alone. You don't have to worry about that."
>
> [Sills said,] "But I never did those things."
>
> I said, "Well, try. Try, try." So it was [like] pulling teeth, she came back, and we started to do the doll, which was the most difficult one because everything was like this: [Gigi gestured mechanically]. She had to coordinate that with all the things. And, just like that—she picked it up.
>
> And then, second act, she said, "Oh, that too, I have to do all those things?" . . . Norman kept saying, "Shh, shh, Beverly. Trust him, trust him. I did the same thing in Mexico, and he was right. Trust him." (Capobianco interview, July 28, 2010)

Gigi explained how she created Sills's makeup for the Olympia role. She made eyelashes from the colorful cellophane ends of hors d'oeuvres toothpicks. They clicked when she blinked. Gigi also had Sills wear red round pasties on her cheeks. Thinking over the entire experience, Gigi said: "So we had a ball with that. But after that, she never complained about anything. And she had a ball. And, she had an ovation" (ibid.).

Sills also commented on her struggle to come to terms with the Capobiancos' conception of Olympia. She said: "I was all apprehension and reluctance" (1987, 156). They continued to push her. When they came to the courtesan role of Giulietta, they asked her to wear a long skirt slit nearly up to her panties with a top cut practically to her navel. In addition to the costume, the movements they developed also filled her with dread, but as she said, she did them, "and they worked" (ibid., 157). When asked if they had first worked with Sills on a different opera whether they would have met with such a fiery clash of wills at the onset, Tito and Gigi were convinced that it would have been the same. To illustrate his point, Tito pulled out a black-and-white photo of Sills as Violetta before they met (photo section page 1). She was stunningly beautiful, but she presented an air of a certain impenetrable distance. Then Tito showed another photo of Sills after they began their fifteen-year-long artistic collaboration. Shots of Sills in performance from the period following her partnership with the Capobiancos often capture an intense, dramatic engagement. The difference was striking. When they first began to work with her, Tito and Gigi saw potential for tremendous emotional and artistic expression in Sills, but she needed direction and hard work to bring it forth. Sills's experience working with the Capobiancos on *Hoffmann* provided her with significant artistic growth. In pushing her beyond her comfort zone, it seems they helped free her to give completely of herself in performance.

Sills and Treigle recognized that Capobianco's *Hoffmann* production was sensational and wanted to bring it to the New York City Opera right away. They convinced Julius Rudel, and he programmed it for October 1965, less than three months after the Cincinnati performance run finished. This work became Tito and Gigi Capobianco's NYCO debut. Harold Schonberg termed the show "imaginative, fantastic (in the sense of fantasy), [and] brilliantly produced." He concluded: "As done by the New York City Opera, it is by far one of the best shows in town. . . . The audience last night responded with enormous enthusiasm" (*New York Times*, October 15, 1965). While the *New Yorker*'s Winthrop Sargeant was less enthusiastic about the production, he noted Sills's emerging gifts as a total performer: "Beverly Sills, whose talents I still don't seem to have completely fathomed, undertook all three female roles—a feat not often attempted—and, though her voice is a little light for Act II, did them in a memorable manner (her coloratura in Act I was particularly impressive, and she has a real trill, not a mere approximation of one)" (1965b, 152).

A few days after the second New York performance of the Capobianco production, Gigi penned a letter to Sills in which she thanked her for making Tito's artistic vision a reality. She opened her letter: "How we need you! And Norman! Oh God! . . . My husband has been more than lucky in finding artists like you and Norman to prove *his* talent. Not all the directors get *that* chance."[19] Thus, a scintillating and mutually beneficial collaboration was formed. In her first autobiography, Sills noted that Tito Capobianco staged all of her major triumphs and that she worked with the Capobiancos "better than with any other director and assistant" (1976, 104).

Although opera singers today are under a great deal of pressure to be conventionally beautiful (that is, thin and toned) and to have a dynamic dramatic presence on stage, this is a relatively recent development.[20] No doubt the increasing popularity of video recordings and television broadcasts in the 1980s, and the Metropolitan Opera's high-definition live broadcasts into movie theaters beginning in December 2006, have contributed to the rise of the demand for this physical and theatrical aesthetic. These standards for physical beauty and realistic acting were not the norm during Sills's career. The "park and bark" style of performance was still common.[21] Sills's collaborations with innovative directors such as Tito Capobianco and Frank Corsaro, and the entire NYCO creative team, were groundbreaking. Certainly this was a significant factor contributing to Sills's popularity. She did things that most divas were not physically willing or capable of doing. Legendary bass Samuel Ramey contextualized this well:

> She was such a magnetic performer and was one of the few at that time. Of course, this was a characteristic of the New York City Opera. They were presenting opera as drama. The emphasis on acting in opera was placed very high at the New York City Opera. The productions were always geared that way; the directors wanted the singers to act. It was not a stand-and-sing opera company. That's what always impressed me with Beverly. She was such a total performer. She would sacrifice the sound of the voice for the necessary dramatic effect. She wasn't about just making beautiful sounds. That's where I think, at that time, she was really unique. (Ramey interview, June 18, 2012)

In the company of Treigle and the Capobiancos, and with the support of Rudel, Sills was now on her way to becoming one of the finest singing actresses of her generation. In his 1973 book, *Divas,* Winthrop Sargeant went so far as to say: "Miss Sills is, in my opinion, the greatest actress currently on the operatic stage; in fact, I would go further and say that she is a greater actress than even the fabled Maria Callas" (1973, 78). He continued: "Miss Sills is that rarity, an intellectual singer. She approaches her work with a thorough grasp of historical subject matter and a clear idea of exactly what she is going to do on the stage. She can move an audience to tears with no apparent effort at all, and bring it back to laughter in the same way" (ibid.).

CHAPTER 3

From Breakthrough to Stardom

Everything would change for Beverly Sills when the New York City Opera opened the fall 1966 season in its new Lincoln Center home with Handel's *Giulio Cesare.* Sills sang the glamorous role of Cleopatra with its fiendishly difficult filigree; her close friend and scintillating stage partner Norman Treigle played the Roman emperor. *Time* listed Sills's performance in this opera as one of ten "Top of the Decade" events in classical music in its December 26, 1969, issue.

The close-knit members of the NYCO were energized by their recent move from the cramped stage and cavernous auditorium of their former home in the City Center's Moorish temple on Fifty-Fifth Street. The company had made its New York State Theater debut in February 1966 with the North American premiere of Ginastera's *Don Rodrigo* starring Plácido Domingo as Rodrigo in a Capobianco production. In fact, they devoted their entire first season in the new venue to the performance of twentieth-century operas, including *The Ballad of Baby Doe* with Sills in the title role, Weill's *Street Scene,* and Menotti's *The Consul.*

As Julius Rudel pondered how to kick off the fall 1966 season, which would come less than two weeks after the gala opening of the new home of the Metropolitan Opera just across the Lincoln Center Plaza, he aimed to stage something unique. With *Giulio Cesare,* Rudel turned the company's innovative spirit in an entirely new direction. Staging a baroque opera was revolutionary for a professional American opera company in the mid-1960s. The Met, for example, did not take on a Handel opera until 1984 with its production of *Rinaldo*; it did not mount *Giulio Cesare* until 1988.[1] Rudel's inspiration came in part when he heard

Norman Treigle sing several Handel arias. He saw the opera as an opportunity to showcase the NYCO's star bass-baritone—whose most profound successes had been mainly as dark or evil characters—in a heroic title role.

Members of opera's inner circle and well-informed fans know something of how Sills came to be cast as Cleopatra. As Sills told it, she was furious when she learned that Julius Rudel had invited Phyllis Curtin to sing the role of the Egyptian queen. Curtin joined the NYCO in 1953, but had left the company at the end of the 1959–60 season for engagements with the Metropolitan Opera, the Vienna State Opera, and other prestigious venues. Sills claimed she felt that by bringing someone in from the Met to sing this sensational role on such an important occasion was essentially making the statement that none of the company's own sopranos were capable of tackling Cleopatra. She threatened Rudel with her resignation. According to Sills, she told Rudel that if he did not give her the part, her wealthy husband would rent out Carnegie Hall where she would give a recital featuring all of Cleopatra's arias. She would make Rudel "look sick" (Sills 1987, 161).

Rudel recalls their encounter rather differently. As he remembers it, Sills and he had a polite breakfast at his home during which they discussed the Cleopatra situation. Sills stated that she had looked over the part and found that it suited *her* voice perfectly. She did not threaten to rent out Carnegie Hall; instead, she said she would go home to her family in Boston and not return, even though she was already scheduled to do four central roles during the fall season (Williams 1991, 32). Although Sills portrays herself as angry and forceful during their meeting, Rudel recalls it "was all very friendly. Her approach always was one with a smile."

What exactly transpired between these two dynamic artists will forever remain a Rashomon-esque mystery. The result, however, was that Rudel halted negotiations with Phyllis Curtin and withdrew his offer.[2] Sills sang the part and skyrocketed to fame as a result. The coloratura tour de force of Cleopatra did indeed fit her voice perfectly. Outside of her performance of Philine in Thomas's *Mignon* ten years previously, Sills had never been given the opportunity with the NYCO to sing a role that demonstrated her unparalleled strengths as what *Time* later proclaimed to be "the fastest voice alive" (1971, 74).

The summer before the opening, Sills had only a few performing obligations. Her focus was on preparing her Cleopatra. She invited Julius Rudel and his family to the Greenoughs' home on Martha's Vineyard where the two of them spent the mornings shaping her part. According to Rudel, he spent the first hour of the mornings alone working out "ornamentations and coloratura stuff for her" (Williams 1991, 33). She would join him and together they would refine her musical lines. Rudel mentioned in our interview that in some cases, he simply mailed the parts out to the singers involved in the production. When there were dual cadenzas, for example, the two singers' parts needed to be carefully coordinated. He said that the whole creative process brought him a great deal of personal satisfaction and joy (interview, October 6, 2009). The question remains, however, of how much of the Cleopatra ornamentation was authored by Rudel and how much by Sills's vocal coach Roland Gagnon. In *Beverly*, Sills attributes Gagnon with its authorship. Taking a rather defensive posture (or at least an emphatic position), she writes: "Roland wrote all the ornamentation for everything I sang from the moment we began working together in 1962. . . . When Julius and I started working on *Julius Caesar* the summer before its premiere, Roland taught me how to sing Cleopatra. He wrote all the ornamentation and showed me how to throw myself into a role musically, to convey as much dramatic intensity with my voice as I did with my body" (Sills 1987, 163).

Again, Sills's and Rudel's memories diverge rather significantly. As something of an objective observer, Charles Wendelken-Wilson, assistant conductor of the NYCO at the time of the *Giulio Cesare* premiere, explained in an interview that he believed Julius Rudel wrote some of the roulades and the decorations, but that the rest were probably Gagnon's work (Wendelken-Wilson interview, August 1, 2008).

The production was devised and directed by Tito Capobianco. As was so often the case, Tito's project became the joint passion of both Tito and Gigi. With no practice of staging baroque opera in New York, and virtually none in the United States, they were free to conceive of the work in completely new terms. They worked together researching baroque performance practice; in the end, they conceived of their production in balletic terms. Every movement would be graceful and beautiful. To this end, Gigi, who had been a prima ballerina in her native Argentina, held dance rehearsals with the cast every day.[3] It is important to note that one of the unique strengths of the Capobiancos as a creative team was their attention to the body and to the singers' dance-acting movements. There is no tradition of training singers' bodies in Western opera as there is in other great musical-theater traditions such as Peking opera or Kabuki. It was the Capobiancos' intensive focus on the body as it moves and as a key element of the singers' expressive tools that helped shape Sills into the one of the most riveting and powerful singing actresses of her generation.

Under Gigi's tutelage, the *Giulio Cesare* cast members donned tights (except for Sills, who refused, joking that Dominic Cossa had better legs than she did) and worked at the barre. As Cossa recalled, "*All* of the show was choreographed. Everything had to be timed. And so it was a thing of beauty. Everything, even the fight scenes, was done in such a way that it was beautiful" (Cossa interview, December 3, 2010). The set as designed by Ming Cho Lee was very simple, basically taking the form of an *X* with staircases up each side with several platforms, including one separating the intersecting point of the two sides of the *X* shape.

Action was staged on the staircases, platforms, and the large open space beneath and in front of the X. Different backdrops and scrims served as changes in scenery. Against this sparse setting, the elegant costumes designed by José Varona "shone like jewels," wrote Winthrop Sargeant of the *New Yorker*. Sargeant went on to comment that the total effect of all of these elements "constituted the finest staging of its sort that I have ever witnessed in any opera house" (1966a, 119).

Opening night remains a clear memory for many interviewed for this book. Silence—the audience's rapt attention—represents one of the most profound impressions these artists immediately recall of the evening. Spiro Malas, who performed the role of Ptolemy, mused: "Beverly had those magic arias that she could just ... you could hear a pin drop. It was incredible" (S. Malas interview, October 9, 2009). Both Spiro Malas and Dominic Cossa mentioned watching and listening to Sills from the wings. Cossa told of being especially moved by her "Piangero la sorte mia"; he reminisced that often when she sang this heartbreaking aria, and not just on opening night, people in the wings would stop and listen—some would tear up (Cossa interview, December 3, 2010).

Sharing her own recollection of opening night, Sills reflected on her singing of Cleopatra's other poignant aria, "Se pietà di me non senti," which comes near the end as Cleopatra laments that she is ready to die if heaven does not take pity and allow her to be with Caesar. When she began to sing, "an absolute hush came over the audience. People were hanging on every note" (Sills 1987, 166). She glanced into the wings when she finished and saw Gigi weeping. The audience remained absolutely still as the curtain came down; suddenly it broke into a roar of applause. Sills mused that this was the "single most extraordinary piece of singing" that she had ever done (ibid.). Breath—both Sills's as she sang and the audience's as they held theirs—is key to how this evening is remembered. The memory is a thoroughly embodied one. Sills aimed to sing as though she had no need to breathe. Listeners recall the sensation of being breathless as she sang.

In developing her musical characterization of Cleopatra, Sills chose to sing these two melancholic arias using a style and technique called *fil di voce* (thread of voice), which New York–based voice teacher and Sills aficionado Gerald Martin Moore says is "most often used in high-lying passages to depict a fragile pianissimo" (e-mail, January 21, 2013). Sills explained: "It was a risky thing to do, because you have to sing very high and very soft for a very long period of time, which takes a lot of breath control and tremendous technique. You have to sing that aria as if you're not breathing; the audience must *never* be aware that you're actually taking time out to breathe" (1987, 166). In the opinion of Moore, *fil di voce* should be used emotionally, never for purely virtuosic show. For him, Sills's "ability to float that head voice sound with such emotional intensity" was the single most extraordinary feature of her singing (although he feels that her astonishing agility in coloratura runs a close second) (e-mail, February 14, 2013).[4] As chapter 9 details, Sills's ability to communicate great depth of feeling through her voice was one of the characteristics of her artistry most cherished by her admirers. The Cleopatra role provided Sills with a vehicle to display both her fast, fluid, and precise coloratura as well as her ability to spin high and delicate pianissimo phrases of tremendous pathos.

Writing for *Newsweek,* Hubert Saal recognized the magnitude of what unfolded the evening of the premiere. Saal observed: "The tall 37-year-old soprano had one of those nights singers dream of. She breathed the spirit of the baroque while developing her Cleopatra from a shallow girl into a queen in love. Her sparkling coloratura voice negotiated every trill and tremolo with ease, clarity and melting beauty. Her every entrance sparked a stir of excitement in the audience as she built, aria by aria, her own pyramid of Cleopatra" (1966, 100).

In his *New York Times* review, Harold Schonberg wrote that the cast "rose nobly to the occasion," but for Sills, the evening was a personal triumph. "She not only could turn a neat trill and handle most of the coloratura, but in addition she sang with melting tone and complete artistry. Coloring her phrases, occasionally using a haunting pianissimo, she sang the words and outlined the melodies with meaning. She always has been an attractive singer, but last night she added quite a new dimension to her work" (September 28, 1966).

Of the opening night, Gigi recalled that choreographer George Balanchine and actor Peter Ustinov both came backstage after the final curtain call. Balanchine said, "This is a dream." That was precisely the reaction the Capobiancos, Tito and Gigi, were seeking in crafting the production; they aimed to transport the audience to a different world—and they succeeded. On an emotional high after the performance, Gigi said that they needed a full two hours to return to reality. The Capobiancos, Sills and her husband, and the Treigles went together to a nearby diner where they waited until four o'clock in the morning for the *New York Times* review to appear on newsstands. During our interview in 2010, Tito spontaneously remembered the essence of the last line of Harold Schonberg's glowing *New York Times* review: "What a stunning, creative production . . ." Schonberg also commented on the magical atmosphere: "It did not take long for the music and the production to exert a spell. By the time the first act was over, waves of love were washing out from the audience to the stage" (September 28, 1966).

Most reviewers were wildly enthusiastic about the opera's music, Rudel's interpretation, and the singers' execution of it. Schonberg wrote: "And the music! It was sturdy, masculine, sometimes even actually sensuous (and sensuosity is not a quality normally associated with baroque music)" (ibid.). Recognizing the challenges of presenting an unfamiliar work from a distant period in operatic history, Schonberg explained that any Handel opera "needs adaptation" given that instruments, pitch, and performance practices had changed dramatically since Handel's day. He noted that Rudel arranged the score, and cut some material while adding excerpts from other Handel operas, which was, of course, normal practice in Handel's day. Winthrop Sargeant credited Rudel with conducting the opera with "masterly understanding" (1966a, 119).

Exhibiting how little was understood of Handelian performance practice in 1966 New York, Sargeant also wrote that "traditional vocal ornamentation of Handel's day [were] scrupulously observed" (ibid.). In fact, very little scholarly research had been done on Handel opera or baroque opera seria generally at the time of the New York City Opera performance of *Giulio Cesare*. There had certainly been no continuous performance practice. *Giulio Cesare* was very popular at the time of its premiere in 1724, and it received several revivals shortly thereafter, but it was not performed for 185 years following its last performance during Handel's lifetime in 1737. In fact, between 1754 and 1920, not a single Handel opera was staged anywhere in the world. In the 1920s, a revival of interest was sparked initially in Germany. His operas were brought back to the stage in forms that Handel would probably have found perplexing. For example, squeamish about heroes singing in alto and soprano ranges, early twentieth-century revivalists typically transposed down an octave into the bass-baritone range male roles that Handel had originally written for castrati or female singers (as was Treigle's Julius Caesar and Tolomeo's and Nireno's parts in the NYCO production).[5] One of the earliest prolific Handel opera scholars, Winton Dean, opined that the early twentieth-century revivals were "grievously distorted on every level by cuts, insertions, transpositions and reorchestration, in a misguided attempt to bring them into conformity with later operatic practice" (Dean 1988). Dean termed the NYCO's handling of *Giulio Cesare* a "travesty," citing the shifting of Cleopatra's "Piangero" to the first scene of act 1 as one of the most egregious offenses (Dean and Knapp 1987, 526). And yet, Sills's performance of the aria, regardless of its placement in the drama, or her singing of what decades later would be judged anachronistic ornamentation, had a tremendously positive affect on her audience—it took away their collective breath. Dean's position was "profoundly modernist," an ideological position that musicologist Richard Taruskin identifies as decreeing "that the work of art is not to be described or valued for its effects (e.g., on an audience) or its human interest (e.g., with respect to its creator), but strictly on its own formal, quasi-mechanistic or quasi-organic terms" (1984, 7). In his essay that accompanied the LP release of the production, Rudel stressed that in crafting the production and its music, they "sought authenticity . . . in the spirit and intent rather than in literalness. We have, as I believe Handel would have wanted, performed his *Julius Caesar* for your enjoyment rather than for your reverence." This would not be the last time Sills performed an edition of an opera that electrified her audience while at the same time drawing the disdain of positivistic musicologists.

With this single stunning performance, Sills established herself as the reigning prima donna of the New York City Opera, a title she would hold until her retirement from singing fourteen years later. Her success drew the notice of opera company administrators and concert programmers everywhere. Invitations poured in from around the country and the world. Meanwhile she finished out the NYCO's fall 1966 season with three more performances of *Giulio Cesare,* roles in three different Mozart operas (Donna Anna in *Don Giovanni,* Constanza in *The Abduction from the Seraglio,* and *The Magic Flute*'s Queen of the Night), as well as two performances of all three heroines in *The Tales of Hoffmann.*

Sills's performance schedule in the fall 1966 season illustrates the repertory nature of the NYCO. Writing in late October 1966, Winthrop Sargeant observed that the NYCO could no longer be considered inferior to the Metropolitan Opera. He noted that in the past, critics sometimes gave the NYCO a sympathetic pass if a production failed or a singer was weak since the company was working with a small fraction of the financial resources of the Met. However, with the move to Lincoln Center, the NYCO was capable of outshining the Met in certain respects. Sargeant observed that the Met's strength was in presenting standard repertoire generally well sung by visiting international singers. The NYCO's main strength was in presenting "productions in which a risk has been taken to present something very special." The repertory nature of the company offered its audience the opportunity to witness the same team members singing in all kinds of operas. He noted: "You grow fond of singers like Beverly Sills and Norman Treigle (who would stand at the top in any institution) and you are curious to see how they will cope with one role or another. This company is a true repertory outfit. Its audience is well acquainted with its principal singers; it loves them, in fact" (Sargeant 1966b, 237).

Suor Angelica: Life and Art Intersect

Following the close of NYCO's fall 1966 season, Sills did three more performances as the Queen of the Night in Houston, followed by a concert in Fort Lauderdale and three performances of *The Tales of Hoffmann* with the Baltimore Civic Opera Company. She had a light schedule with the NYCO during its spring 1967 season, largely a result of her overseas appearances. She did two matinees of *The Abduction from the Seraglio,* but then took on all three leading female roles in Puccini's *Il Trittico.* She had never before performed any of these roles. For one singer to sing them all is rare. Typically, Giorgetta in *Tabarro* is sung by a dramatic soprano, *Suor Angelica* by a lyric soprano, and *Gianni Schicchi*'s Lauretta is usually taken by a light soprano. As Sills's career continued to develop, she often chose her roles because of the dramatic challenges that they presented, not because they perfectly fit her natural vocal talents. *High Fidelity* quoted her as saying: "My voice . . . is a coloratura, but my soul is that of a dramatic soprano" (Gelatt 1969, 27).

Although she learned the roles in all three of the short operas, her performance of them on the evening of March 8, 1967, would be her last. That night art mirrored life with an unbearable likeness and Sills could not face the role of Suor Angelica again. *Suor Angelica* is the story of a young noblewoman sent to a convent as punishment and in atonement for giving birth to a child out of wedlock. She has been in the convent for seven years without a family visitor when her aunt, the coldhearted La Zia Principessa, arrives. She has come to ask Angelica to sign away her substantial inheritance. When Angelica inquires about her son's well-being, her aunt reluctantly informs her that the child has been dead for two years. Angelica collapses in tears; after collecting Angelica's signature, the Principessa leaves. At this point in the drama, Angelica sings the opera's most famous aria "Senza Mamma" ("Without a mother, my baby, you died!"). As a specialist in mixing herbal remedies, Angelica then prepares a poisonous potion. After drinking it, she suddenly awakens from her grief-induced state of half-consciousness with the realization that suicide is a mortal sin, one that will separate her forever from her son. She begs the Madonna for forgiveness. Just before she dies, she has a vision of both the Madonna and her son, who runs toward her.

Just days prior to this performance, she and her husband institutionalized their son Bucky.[6] They did so knowing that he would never return home. At age six, autistic and severely mentally disabled, he was self-injurious and had begun to suffer grand mal seizures. The care he required was beyond what the family could give at home. Furthermore, if his life was to improve, he needed specialized training and education. The Greenoughs placed him in the same home where Peter's youngest daughter was already a resident.

Suor Angelica's pain of separation and loss became Sills's. Director Frank Corsaro, who attended the performance, was cited in *Time* as saying it was the only hysterical performance he ever saw Sills give (November 22, 1971). Decades later, when asked in an interview if he still remembered the performance, Corsaro became animated: "Oh, oh, oh, yes! There was something so private about it that it was a little frightening. . . . It was alarming, and yet startling and effective. I had never seen quite that degree of personal angst from her in her performances. . . . I think, by the way, at the time, vocally, one felt that she was not going to be able to get through it, but she did. She had enormous stamina and beyond that a control of her vocal instrument. It was quite extraordinary" (Corsaro interview, May 13, 2013).

In one of Sills's scrapbooks now held in the Library of Congress, Peter Greenough (who compiled most of the scrapbooks and occasionally wrote in annotations) penned the following beneath one of the published reviews of the performance: "Bucky went off to school this March and part of B. S.'s emotional outlet went into this evening, notably Suor Angelica." Anthea de Forest, who sang the role of one of the novices, recalled: "She got through *Il Tabarro* without incident, but, it was the *Suor Angelica* that suddenly brought it all home to her. I don't think she was prepared, emotionally, for it. She was trying so hard to be brave and it took her unawares" (e-mail, January 29, 2013). Frances Bible, who sang the part of Angelica's aunt, told her friends that Sills was crying so hard when she came into the wings at the opera's end that she was frantic. Bible had to smack Sills to bring her around so that she could prepare herself to go back out and sing Lauretta in *Gianni Schicchi* (K. Ames interview, December 27, 2010).

A bootleg recording (or "private" recording, as they are discreetly referred to in the opera world) of this performance still circulates among opera fans. Although the sound quality is rather poor, the intensity of the performance is unmistakable. It is impossible to tease apart with certainty which aspects of the performance are simply Sills in character and which are Sills expressing her own personal anguish; there are, however, certain passages in which her emotional distress is palpable. In the course of research, I was able to obtain a copy of this recording and the following is an attempt to share the listening experience with the reader:

> I first hear the sound of raw emotion when Angelica lashes out at her aunt for casting the news of her younger sister's wedding in terms that denigrate Angelica. Although Puccini's music, especially the crescendo to a forte in the orchestra, calls for this passage to be sung loudly in hurtful anger, Sills also expresses disbelief and betrayal as she nearly screams her line: "Sorella di mia madre, voi siete inesorabile!" (My mother's sister, you are unrelenting!).
>
> Next, Angelica explains that she has offered everything to the Virgin, barring one sacrifice. She cannot forget her son. With her singing of "Mio figlio! Mio figlio, il figlio mio! Figlio mio! (My son! My son, the son of mine! The son of mine!), I hear Sills as crossing a line. It seems she has entered the drama to such a degree that her personal pain is now that of the character she is portraying. Sills is crying out for her own son.
>
> She regains some composure as Angelica begs her aunt to tell her about her child. Once she learns that he has died, her hysteria takes hold. Rather than singing, "È morto? Ah!" (He's dead? Ah!) per Forzano's libretto, Sills cries, "È morto? No!" and then descends into heart-wrenching sobs. She collapses onto the floor; her aunt departs, leaving her alone on the stage. At this moment, the audience reaction as preserved in the private recording offers insight into the mood in the house. As Puccini's orchestral music closes the scene and Sills

continues to weep, the audience erupts into enthusiastic applause. This is not customarily a point in the musical drama at which the audience applauds. I have learned that the recordist was a fan and very close friend of Sills. He, and no doubt people seated next to him, knew of Sills's personal circumstance. I hear the burst of rapid and forceful applause, which those near the recordist led, as signaling support for Sills, who was clearly overwrought.

She begins her "Senza Mamma" with a cracked tone; perhaps weeping has constricted her throat. Several times throughout the aria her voice becomes thin as she struggles to keep the tone flowing, all the while singing of how her son died without his mother's kisses and embraces, and without knowing that his mother had loved him dearly (just as Sills's severely developmentally disabled child may not have known of his mother's love).

At the aria's close, she begs her son, now in heaven and finally able to see her, to speak to her: "Parlami, parlami, amore, amore, amore!" (Speak to me, speak to me, my love, my love, my love!). As Sills attempts to cut off the final long-held A above the staff sung to "Amore," her voice cracks as though she's about to choke. The audience applauds enthusiastically at the aria's end; again I hear their applause as aimed at supporting a struggling Sills. One audience member continues to clap loudly and frenetically after the others, and he is shushed. A cross word is uttered (to the lone clapper?); unfortunately, the recording's low fidelity makes it impossible to discern.

After continuing to labor through the "La grazia e discesa dal cielo" section in which Angelica has a vision of the Madonna descending in a glow of light, Sills finishes the passage with a ringing high C that shimmers above the chorus. One audience member whistles in a spontaneous expression of "wow" after she flawlessly releases her long-held note. Once the chorus concludes their phrase, someone begins to clap vigorously, only to be quickly shushed. Sills sings hauntingly as she narrates Angelica's preparation of her mix of deadly flower poisons. Her voice is sweet, though still registering her emotional instability, as she bids farewell to her sisters, explaining that her son has called her to heaven.

After she drinks the fatal potion, we hear the bowl in which the poison was mixed drop to the floor. The thud brings Angelica out of her transcendental state. With her realization that she has damned herself to an eternity without seeing her son, Sills sings the cries for forgiveness with bloodcurdling passion.

Retired singer and voice teacher David Wylie shared the following upon hearing this recording: "'O Madonna, Madonna, salvami, salvami!' (O Madonna, save me!) sounds as though she has lost control. The last 'O, Madonna, salvami!' sounds helpless to me. The ending 'Ah! Ah!' sound hysterical and beyond her dramatic control within the character" (e-mail, February 19, 2012).

Only a handful of the nearly three thousand audience members in attendance knew of the personal circumstances that gave rise to the emotional intensity of Sills's performance. Nevertheless, they were swept up by this extraordinarily powerful theatrical moment. Ed Rosen, a New York–based opera aficionado and owner of the Premiere Opera Company, shared his memory of the evening in his initial posting to the Facebook page "The Beverly Sills Crazies!":

> In thinking of the great Beverly Sills, one night in particular comes to mind, though there were so many unforgettable nights. It was the night in 1967 where she sang all three soprano roles in the Trittico under very difficult circumstances, which I feel sure are well known to all here. It was absolutely unforgettable, first because she really sang the hell out of these roles. She remains, to this day, by far the finest Suor Angelica I have ever seen, and the ovation at the end of this opera seemed to go on forever, and deservedly so. In going to operas there are some or even many nights that give one thrills. This night was even more than that. You sat there and felt absolutely privileged to be a witness to utter and absolute greatness that put you in a "spot" that can only really happen once in a lifetime. Mesmerizing is too mild a word. Sometimes there are no words, and this was one of these times. (January 23, 2013)

Sills's performance of *Suor Angelica* was the site of a rare public display of her inner anguish, the expression of which she normally kept private. The bootleg recording memorializes and preserves a moment when the misery of real life took artful expression with extraordinary intensity. In public appearances, such as television interviews, and in almost every aspect of her life, she always appeared cheerful. Her toothy smile is the feature most often exaggerated in caricatures.[7] When friends and fans reminisce about their times with her, they frequently mention her infectious laugh. However, she was also often cited as saying: "Happy I'll never be, but I'm as cheerful as I can be" (e.g., *Time,* November 22, 1971). Writing for the *New York Times Magazine,* Joan Barthel surmised that for Sills a "constant cheerful smile" was her "best defense" against what she herself described in reference to her children's disabilities as a "kind of shattering that never goes away . . . a kind of hopelessness that sits on you forever" (1975, 63, 65). Lotfi Mansouri depicted her smiling demeanor as a mask that she would rarely allow anyone to see behind (Mansouri interview, February 15, 2010). On the evening of March 8, 1967, her pain was palpable and displayed before an audience of thousands.[8]

A week following her *Il Trittico* performance, Sills began a dizzying several months of touring. She did two performances of *La Traviata* with the Tulsa Opera before heading to Europe for a concert appearance in Salzburg, Austria; a recording session for the West German Radio in Cologne, Germany; and one performance as the Queen of the Night with the Vienna State Opera. A little over a week after her Viennese appearance, she sang three performances of Mendelssohn's oratorio *Elijah* in Lima, Peru, after which she returned to the United States for two nights performing all three heroines in *The Tales of Hoffmann* in New Orleans with Norman Treigle and John Alexander. She had two weeks at home before heading back to Europe for two appearances as Donna Anna at the Theatre de Beaulieu in Lausanne, Switzerland. In the month of June, Sills performed in Puebla, Mexico, and at the Caramoor Festival in Katonah, New York. She finished the summer by spending July in Cincinnati with a run as Violetta in *La Traviata* and then as Rosalinde in an English-language version of *Die Fledermaus*. Finally, she made two appearances in August as Constanza in a concert version of *The Abduction from the Seraglio* at Grant Park in Chicago.

A self-professed workaholic, Sills rarely took more than several consecutive weeks per year away from the stage, even when recovering from a life-threatening illness. Certainly one factor that drove her to maintain such a hectic schedule was the fact that she was already thirty-seven years old when suddenly, and finally, she found herself in the limelight with invitations making demands on her every waking minute. Another factor was her need to keep busy; time spent in rehearsal and in front of an audience was time not spent worrying about her children's ailments. Joan Barthel offered yet another view of Sills's "crazy schedule," asserting that it was "explainable only in terms of desire, a yearning to succeed so overwhelming that it probably isn't explainable at all. A man who knows her well calls it the 'killer instinct'—the urge, indeed the need, to conquer, a need that overcomes fatigue, laryngitis, genuine illness" (1975, 68).

From this period forward through the end of her singing career in 1980, Sills kept up an extremely rigorous schedule of operatic, recital, concert, and television appearances.

CHAPTER 4

From Stardom to Retirement

Beverly Sills gave a staggering number of performances during the years between stardom and retirement. This chapter focuses on her most notable roles after reaching stardom. It considers general patterns in her artistic development and important life events, but both only insofar as they intertwined with her career trajectory. Roles include her performing in Rimsky-Korsakov's *Coq d'Or,* Massenet's *Manon,* Gounod's *Faust,* Donizetti's *Lucia di Lammermoor,* and playing three Tudor queens in Donizetti's *Roberto Devereux, Maria Stuarda,* and *Anna Bolena.* Career events include making her debuts at La Scala, Covent Garden, and the Metropolitan Opera, as well as concertizing. Life events include her health problems, vocal decline, and retirement from singing, as well her administrative and fund-raising work.

Queen Shemakha, Manon, and Marguerite

The New York City Opera's fall 1967 season saw Sills giving repeat performances of the Queen of the Night and also Cleopatra.[1] The highlight of the season came in a new production of Rimsky-Korsakov's *Coq d'Or,* which John Chapman of the *New York Daily News* identified as the "prize attraction of Lincoln Center" following its opening night (September 22, 1967). Sills played the seductive enchantress Queen Shemakha alongside Norman Treigle's doddering and fatuous King Dodon. The same artistic team that created the *Giulio Cesare* sensation—headed by Julius Rudel, Tito Capobianco, Ming Cho Lee, and José Varona—turned Rimsky-Korsakov's rarely performed "bitter fantasy" into a "sugar-coated delicacy" (Saal 1967b, 86). As part of the Capobiancos' conception of the Queen as both sexy and comical, Gigi choreographed and trained Sills in the execution of the dance she performed while singing "Hymn to the Sun." The dance—which Sills performed in harem pants, a bra-like top with her midriff covered in skin-toned mesh, and a five-layered, bejeweled headpiece—incorporated belly-dance moves. Of her performance, Patrick J. Smith of *High Fidelity* commented: "Sills's coloratura continues to be an incredibly warm and flexible instrument, and her breath control and legato sense is little short of phenomenal." He declared the "beautiful interaction" between Sills and Treigle as "one of the most convincing love scenes" he had recently seen in opera (1967, MA 11).

While Rudel staged *Coq d'Or* as a vehicle to highlight Norman Treigle in the leading role of King Dodon, he offered Sills a new production of her choice for the 1968 season. She immediately selected Massenet's *Manon*. This role became one of the most acclaimed of her career. Sills was fluent in French and her voice was especially well suited to the language. Writing in 1987, she recalled that her voice teacher Estelle Liebling was never more satisfied than when her prized student sang French repertoire (Sills 1987, 174). Sills had studied the role with Mary Garden, sung it semiprofessionally in Baltimore in the early 1950s with Rosa Ponselle's coaching, and performed it twice in 1962 under Sarah Caldwell's direction in Boston. Even with these experiences, she felt that she had not thoroughly grasped Manon's character. Together she and the Capobiancos developed a multifaceted character who deeply engaged the audience as she transitioned from a not-so-innocent country girl into a glamorous Parisian courtesan. Especially electrifying was her execution of the Saint-Sulpice scene, in which Manon seeks to win back her lover, Des Grieux, who was so thoroughly devastated by her betrayal that he withdrew to a monastery. Rather than portraying Manon as a self-interested whore (as in Laurent Pelly's 2012 production at the Metropolitan Opera starring Anna Netrebko), Sills played her as an adventurous young woman whose thirst for wealth leads her astray and whose confident sensuality is impossible to resist. As she sings to Des Grieux asking for his forgiveness in the Saint-Sulpice scene, she uses her chiffon scarf to draw him to her as she practically wraps herself around him. Powerless to resist, his face is buried in her scarf. They embrace; overwhelmed, he kisses her breast (much to her delight). They join hands and flee the monastery to make love posthaste. Hubert Saal reported in his *Newsweek* review that a "goggle-eyed" woman in the audience grabbed her husband, "crying, 'Sam, Sam, she's making him crazy'" (1968, 108). Of the Saint-Sulpice scene, Winthrop Sargeant wrote that Sills's singing and acting were "memorable for femininity, subtlety of vocal nuance, and conviction. There were people in the house who wept. I am not a weeper, but chills went up and down my spine. . . . I have been going to opera for many years. I do not remember as fine a Manon in all my experience" (1968a, 120). Summing up Sills's Manon, Harold Schonberg declared: "She was everything—handsome, a fine actress, a sex symbol, petulant, merry, naïve, and terribly, terribly knowing" (*New York Times,* March 22, 1968). Even Peter Davis, who was typically one of Sills's harshest critics—right up to her death—wrote that her Manon was a "superbly detailed characterization, limned in pathos, light comedy and sheer sex appeal, while the voice arched through Massenet's bitter-sweet melodies as if the music had been written especially for her" (Davis 1975). When Sills returned to the role for three performances in the spring of 1969, Winthrop Sargeant paid a bold compliment to the Brookyn-born diva. His "Musical Events" contribution for the *New Yorker* carried the subtitle "Civic Wonder" and opened: "If I were recommending the wonders of New York City to a tourist, I should place Beverly Sills as Manon at the top of the list—way ahead of such things as the Statue of Liberty and the Empire State Building" (1969a, 105).

Although Marguerite in Gounod's *Faust* is not one of Sills's most famous roles (she did not record it; she performed it less than two dozen times as compared to more than one hundred performances of *Lucia,* for example), her participation in the production directed by Frank Corsaro at the New York City Opera in the fall of 1968 deserves mention. Frank Corsaro and Tito Capobianco were two of the most innovative operatic stage directors in the United States in the 1960s and '70s.[2] Both took the drama of the works under their direction as being as equally important as the music. Their presence was integral to the creation of the New York City Opera's culture of singing actors, which was a cutting-edge development in operatic performance at the time. The 1968 *Faust* was Sills's single experience working with Corsaro in the staging of a new production. Several of her former colleagues interviewed for this book pointed to this engagement as forming yet another milestone in shaping Sills's thespian talents. In his *Faust* review, Winthrop Sargeant (who was fond of food analogies), put her artistic evolution in humorous terms: "Beverly Sills, whom we have all watched grow to a magnificent maturity, is now a real lobster-supper diva from whose slipper her devotees would have quaffed champagne a hundred years ago" (1968b, 200).

Sills had performed in no less than four different productions of *Faust* prior to Corsaro's. Lore has it that she arrived at the first rehearsal with Corsaro and said: "Well, here I am—my only problem is do I wear the pigtail on the left side or the right side?" (Rudel interview, October 6, 2009). Corsaro pointed out that Marguerite murders her mother, gets herself seduced on a first date, drowns her illegitimate child, causes the death of her brother, and goes to her execution in the end. By opening night, Sills's Marguerite was a dramatically coherent, edgy, and deeply tragic character. As Harold Schonberg commented: "She acted magnificently" (*New York Times*, 18 October 1968).

The *La Scala* Debut

In April 1969, Sills made her debut at one of the world's most prestigious opera houses, the Teatro alla Scala in Milan, Italy. She was called in with four months' notice to replace a pregnant Renata Scotto to play the role of Pamira in the rarely performed Rossini opera *L'assedio di Corinto*. Sills's performance was an unmitigated triumph, earning her both the affection of La Scala's audience, for whom opera can be a blood sport, as well as further acclaim at home, including a *Newsweek* cover story. With her Cleopatra breakthrough performance less than three years prior, Sills's voice was at its peak. As a recording kept in circulation by bootleggers of the La Scala radio broadcast attests, Sills's voice was pure: her coloratura was stunning in its speed and accuracy; her floating of long, pianissimo, pathos-laden lines was breathtaking. Interestingly, the reviews, which were almost universally positive with only a few minor caveats, identify most of the themes that would reappear, in changing proportions, across the body of reviews throughout the rest of her singing career. The following are representative examples.

Peter Hoffer, in his review for *Opera News,* points to three key themes that would underlie much of the reception to Sills's singing. First, he commented on the size and vocal quality or timbre of her voice—some critics and opera aficionados found Sills's voice lacking in body and color, especially when compared to contemporaries Leontyne Price and Joan Sutherland. Second, Hoffer pointed to her extraordinary, innate musicality and her solid vocal technique. Third, he noted her ability to move her audience to tears through her voice's communication of pathos.

> Miss Sills does not have a voice of unmitigated beauty, and one noted some cutting shrillness. However, her musicianship and vocal technique are of such high order that this weakness does no more than remind one that she, too, is human. Her *mezza voce* was a tour de force, and her Pamira produced tears in the eyes of many listeners. (Hoffer 1969, 28)

Andrew Porter's assessment for the *Financial Times* of London echoed the main themes identified by Hoffer.

> [S]he certainly revealed a prodigious facility in rapid singing: her divisions, her graces, her scales, her leaps, were all surprising, while the treatment of long, slow phrases showed considerable feeling for line. The roulades (the music had been decorated up the hilt) were amazing; the andantino air "Du séjour"—one

of those simple melodies touched with sudden, delicate *fioriture*—was deeply moving. Miss Sills looked well, tall and romantic. Reservations must be about [*sic*] the lack of solidity, of firm centre, in her tone. (May 15, 1969)

Reviews in the Italian press were generally exuberant. Francesco Canessa, writing for the newspaper *Roma,* praised both Sills and Marilyn Horne, especially for their performance in act 3, which he termed "truly formidable, a competition of bravura, taste, vocal beauty, and of generous musicality" (il loro terzo atto è davvero formidabile, una gara di bravura, di gusto e bellezza vocale, di musicalità generosa) (April 12, 1969). In commenting specifically on Sills, he wrote: "Sills's Italian debut was certainly a surprise, a big surprise. In substance, she is a coloratura soprano, of spun and subdued sweetness of tone, and of surprising agility while maintaining a full-bodied and expressive tone. Also, she had an outstanding presence and impeccable style" (per la Sills, al suo esordio italiano, è stata certamente una sorpresa, una grossa sorpresa. È, in sostanza, un soprano-coloritura [*sic*], dai filati soffusi, dolcissimi, dalle agilità sorprendenti, cui si aggiunge un centro corposo ed espressivo. E la personalità è notevole, lo stile impeccablile) (ibid.).

Mario Pasi of Milan's *Corriere d'informazione* commented similarly: "The debut of Beverly Sills (Pamira) was magnificent: her voice is splendid, agile, rich, pleasurable to the ear, and with good phrasing. Her stage presence was beyond remarkable" (Il debutto del soprano Beverly Sills (Pamira) è stato magnifico: la voce è splendida, agile, ricca, piacevole a udirsi, il fraseggio è buono e la presenza scenica più che notevole) (April 13, 1969). Alcco Toni, writing for Milan's *La Notte,* expressed an almost polar opposite view to Pasi's. Although he termed Sills a "virtuoso to the max" (virtuosa al massimo), Toni described her voice as sometimes lacking in clarity and sonority (ma non sempre con voce chiara, brillante di rotonda sonorità). Furthermore, he found her expressivity mannered and boring (espressiva [*sic*] piùttosto manierata e lagnosa) (April 12, 1969).

Writing as a foreign correspondent for the *New York Times,* musicologist and composer Everett Helm touched on the key issues identified by other reviewers. Furthermore, he introduced an important observation on how Sills's commanding performance transcended the serious failings inherent in Thomas Schippers's performing edition of *L'assedio.*

> The many weaknesses of score, libretto and story were forgotten in a performance that was close to spectacular. Major interest centered of course on the interpreter of the leading role, Beverly Sills, whose name is not yet very well known in Europe. Now Italians know what Americans have known for a couple of years: Beverly Sills is a fine artist with a glorious coloratura voice which she handles magnificently. Especially in the high registers (the higher the better), she sang with such purity and control as to bring down the house repeatedly.

Apart from a few harsh tones in the middle register, she demonstrated flawless coloratura technique in which every note of the embellishments was clear, and a marvelous bel canto in the quieter numbers. (April 20, 1969)

As Helm pointed out, the score and libretto used for the La Scala *L'assedio di Corinto* were highly idiosyncratic. Conductor Thomas Schippers, working with Randolph Mickelson, concocted a performing edition that drew on no less than three different, but related, Rossini operas: *Maometto II* (written for its premiere in Naples in 1820), *Le Siège de Corinthe* (Rossini's earliest French opera written in 1826 and based on a revision of Maometto II), and *L'assedio di Corinto* (a problematic Italian translation of *Le Siège de Corinthe*) (Gossett 2006, 119–20). Schippers drew most of his materials from the florid Naples work and about 20 percent from the more austere French opera (ibid.). The "ludicrous result," to borrow Rossini scholar Philip Gossett's words, was an edition that was inconsistent in style and enormous in size (ibid., 121). As an example of the unevenness, Gossett pointed to the inclusion of a cabaletta for Pamira borrowed from *Ciro in Babilonia*, an early Rossini opera whose orchestration was strikingly different in style from that of *Maometto II*, which was composed a decade later (ibid., 121). Gossett noted, however, that "[d]espite this travesty of the music of Rossini, the ladies [i.e., Beverly Sills and Marilyn Horne] sang their hearts out and *L'assedio di Corinto* was a triumph for the prima donnas" (ibid., 122). In concluding his critique of the Schippers edition, Gossett touches on an issue that continues to invigorate debate surrounding the performance practice of Italian opera, and which was a recurrent theme in the critical reception of several of the productions, such as Handel's *Giulio Cesare*, in which Sills was involved. Namely, this is the question of balance between attempting to strictly honor a composer's intentions (based on all available scholarship) versus allowing a performing artist a good deal of interpretive or creative freedom. Gossett asserts that the Schippers edition represented an example of the later stance in which "an opera is an entertainment and can be freely manipulated as long as the result is a good show" (ibid., 122). As if in response to the position represented by Gossett, Helm concluded: "The procedure may be reprehensible from the musicologist's standpoint, but it proved to be a blessing for the audience. . . . The moral of the evening: if you insist on fishing for old operas, be sure you have the best possible bait. It was the performance, not the music, that made this revival memorable" (*San Francisco Sunday Examiner and Chronicle*, May 18, 1969).

Sills's La Scala debut was an enormous success; however, that success was made almost entirely on the strength of her singing. Her character, the two-dimensional Pamira, allowed for little dramatic development. As Sills wrote: "Dramatically, the role was unsatisfying—no acting was asked for or needed; *The Siege of Corinth* was one of the few stand-up-and-sing operas I ever did" (1987, 176–77).

Lucia di Lammermoor
and the Covent Garden Debut

While Pamira provided only a limited scope for theatrical engagement, Sills was in the process of discovering that other bel canto roles (here meaning Italian operas written during the time of Rossini, Donizetti, and Bellini)—which allow their singers a good degree of freedom to act with the voice—suited her evolving talents as a singing actress. Sills's ability to communicate emotion through subtle shadings of expression was one of her greatest gifts. The nature of bel canto—which calls for vocal agility, legato phrasing, and a light tone in high registers, while permitting a degree of melodic interpolation—drew Sills like a moth to a flame. Even prior to her high-profile appearance in Rossini's *L'assedio,* Sills was beginning to shape her interpretation of Donizetti's *Lucia di Lammermoor.* Before Maria Callas brought Lucia and other bel canto heroines to the stage in the 1950s, these roles were typically sung by songbird-like coloraturas who took the works primarily as vehicles for showcasing their light-toned vocal acrobatics. Callas showed that these operas—composed at a time when singers were given far more interpretive freedom than composers of the later half of the nineteenth century allowed—presented something of a blank canvas onto which the singer could cast her musical and dramatic interpretation.

Lucia di Lammermoor became Sills's first fully developed bel canto role. During the course of her career, she would sing Lucia more than one hundred times. She made her role debut in Fort Worth on April 5, 1968, followed by performances in Cincinnati, Edmonton, and Boston before bringing her Lucia to the New York City Opera stage on October 9, 1969. A comparison of bootleg recordings from the first Fort Worth performance and the first New York City Opera performance document the evolution of her interpretation both musically and dramatically.

Rather than singing Estelle Liebling's published Lucia cadenzas, Sills's vocal coach, Roland Gagnon, composed new cadenzas for her as well as new interpolations and ornamentation in early 1968. In *Beverly,* Sills discussed the creative process employed by her, Gagnon, and the Capobiancos as they worked together to develop her interpretation.[3] She and the Capobiancos pored over the libretto, discovering that the cuts that had become standard severely distorted the drama. They would present the full opera for the first time in New York in a century. Raymond Ericson, music critic for the *New York Times,* commented that opening the cuts was a "major virtue" of the production because the full version "has a more varied, continuing theatrical pulse superior to its chopped-up predecessors" (October 10, 1969). Based on her new understanding of the role, she and Gagnon trimmed some of the more florid ornamentation that we hear in the bootleg recording of the Fort Worth performance. As a result, her Lucia became less of a sweet and young innocent who simply snapped under pressure, and more of an emotionally intense young woman who was psychologically unstable from her very first scene. Her *fioritura* took on dramatic function rather than simply serving as melodic ornamentation. For example, Sills recalled how she sang Gagnon's mad-scene cadenza to different characters as if she were speaking to them (Sills 1987, 196). Gigi Capobianco explained that Tito expected his singers to "use coloratura as if they were words. They can be laughter, they can be sorrow, they can be rage. In *Lucia*, every cadenza with the flute was one member of the *coro* who tried to come to talk to her; she's in such a state, she just pushes like that [Gigi gestured a full-body shove]. 'No. Not you. Not you. It's not Edgardo.' The cadenzi are all used like that. So they make sense; it's not just listening to singing. No!" (Capobianco interview, July 28, 2010).

Tito continued: "One of the secrets of the director of an opera is to make you forget that they are singing. No, they are not singing. They are telling you something" (ibid.). Much of the ornamentation chiseled out in her sessions with the Capobiancos and Gagnon became fundamental to her characterization of Lucia and remained central to her interpretation regardless of the production.

Winthrop Sargeant's review of the opening night narrowed in precisely on Sills's development of Lucia's character and her adept use of coloratura for dramatic purposes:

> Her interpretation was a revelation of all the emotional and psychological factors that can color Lucia's character. One heard and saw all the changes of mood—from innocence to despair and madness—that can be extracted from the role. As has happened before, Miss Sills brought her audience to the verge of tears, this time with Lucia's mad scene, which was done with such warmth and personal involvement that one could almost forget the athletic aspects of her coloratura technique. And yet the technique was there in brilliant quantity, and every high E-flat was hit squarely and without apparent effort. . . . Again, she was setting a new standard—throwing off the *fioritura* not as if it were an athletic stunt but as if it were an integral ingredient in a very human character.[4] (1969b, 170–71)

When the NYCO took its annual tour to Los Angeles in December 1969, William Murray of the *Los Angeles Magazine* also commented on how Sills infused her voice with meaning in her dramatic portrayal of Lucia.

> She is the sort of artist who is incapable of singing a single note that has not been dramatically conceived and motivated. She manages to convince us that we are witnessing a young girl actually in the process of losing her mind, so that we, like the on-stage chorus, become witnesses and participants in a profoundly horrifying and distressing event. Hers is a dramatic achievement that deserves, but will not get, a Tony award. (Murray 1970, 51)

Between October 1969 and August 1974, Sills performed *Lucia di Lammermoor* thirty times with the NYCO. Lucia remained in her repertoire up through her last performance of the role in January 1977 at the Metropolitan Opera. She sang Lucia in many locations within the United States, including Philadelphia, Houston, and New Orleans, and abroad. She appeared with Luciano Pavarotti as her Edgardo in Mexico City shortly after her NYCO role debut in October 1969; they played the star-crossed lovers again in November 1972 in San Francisco. Sills took her Lucia to La Scala in March 1970, to London's Covent Garden in December 1970 through January 1971, and to Buenos Aires in July 1972 with Alfredo Kraus as her Edgardo.

Of all of her foreign performances, she felt that she met with the least positive reception in London. In her memoirs, Sills attributed her cool reception at Covent Garden in part to a general feeling of loyalty in the house to Joan Sutherland. After all, it was Sutherland's performance of Lucia at Covent Garden in 1959 that launched the legendary singer to international fame. Sills appeared in the same Franco Zeffirelli production and with the same conductor, John Pritchard, as did Sutherland. The two singers' approach to the role (and to performance generally) could hardly have been more different. Sutherland possessed a phenomenal voice with its rare combination of lush tone, huge size, and extraordinary coloratura. In fact, Sutherland was dubbed "the voice of the century." However, she was not particularly invested in acting. She often sacrificed drama and diction in the production of her stupendous sound. Sills, on the other hand, did not have what opera aficionados typically regard as a beautiful voice. And Sills, like Callas, was quite willing to sacrifice vocal beauty if she felt it dramatically appropriate. The stage was set for Sills to be compared unfavorably to the local favorite. Arthur Jacobs, writing for *Opera*, addressed this inevitable comparison directly by stating that Sills's appearance did not create an "audience electrified" or an "evening of emotion" like Sutherland's first appearance in the role in 1959 (Jacobs 1971, 165). In fairness, he declined to judge which performance was "better," reasoning that twelve years earlier, when Sutherland performed *Lucia,* the opera was unknown to most audience members. Furthermore, "what helped to rouse the emotion then was the audience's feeling for 'its own' emergent star" (ibid., 166).

Private recordings of two of Sills's seven Covent Garden performances remain in circulation. The fidelity of both is poor; it sounds as though the recordists were a great distance from the stage. These imperfect recordings suggest a Sills who was a good bit more timid than we typically hear in other recordings of her live performances, especially those with the NYCO. Several reviewers suggested that she might have been holding back because of nerves as it was her first performance in this prestigious house. However, there is no such hint of nervousness in the bootlegs from La Scala, an equally venerable house. Perhaps rather than being intimidated by the venue, she did not feel comfortable falling as deeply into her character as she typically did when surrounded by friends and familiar colleagues—in a production that she helped create—at the NYCO.[5] Although the absence of intimacy and security that comes with performing in a repertory company did not hamper Sills when portraying the shallow character of Pamira at La Scala, the execution of her vulnerable Lucia was an entirely different matter.

Generally, the reviews of the Covent Garden *Lucia* are positive. A few critics found her voice lacking in "amplitude, richness and range of tone color," such as Frank Granville Barker of *Opera News,* who also commented that "the voice soon lost its brightness and bloom under pressure" (Barker 1971, 30). Stanley Sadie opined that while he found her voice warm, it was "not quite big enough to carry at some of the crucial moments." He also commented, though, that while he had heard "more brilliant, more thrilling" Lucias, he had encountered "none so complete. Miss Sills is an absolute professional, and her professionalism comes through in all she does. None of her stage movement is exiguous: every step, every gesture has point. No inflexion of tone or phrase is empty or without meaning: it is all closely keyed to the words and to the emotion behind them. Her vocal decoration, which is liberal, is always dramatically functional" (*Times,* December 24, 1970).

During her Covent Garden performance run, which spanned from just before Christmas to the last week in January, Sills gave two performances on the continent. Lorin Maazel invited her to Berlin where she did a single Violetta with the Deutsche Oper on January 6, 1971; on January 22 she gave a concert at the Salle Pleyel in Paris. After this prolonged time away from home, she would only accept one final European engagement—with Venice's Teatro La Fenice where she gave three performances as Violetta in June 1972.

Sills wrote that she did not especially enjoy foreign touring because she missed her family (1987, 222–23). When she performed at Covent Garden, Peter and Muffy accompanied her to England, but returned home well before the end of her engagement. Others have commented that Sills did not do well alone. She especially disliked being separated from her husband, who, in many ways, supported and shielded her from harm, sometimes quite literally. If they were in a space with someone who was obviously suffering from a cold, Peter would put himself physically between the sick person and his wife. He also protected her professionally, most often through his connections with the press, as the unfortunate souls who crossed her sometimes learned. Sills was an extraordinarily strong woman, but Peter was her rock. Although her career often took her on the road, she returned home to her family as quickly as she could. For Sills, touring to Europe and other distant locations lost its luster once she had sung in the major opera houses. Her last engagement outside of North America was a series of four performances of Lucia in June and July of 1972 in Buenos Aires at the Teatro Colón.

The Three Tudor Queens

The benefits that her position as the reigning prima donna of the New York City Opera afforded Sills contributed to her unwillingness to endure the rigors of foreign touring. Within her home company, she had the freedom to choose the repertoire she wanted to tackle and the luxury of bringing new roles to the stage in productions newly created for her by her closest artistic cadres headed by Tito Capobianco. The apex of this came with the NYCO's mounting for Sills of Donizetti's three operas, *Roberto Devereux, Maria Stuarda,* and *Anna Bolena,* the so-called Tudor trilogy.[6]

Of all of the more than sixty roles that Sills performed over the course of her operatic career, none was more controversial than her Queen Elizabeth I. The debate centered on the innate quality of her voice and its suitability to the role. Because of its vocal weight, size, timbre, and tessitura, Sills's voice is best classified as a lyric coloratura following the *Fach* system of voice and role categorization.[7] Examples of lyric coloratura roles include some of her most celebrated portrayals such as Baby Doe, Marie (in Donizetti's *La Fille du Régiment*), and Olympia (in Offenbach's *Les Contes d'Hoffmann*). It is the opinion of voice teacher Gerald Martin Moore that Sills pushed her voice into the heavier dramatic coloratura realm by virtue of her acting (e-mail, March 4, 2013). Roles in this category include Lucia, Violetta, Elvira (in Bellini's *I Puritani*), and Maria (in Donizetti's *Maria Stuarda*).

The *Fach* classification system is, of course, a social construct. As such, it is subjective and evolves over time. It was first codified in Germany in the early twentieth century by singers' unions as a means of protecting individual singers from being assigned by opera houses to roles that would be unsuitable and possibly damaging to their voices (Cotton 2012, 155). The system parsed roles into categories; individual singer's contracts specified his or her *Fach.* It is essential to keep in mind that the *Fach* system is a twentieth-century invention; the careers of many legendary singers of the nineteenth century would have defied tidy classification. The career of the great Giuditta Pasta (1797–1865) exemplifies the diversity of roles undertaken by singers in the past. While perhaps overstating his point, musicologist and conductor David Lawton observed that in the contemporary environment, "it is inconceivable that the leading soprano roles of *La Sonnambula* and *Norma* could be performed by the same singer, yet Bellini wrote both for Giuditta Pasta" (1988, 158). Donizetti also composed his *Anna Bolena* with Pasta in the title role. Examples of other roles for which she was acclaimed include Cherubino in Mozart's *Le Nozze di Figaro* and the title role in Rossini's *La Cenerentola*, both of which are typically taken by mezzo-sopranos today. Pasta's versatility, like that of other great singers, including Maria Malibran (1808–36) and Adelina Patti (1843–1919), could not have been contained in any single *Fach* category.[8]

Harold Schonberg's reaction to Sills's Elizabeth represents well the opinion that her voice was too light for the role. Reviewing the opening-night performance on October 15, 1970, he wrote that she was not in good voice. "Perhaps she had rehearsed too long and was tired, but whatever the reason she sounded shrill and nervous, and was constantly having pitch problems. . . . As a specimen of bel canto singing it was, unfortunately, far wide of the target" (*New York Times,* October 17, 1970). A bootleg recording of the performance reveals an occasional intonation problem such as her undershooting several pitches. Most of the unsteadiness comes in the opening recitative in her first scene as when she ends the phrase "La mia vendetta!" on an out-of-tune low C. After the first few minutes, however, her voice warmed up and the intonation problems were largely behind her. Her first aria, "L'amor suo mi fè beata," is a study in floating, beautifully contoured phrases, crisp trills, and is capped off with a ringing high B-flat. She executes the florid coloratura passages of her caballeta "Ah, ritorna qual ti spero" with impeccable precision and apparent ease.

At the heart of Schonberg's criticism is the idea that Sills's voice was unsuitable for the Italian bel canto repertoire. Apparently, his negative review of opening night drew significant ire from the public. He elaborated on his specific issues with her singing of Elizabeth in a rebuttal published a month after his initial review: "The Beverly Sills Fan Club is down on me. Ever since my review of 'Roberto Devereux' the letters have been pouring in, accusing me of being tone deaf, insensitive, an atheist, prejudiced in favor of That Other Woman (Joan Sutherland), unfit to serve even as an apprentice in the dog pound. All that to me, who has been one of Sills's admirers from the beginning" (*New York Times,* November 15, 1970).

Schonberg situates his criticism within the well-worn debate between opera aficionados who place beauty of voice above drama and those for whom the voice is a vital medium in conveying emotion and drama, even if beauty of tone must be sacrificed when dramatically appropriate. Schonberg identifies these opposing orientations as either "music-oriented" or "drama-oriented." Several questions are typically left unexamined in this discussion: What constitutes vocal beauty? What are the limits of musicality? Do we unequivocally leave the realm of music when a singer shouts rather than sings a word? More specific to Schonberg's argument, what are the acceptable limits of bel canto performance?

Schonberg hears Sills as a "coloratura *manqué,* who, in basic matters, cannot fully match the requirements of the roles she undertakes." Although he praises her Cleopatra and Manon, he lists shortcomings that make her unsuitable for the bel canto repertoire, such as "gaps in her middle range" and a trill that he claims becomes unfocused and off pitch above the staff. Generally, he feels "strain and even desperation as she tries to maneuver her voice into areas for which it was not intended," which leads to "frequent shedding of tone and loss of quality." In his opinion, this "loss of quality is fatal in bel canto opera." Finally, Schonberg rejects the notion put forth by Sills and her supporters that she "purposely sang roughly in order to bring out the character of Queen Elizabeth" (ibid.).

Criticisms similar to Schonberg's echoed across numerous reviews, including those of Irving Kolodin and Peter Davis. Writing for the *Saturday Review,* Kolodin noted that although Sills "pours out scales and skips, flourishes and embellishments with a well-bred disdain for error" and effortlessly sung a dozen high Ds, he found her tone "thin and rather colorless" in recitative passages and moments of high drama. Especially troubling was her middle register: "It just doesn't have the weight for drama on the order of Donizetti's requirements in this role" (Kolodin 1970, 41).

In one of his more acerbic attacks on her career trajectory in his 1975 article "Beverly Sills—Media Heroine or Genuine Superstar?," Peter Davis claimed that Sills "punished her light, lyric voice which by its very nature is not suited to music of this sort." Davis wrote that in the confrontation scenes and in the histrionic finale "it sounded rather as if a girl had been sent to do a woman's work—and the effort it cost may well have damaged Sills's voice." Like Schonberg, Davis credits Sills with giving a riveting dramatic performance, but concludes, "one often had the impression that Sills was getting through the part on sheer will power" (Davis 1975).

The opinions of Schonberg, Kolodin, and Davis contrasted sharply with those of critics who were more "drama oriented." Winthrop Sargeant and Martin Bernheimer (chief music critic for the *Los Angeles Times*) belonged to the latter camp. Sargeant's *New Yorker* review of the opening-night performance places Sills's performance in historic terms:

> Not since Maria Callas has the art of acting been as splendidly displayed on the operatic stage as it was by Beverly Sills as Queen Elizabeth in the New York City Opera's production of Donizetti's "Roberto Devereux." . . . Every gesture and mood of the famous queen, from regal imperiousness and feminine impatience to brokenheartedness, was made real as Miss Sills developed the character before her audience. Certain scenes—the whole of Act II and the final episode of grief and remorse—were almost overwhelming in their power. What she did with her role purely from the histrionic standpoint was

something one is privileged to witness only a few times in a lifetime—and to say that her audience was stunned is to state things in a humdrum way. She *was* Elizabeth, from the extreme pallor of her makeup, which one remembers from old portraits, to the royal sweep of her train, the conflicts of emotion that history has recorded, and the nervous movements, whether of her fan (which revealed by its rapid motions what was going on inside the woman) or of her whole body convulsed in wrath as she pounded the table in front of her. This was great theatre judged by any standards, and it was a characterization that I shall never forget.

To add to all this, there was the Sills voice—in its conventional uses a familiar thing but here made to convey every shade of feeling, even sometimes made deliberately ugly to express fury or despair. No reader of this column need be reminded that it is a voice of extraordinary beauty, capable of overcoming the most terrifying coloratura hurdles. The hurdles provided by Donizetti in this score are difficult enough to require the entire concentration of an ordinary singer. Yet here was Miss Sills not only singing the scales and arpeggios and high notes with accuracy but coloring them with all manner of emotion and presenting the visual impression I have described besides. It is not surprising that the audience gave her a standing ovation at the end of the second act and that the curtain calls lasted far into the night. The combination of skills she brought to her role made this a historic moment. Though I had long before praised her to the skies, I had not realized the extent of her dramatic powers. (1970, 161)

Martin Bernheimer's assessment of Sills's performance when the NYCO took *Roberto Devereux* to Los Angeles in November 1971 (a little over a year after the show's opening in New York) resonates strongly with Sargeant's:

Beverly Sills as Queen Elizabeth I, enthroned at the Dorothy Chandler Pavilion Sunday, is still the eighth wonder of the world, and, perhaps the first operatic one. This is, in every respect, a brilliant characterization, a thoughtful characterization, a poignant characterization. . . .

She brings stunning serenity and a shimmering pianissimo to the introspective moments, equally striking intensity to the dramatic outbursts. She copes with the quiet, lyric passages with melting bel-canto purity. But she has no qualms about sacrificing surface beauty for expressive impact when the violence bursts through the old Queen's thin veil of composure.

The perilous coloratura flights, of course, are unflinchingly accurate and unfailingly expressive.

Furthermore, Sills' Elizabeth remains as triumphantly virtuosic histrionically as vocally. Every halting step, every twitch of a hand or droop of an eyebrow has its own inner meaning. Yet no gesture, no tremor, seems calculated or self-conscious. (*Los Angeles Times*, November 23, 1971)

As it happens, Sills was initially uninterested in the role when Tito Capobianco and Roland Gagnon suggested it as a possibility. She had heard a private recording of a concert version with Montserrat Caballé singing Elizabeth and found it dull.[9] Roland was insistent. He sent Sills a nine-page letter (which she kept tucked in her *Roberto Devereux* score well past her retirement) detailing its merits (Gurewitsch 2000). It was only after Roland convinced her to carefully read the libretto and score that she began to change her opinion. One portion of text in particular drew her in: "Pria che il sen di fiamma rea t'accendesse un Dio nemico, pria d'offender chi nascea dal tremendo ottavo Enrico, scender vivo, nel sepolcro, tu dovevi, o traditor!" (It would have been better for you to incite the wrath of God than to incite the wrath of the daughter of the terrible Henry the Eighth, better had you descended alive into your grave, oh traitor!). Many years later, in an interview for the *New York Times,* Sills said: "I couldn't wait to turn around and deliver that line. It's like shooting off a cannon" (ibid.). It is fair to surmise that ultimately it was the role's dramatic possibilities that Sills found impossible to resist.

Important to note is that Sills's voice teacher, Estelle Liebling, was vehemently opposed to her singing Elizabeth because she believed that it would take "a terrible toll" on Sills's voice (Sills 1987, 186) and refused to work with her on the music. Years later, Sills admitted that the role took several years off her singing career.[10] She always claimed, though, that she would rather have had a few exciting years than many dull ones. In the end, she claimed that *Roberto Devereux* was the "greatest artistic challenge and finest achievement" of her singing career (ibid., 217).

In March 1972, Sills and the NYCO mounted *Maria Stuarda,* the next installment in their Tudor queen trilogy. None of the operas had been staged previously in New York.[11] Sills attributed Roland Gagnon with the idea of her performing the roles of all three queens. Of the three leading roles, Maria Stuarda (Mary Stuart, Queen of Scots) was the best suited to Sills's voice in terms of size and tessitura. Unfortunately, the role was also the least dynamic dramatically. Besides the explosive confrontation between Queen Elizabeth and Mary Stuart at the end of act 1, Mary's turmoil is largely introspective,[12] and therefore, expressed within a rather limited dramatic range. She has no mad scene or intimate love duet. The general feeling at the NYCO was that *Maria Stuarda* was a weaker work compared to Donizetti's other Tudor queens; this was evidenced in part by Rudel's turning the orchestra over to staff conductor Charles Wendelken-Wilson. In Sills's opinion, "Mary Stuart was the weakest character and had the weakest music of the three queens" (1987, 237). While quite positive, the reviews for *Maria Stuarda* were also much milder than those for *Roberto Devereux,* which, as witnessed above, drew both passionately laudatory and harshly critical responses.

The NYCO brought *Anna Bolena*—the final opera in its "Elizabethan Ring," as Julius Rudel called it—to the stage in October 1973. Sills's performance of the title role is the focus of chapter 8. Her performance history of the three operas confirms her preference for *Roberto Devereux,* which she staged thirty-eight times between October 1970 and July 1975. The last two times she performed her Elizabeth I were at Wolf Trap and followed a ten-month-long break from the role. It is the first of these two performances that is memorialized in a commercially released video (*Roberto Devereux,* Video Artists International [VAI] DVD 4204). She played Mary Stuart eighteen times over two-and-a-half years and Anne Boleyn sixteen times over just a year and a half. Once these operas entered the repertory, she occasionally performed two different queens in the same week; twice she did all three within a little over three weeks.[13]

During the period in which Sills developed her Tudor queens, she also brought several other new roles to the stage, including Donizetti's comedy *La Fille du Régiment* and Bellini's melodious *I Puritani.* She performed her zany Marie (which she described as a Lucille Ball–like character with high notes) nearly fifty times between 1970 and 1978 throughout the United States and in Edmonton, Alberta. In 1973, Lotfi Mansouri directed a new production cosponsored by the Houston Grand Opera and San Diego Opera companies. Sills would play Marie in the production when it traveled to Boston, Philadelphia, San Francisco, and the NYCO. It also made it to Wolf Trap from where it was broadcast nationwide on PBS.

Recitals and Concertizing

Beginning in 1969, Sills began to appear in recital with increasing frequency. By the end of her singing career, she had given more than ninety recitals in major cities and small towns across the United States. Roland Gagnon acted as her accompanist for five recitals in 1969. However, he did not particularly enjoy performing publicly or traveling, and asked Sills to find someone to replace him. Edgar Vincent introduced Sills to Charles Wadsworth, who became her main collaborator. They began working together in early 1970, though Gagnon occasionally filled in, such as when she gave her White House recital in February 1971. Sills and Wadsworth became good friends, compatible traveling partners, and a dynamic musical duo. She insisted that he be listed not as an "accompanist" on their programs, but as "pianist" or "at the piano" or some other designation that paired them more equally. On a very few occasions, when neither Wadsworth nor Gagnon was available, Sills performed with other pianists, including Samuel Sanders.

Her appearances as a concertizing soprano began much earlier than her career as a recitalist. Sills's first major concert appearance dates back to her Carnegie Hall debut on February 3, 1956, with Leonard Bernstein conducting the Symphony of the Air Orchestra (formerly Toscanini's NBC Orchestra). She sang the part of Sophie in excerpts from Richard Strauss's *Der Rosenkavalier.* Prior to 1970, she had already soloed with the New York Philharmonic under André Kostelanetz, the Boston Symphony with Erich Leinsdorf conducting, and the Chicago Symphony under Aldo Ceccato, among others. The height of her activities as a concert guest artist was in 1974 when she gave at least twelve performances, ranging from engagements with the Los Angeles Philharmonic under Zubin Mehta and the Philadelphia Orchestra with Eugene Ormandy conducting to the Denver Symphony under Brian Priestman and the Milwaukee Symphony with Kenneth Schermerhorn conducting.

Cancer Surgery and Its Physical Toll

The 1974 concert count may have been even higher if Sills had not fallen seriously ill in the autumn. During a performance of *Maria Stuarda* in early September, she was suddenly struck by a searing, sharp pain as she was holding a sustained high note (Sills 1987, 256). She dropped the note and made it quickly to an onstage bench where she sat until the pain subsided. She finished the performance, but called her brother Sydney, a gynecologist, the next morning. After a series of tests, her doctor, in consultation with her brother, agreed that she could finish her performing commitments through November, but would have a hysterectomy in early December. Although she does not mention it in her autobiographies, she had been quite ill at least a week prior to the *Maria Stuarda* episode. She was nauseated during a performance of *Anna Bolena,* and Gigi Capobianco ran from one side of the wings to the other putting buckets around so that Sills could walk offstage and vomit. Susanne Marsee recalls Gigi telling the tenor that he would have to hold Sills up as she leaned into him, otherwise she would never make it through the performance.[14] Nevertheless, Sills finished out the NYCO season, which included three performances of *I Puritani* and a *Roberto Devereux.* Before the end of October, her concert and recital obligations took her to Philadelphia, Syracuse, Minneapolis, and Evansville, Indiana.

Sills left New York on October 21 for Dallas, where she was to make her role debut in Donizetti's *Lucrezia Borgia* on November 1. Rehearsals on the twenty-second turned out to be impossible as she was in severe pain and hemorrhaging. Before long, she received a call from her brother telling her to return to New York immediately. The results of a biopsy were back; she had ovarian cancer. She returned on the twenty-third and went directly from the airport to the hospital. The next day, doctors removed a grapefruit-sized tumor. In violation of her doctor's advice, she was on the stage for a dress rehearsal for *La Fille du Régiment* in San Francisco on November 17. In *Beverly,* she wrote that, in retrospect, going back so soon "was a dumb move" (1987, 259). Press photos confirm that she was gaunt. Although she had been dieting prior to her diagnosis, all in all, she lost forty or so pounds over a relatively short period. Everyone at the San Francisco Opera was aware of her fragility; she eliminated much of her stage action due to her weakened state. In self analyzing what drove her to push her recovery, she said she was afraid that people would think she was on her deathbed; she worried that if she canceled, *she* would feel that she was dying. She needed to overcome her fear by singing through the pain. Another explanation is that Sills desperately needed to get back onstage as performance had by then become a familiar safe zone in which she took refuge from her real-life problems. She sang all five *La Fille du Régiment* performances in San Francisco over a short span of twelve days.

Abdominal surgery is potentially damaging for a singer because the procedure involves cutting some of the muscles used in breath support. With the loss of her ovaries, Sills was thrust into menopause, which can also be menacing. A scientific study, which builds on the experience of classically trained singers, found that some women's voices undergo changes around and after menopause, such as loss of power, diminished vocal control, and difficulty in the highest reaches of the range (Boulet and Oddens 1996). Both menopause and diminished strength in her abdominal muscles likely contributed to a noticeable vocal decline in the year following her cancer surgery. Her dramatic weight loss may also have negatively affected her singing. The key issue is that a major change in body weight means a shift in the singer's center of support. Sills did not take the time to retrain her muscles. Furthermore, she did not work with a voice teacher again after Estelle Liebling passed away in 1970. Essentially, Sills needed to retrain her body after the trauma of surgery, hormonal changes, and weight loss, and had nobody systematically guiding her through this challenging adjustment process. Lastly, Sills's insistence on not resting properly following her surgery also likely affected her physical stamina.

Three days after her last San Francisco performance, she was on the stage of the Dorothy Chandler Pavilion in Los Angeles singing *I Puritani* with the NYCO in the last week of its fall tour. She was to have sung *Lucia di Lammermoor* as an opening night benefit on November 13. Sills's friend Birgit Nilsson came to the rescue by performing *Tosca* in what was Nilsson's NYCO debut. The day after her *I Puritani* performance, Sills appeared on the *Tonight Show* with Johnny Carson. Her singing of two numbers on the show represents the only known video record of Sills's performance in the period immediately following her surgery. As she always did when she appeared on the show, she traded humorous anecdotes; she even joked about her cancer, recalling that her doctor told her that she was a very healthy woman except for having "a touch of cancer." When she first came out, she sang an English-language version of "Vilja" from Lehar's opera *The Merry Widow*. She may have chosen to do this number because she sang it during a previous *Tonight Show* appearance and could avoid the need for rehearsal. Her second number was Manuel M. Ponce's song "Estrellita," which she asked to do with guitar accompaniment. *Tonight Show* guitarist Bob Bain recalls that when Sills arrived in the studio before the show she was tired and preferred to lie down rather than to rehearse.[15] She was uncertain if she would do the second number; she expressed confidence that Bain would be able to follow her, if she felt up to performing.[16] Her voice broke several times as she sang "Estrellita" with a rather strident tone and a previously uncharacteristic wide vibrato. At moments, her facial expression mirrored the text: "Estrellita del lejano cielo" (Little star of the distant sky), "Que miras mi dolor" (You see my pain), "Tu sabes mi sufrir" (You know my anguish). Completing this herculean, postoperative marathon in her weakened state may well have contributed to a general loss of stamina, which marked the last few years of her singing career.

With her final performing obligations of 1974 completed, Sills and her family took a vacation to Puerto Vallarta. After a month of rest, she was back touring as a recitalist and she appeared four times as Lucia, twice with the Omaha Opera and twice with Milwaukee's Florentine Opera Company. Once the NYCO's winter 1975 season started, she did three performances of *I Puritani* and three *Anna Bolena*s. Also occupying her time in New York were the rehearsals for her long-overdue Metropolitan Opera debut, which came just six months after her cancer surgery.

The Metropolitan Opera Debut

Negotiations with the Metropolitan Opera for her debut began as soon as Rudolf Bing retired in 1972. Bing had made Sills several offers previously, but always managed to propose dates on which she had well-publicized prior engagements, such as her Covent Garden debut or the NYCO premiere performance of *Roberto Devereux*. In early 1972, Goeran Gentele, who took over from Bing, invited Sills to lunch, during which they began to discuss possible debut vehicles. Sills was most interested in doing *I Puritani,* a work that she had not yet performed in New York and that she had just sung brilliantly with Luciano Pavarotti and Paul Plishka in Philadelphia. Gentele initially agreed and proposed a new production for Sills for April 1975. Before long, however, he learned that Bing and Sutherland had already discussed Sutherland's doing *I Puritani.* Her agent threatened that she "would never set foot in the Metropolitan again" if Sills were to do *I Puritani* (Chapin 1977, 331).[17] Next, in consultation with Edgar Vincent and others, Sills floated the idea of doing either *L'assedio di Corinto* or *La Fille du Régiment.* In the end, they settled on a revival of the La Scala *L'assedio* with Thomas Schippers conducting.

Justino Diaz returned to his role as Maometto II; Shirley Verrett replaced Marilyn Horne as the Greek warrior Neocle; and Harry Theyard took over the role of Pamira's father Cleomene. The Met hired the same directing team as was employed in La Scala; the sets and costumes were similar to the earlier production. The music was changed substantially, partly to add two additional cabalettas for Sills and partly to sidestep proprietary claims asserted by Randolph Mickelson. In searching for suitable materials to add, Jack Mastroianni, who was assisting Schippers, extended his sources to include a revision of *Maometto II* for a Venetian performance and a score for a later Venetian performance of *L'assedio*.

The choice of this work as her debut vehicle is just one facet of the entire absurdity that was Sills's long road to the Metropolitan Opera. This opera was certainly not one of Rossini's finest, especially not in terms of drama, and Schippers's performing edition was no masterpiece. The drama is ultimately a moribund ode to filial and patriotic duty peopled by static characters. To make matters worse, as Martin Bernheimer observed, stage director Sandro Sequi's "nonstaging—he apparently regarded the drama as a frozen oratorio—proved an embarrassment" (*Los Angeles Times,* April 27, 1975). Evidence of Sills's disdain for her character, the priggish Pamira, abounds in the pages of her personal score, now held by the New York Public Library for the Performing Arts in Lincoln Center. For example, at the opening of act 2, Pamira is distraught as she only recently learned that the man she is about to marry, Almanzor, is really Maometto II, the Turkish leader and enemy of her fellow Greeks. When the young Greek officer Neocle (to whom Pamira's father has promised her) breaks into the Turkish camp to take her home, Pamira decides she would rather die than to live with the enemies of her compatriots. As she makes her intentions clear to Maometto, Neocle exclaims, "Io trionfo, io trionfo!" (I triumph! I triumph). After Neocle's words, Sills penciled in her score, "cretino" (cretin). On the next page, above her lines "Oh mio padre! No, la morte!" (Oh my father, No, I die! [rather than marry Maometto]), Sills sums up her feelings about Pamira: "She is really a lunatic." The act closes with Pamira singing of patriotism and honor: "Tutta l'alma al pensier si riaccende di morir per la patria e l'onor" (My whole soul is rekindled at the thought of dying for the fatherland and honor). Taking a jab at Pamira's blind obedience, Sills circled the words "di morir per la patria e l'onor," writing above them, "balloni" (a play on "baloney").

As a "stand-up-and-sing" role, Pamira was not the best choice for Sills at this point in her career. A comparison of her key arias recorded during her La Scala premiere in 1969 and those from her Met debut six years later reveal rather dramatic changes in her voice. While her coloratura still retained its stunning accuracy and speed, she no longer reached her highest notes effortlessly. The pure, melting legato spun so ethereally at La Scala now suffered from a hardening of tone and a slow, wide vibrato. Very few reviewers commented negatively on her singing on the occasion of her celebrated Met debut. Harold Schonberg was an almost singular exception, although he was gentle in his criticism.

> Her voice these days has a few problem areas, and she does have trouble with long-held high notes. But she sang to strength, and her cadenzas and other interpolations were largely successful, playing to strength.
> Those strengths include brilliant passage work, tightly controlled trills in the middle register (they break up above the staff), beauty of tone and infinite feeling. There were a few unfortunate encounters with high notes in exposed positions. Miss Sills's public expects her to take those high notes, and she gallantly tries, although her singing would be so much better off if she modestly took a low option. (*New York Times,* April 8, 1975)

An examination of her performances in *L'assedio di Corinto,* as captured in bootleg recordings, provides a good vehicle for tracking Sills's vocal decline. The recording of the Metropolitan Opera Saturday matinee radio broadcast on April 19, 1975, finds her voice in rather poor condition. Between this performance and her earlier debut on April 7, she sang *L'assedio* three times (on April 10, 12, and 15). However, on April 10, she also did a matinee performance for the filming of *Danny Kaye's Look-In at the Metropolitan Opera* with Robert Merrill and conducted by James Levine.[18] This performance was repeated on April 11. By the time of the Met radio broadcast, she had laryngitis. In his *Los Angeles Times* article, Martin Bernheimer revealed: "Reliable spies backstage reported that she was, quite literally, speechless" (April 27, 1975). Yet, in the spirit of "the show-must-go-on tradition," she insisted on performing. Bernheimer noted that she was no doubt physically exhausted as this was her fifth performance of *L'assedio* in two weeks and she had given two performances on the Danny Kaye "television spectacular" in between. Bernheimer found her "tone was fluttery and opaque, the markmanship with high notes inexact, the delivery strained." With no announcement being made during the broadcast about her laryngitis, radio listeners were left wondering "what all the fuss was about." As Bernheimer commented, "it wasn't fair" (ibid.). But Sills drove herself, often to exhaustion. She rarely canceled and she seemed to think nothing of performing with laryngitis.[19]

L'assedio opened the fall 1975 season, thus winning Sills's the most prestigious date on the Metropolitan Opera calendar. By this time, however, it became apparent to Sills that her part (which Schippers and Mastroianni had expanded from the La Scala performing edition to give her two additional caballetas) was simply too taxing given her declining physical stamina. Mastroianni reports that they cut all of her caballetas in half (Mastroianni interview, March 19, 2011). Unfortunately, there is no known recording of the five fall performances. However, a recording of a January 17, 1976, radio broadcast still circulates. In it we hear that she has altered some of her ornamentation and interpolations; in most cases, she has reworked them to avoid singing in the now-difficult upper reaches of her range.

Vocal Decline and Retirement

Sills added four other roles to her list of those she performed at the Metropolitan Opera before retiring: *La Traviata* (1976), *Lucia di Lammermoor* (1976–77), *Thaïs* (1978), and *Don Pasquale* (1978–79). Three contrasting reviews of her first Violetta at the Met in January 1976 give a good sense of the range of audience reactions to Sills in her last four years of singing. Her audience included those for whom Sills's now-unavoidable vocal imperfections marred her entire performance, those for whom her deep engagement in the total performance minimized their attention to her vocal difficulties, and those who idolized Sills and were impervious to her flaws.

Harold Schonberg represents the first of these views. Although he conceded that Sills "presented a convincing dramatic realization of the role," he reported that she had "a great deal of pitch trouble in the first act. Later on she was closer to the note, but even there, one's enjoyment of her performance depended in large part on one's tolerance to pitch deviations" (*New York Times,* January 14, 1976).[20]

The second view was well expressed by Andrew Porter, who was clearly drawn in by Sills's strong stage presence and ability to inhabit the role completely. For Porter, the performance was "one in which all that matters is the present; one during which memories fade, comparisons are forgotten, and any critical faculties are largely suspended; one in which the heroine holds an audience rapt and intent on everything she says, does, thinks, feels" (Porter 1976, 88). He notes that Sills "is not a perfect vocalist," but she and her conductor, Sarah Caldwell, knew exactly what she could and could not do, and "even without full-throated, glorious sound for climaxes, Verdi's music and his drama can be brought to life" (ibid.).

Shirley Eder, writing from New York for the *Detroit Free Press,* captured the third reaction (and perhaps some of the second, too) when she noted that Sills brought the audience to its feet. "She received thunderous applause and cheering and was even bombarded with confetti-like bits of paper as she took her final bows. It all looked like a ticker-tape parade" (*Detroit Free Press,* January 17, 1976).

As Sills came to her final years of singing, she increasingly added lighter, comic roles to her repertoire, such as Rosina in Rossini's *Barber of Seville,* Anna in Lehar's *The Merry Widow,* Norina in Donizetti's *Don Pasquale,* and Fiorilla in Rossini's *Turk in Italy.* These roles were far less demanding in terms of the emotion they required of the engaged singing actress than more taxing roles such the three queens. She termed these her "cream puff" roles. She even returned, if only briefly, to the French repertoire, as Miss Liebling had encouraged her to do when she first began taking on bel canto roles. She did six performances of Massenet's *Thaïs* with the San Francisco Opera in September 1976 and seventeen more with the Metropolitan Opera in 1978. In spring of 1977, she starred in a new production of Charpentier's *Louise* with the New York City Opera; however, she did not return to the role after the six scheduled shows.

By the late 1970s, there were a number of occasions when Sills felt the need to substitute lighter roles, which better suited her vocal condition, for the heavy roles she was contracted to perform. For example, she was slated to sing *Anna Bolena* with the Tulsa Opera in spring 1978. She had announced at a press conference in January that she would be retiring in fall 1980 (*New York Times,* January 10, 1978). Just weeks before the March performances in Tulsa, Sills asked if she could substitute *I Puritani* because she felt it would be more congenial to her voice than *Bolena* and demand less of a change in vocal production relative to the roles she would be singing before and after her Tulsa appearance. Fortunately, several of the singers involved in the production had already performed *I Puritani* and the Tulsa Opera was able to accommodate the change (Williams and Sowell 1992, 47). Very near the end of her career in May 1980, she was to do a concert featuring Victor Herbert songs with the Dayton Philharmonic under Charles Wendelken-Wilson's direction. About a month before the performance she called her former NYCO colleague Wendelken-Wilson and asked to change the program, saying that she could no longer bear to hear her own voice singing "Ah, Sweet Mystery of Life"; she did not want the audience to hear it either. The wobble in her voice (that is, an uncontrollable, wide vibrato), which was most exposed in long-held notes, was now a constant presence. In the place of the Herbert songs, with their long melodies and sustained notes, they substituted a program of flashy, coloratura numbers, including "Una voce poco fa" from the *Barber of Seville,* "O, luce di quest anima" from *Linda di Chamounix,* and "Ah! Chacun le sait, chacun le dit" from *La Fille du Régiment.* Wendelken-Wilson recalled that in the dressing room before the performance she told him: "Charlie, I can't wait until October when I retire. I can hear what I sound like and I hate it" (interview, August 1, 2008).

Other colleagues have also shared stories of Sills's struggle during her final months of singing. Susanne Marsee recalled several poignant moments from their time together in San Diego in May and June 1980 as they prepared the world premiere of Menotti's *Juana la Loca.* Things were very stressful, partly a result of Menotti's failure to produce a completed score prior to the start of their final rehearsal period. During a break one day, Sills turned to Marsee and sang in a half-voice, "Tu, tu Seymour, mia rivale" (You, you Seymour, my rival), a fiery line Sills sang to Marsee when Marsee played Jane Seymour to Sills's Anne Boleyn, after which she said wistfully, "I'm never going to get to say that to you again." In this rare deviation from her normally upbeat public persona, Sills revealed how she truly felt about the loss of her singing career. She also confided to Marsee that she simply did not recognize her own voice any longer (Marsee interview, January 25, 2008). What she could have done years previously without effort or a moment's thought, she no longer could do.

In a feature article published in the Sunday *Washington Post* on November 2, 1980, Sills reflected on the winding down of her singing career.

> I was already making compromises in my repertoire, already making vocal compromises. I am used to being able to tell my voice exactly what to do and if occasionally it didn't do what I wanted, I knew the next time it would. If I had an off night I knew the next night was not going to be one. And now it became unreliable. I found that very offensive. I found myself thinking of my voice for the first time as a separate entity. You know—when it's not behaving. And I decided I could not spend the rest of my life doing recitals by adjusting the repertoire, or doing all this cream puff I was doing: Rosalinda [*sic*], Adele, Rosina, Norina. This was a voice that was used to doing Elviras and Elisabettas and Maria Stuardas. I couldn't go on doing repertoire like those others. It's not me.

Sills went even further in an interview for *Opera News*: "I can't spend the rest of my life on cream puffs. I'm used to walking out of the theater emotionally exhausted from my roles, and now my voice just can't handle the music that's been my life's blood" (Jacobson 1980, 9).

To mark Sills's final appearance on an operatic stage, the New York City Opera organized a spectacular party and concert gala for October 27, 1980, just two days short of the twenty-fifth anniversary of her company debut. The festivities began at 6:30 PM with trumpeters echoing fanfares across the Lincoln Center Plaza as 1,600 guests made their way to a cocktail party at which Sills personally greeted all of those who braved the reception line (*New Yorker*, November 10, 1980, 48). Dinner followed with the seating venue (either Avery Fischer Hall or the New York State Theater) and menu varying according to the ticket prices, which ranged from $250 to $1,000. Sills had been general director of the NYCO since July 1980 and she took her farewell as an opportunity to raise much-needed revenue for the company. Sills was a legendary fund-raiser. She managed to have fashion mogul Mohan Murjani sponsor her entire farewell gala; therefore, all of the evening's one million dollars in proceeds went directly to the NYCO's coffers.

After dinner, the performance began with the ballroom scene of *Die Fledermaus* (the same opera in which she commenced her long NYCO career) performed by NYCO singers with Kitty Carlisle cross-dressing as Prince Orlofsky and Sills as Rosalinde. Midway through the *Fledermaus* scene, Sills's close friend Carol

Burnett burst in wearing a chic, knee-length dress (in contrast to the opera's period costuming), making her entrance down the stage staircase calling, "Where is she? I know she's here. Beverly?" The *Fledermaus* drama ceased; soon, the show became a parade of stars performing their numbers. Among the artists who joined in the procession were Broadway celebrities Mary Martin and Ethel Merman; popular singers Dinah Shore and Bobby Short; and ballet dancers Cynthia Gregory, Heather Watts, and Peter Martins. From the opera world, John Alexander, Dominic Cossa, Plácido Domingo, Eileen Farrell, Donald Gramm, Leontyne Price, and Renata Scotto each sang either a popular number or an aria. Sills and Burnett then took center stage, where, with Sills seated on Queen Elizabeth's throne from *Roberto Devereux* and Carol perched on a stool, they repeated the medley of operatic and crooning melodies that they first did as part of their Thanksgiving Day special in 1976, *Sills and Burnett at the Met*. Near the close of the performance, other notable personalities took to the stage to dance with Sills or simply to embrace her, including Tito and Gigi Capobianco, New York City mayor Ed Koch, Walter Cronkite, Zubin Mehta, Burt Reynolds, and Lady Bird Johnson. The range of personalities who graced the New York Theater stage gives a good sense of Sills's broad appeal.

Sills closed the performance alone on the stage with her longtime musical partner Charles Wadsworth at the piano. She ended her career as she did her recitals—with a simple Portuguese lullaby given to her on her tenth birthday by Miss Liebling. "After the millions of notes she had uttered in that twirling, diamond-studded lariat of a voice, after all of the colossal passions she had reenacted—mad scenes, flamboyant lamentations, suicidal soliloquies—she spent those final minutes in 1980 with a simple, touching tune," wrote Justin Davidson for *New York* magazine (July 9, 2007).

With her singing career behind her, Sills's need to engage with an audience was met by her many appearances as a hostess or emcee on programs such as PBS's *Great Performances* and the intermission features for the Metropolitan Opera's high-definition broadcasts. Meanwhile, Sills went on to become a major force in arts administration. Writing of her long and distinguished administrative career, Mark Swed mused: "She could be tough as nails when she needed to be (although she had the capacity to put on the charm like nobody's business). She expected people to overcome obstacles as readily as she had her whole life" (*Los Angeles Times,* July 4, 2007).

When she took over as the general director of the NYCO, she discovered that the company was five million dollars in debt. Through her endless and mightily successful fund-raising efforts, she brought the company into the black. Among her most lasting contributions was the company's controversial introduction of supertitles, which are now a standard part of opera productions in all major

American opera houses.[21] She stepped down as general director in 1989 following a series of health problems, although she stayed on as the president of the NYCO board. In 1991, she left this position and joined the Metropolitan Opera's board of directors. Three years later, she became the chairman of Lincoln Center. As the organization's head, she helped establish the Lincoln Center Festival, one of the most important forums in New York for the performance of works of art from outside the Western European canon. She held this position until 2002, when she announced that she was finally ready to retire. Rest and relaxation did not suit her. Within six months, she was invited to serve as the chairman of the Metropolitan Opera's board, and she cheerfully accepted. Among her many accomplishments was to keep alive the Met's Saturday-afternoon broadcasts after their longtime corporate sponsor Chevron Texaco withdrew its support in 2004. She launched the "Save the Met Broadcast Campaign" by going on the air during an intermission feature and appealing directly to the radio audience. She also was instrumental in hiring Peter Gelb as general director of the Met, whose legacy is still in the making. Gelb's pathbreaking establishment of high-definition broadcasts of live Met performances into movie theaters around the world is certainly a fitting tribute to Sills's populist achievements.

Beverly Sills's final retirement came in January 2005, when her long-ailing husband, who had suffered a stroke and was in the advanced stages of Alzheimer's disease, was coming to the end of his life. Peter Greenough passed away in September 2006 at the age of eighty-nine. Sills followed at the age of seventy-eight the next July.[22] She is buried in Valhalla, New York, at Sharon Gardens Cemetery with Peter on her left and her mother and father on her right. Borrowing a phrase from the final scene of *The Ballad of Baby Doe,* her epitaph reads: "Loving Wife and Mother, 'Always and Forever.'"

Studio portrait as Violetta in Verdi's *La Traviata*. Charles Wagner tour, 1951. Courtesy of Ron Runyon.

As Tosca in Pucinni's *Tosca* with William Chapman as Scarpia,
Musicarnival, Warrensville Heights, Ohio, 1957. Courtesy of the John L.
Price Jr. Musicarnival Archives at the Cleveland Public Library.

As Cleopatra in Handel's *Giulio Cesare,* New York City Opera, November 1968. Copyright © Beth Bergman 1968, 2014.

(above) As Baby Doe in Moore's *The Ballad of Baby Doe*.
Musicarnival, Warrensville Heights, Ohio, 1958. Courtesy
of the John L. Price Jr. Musicarnival Archives at the
Cleveland Public Library.

(right) As Queen
Shemakha in Rimsky-
Korsakov's *Coq d'Or*
with Normal Treigle
as King Dodon, New
York City Opera,
March 1969. Copyright
© Beth Bergman 1969,
2014.

As Manon in Massenet's *Manon,* New York City Opera, February 1969.
Copyright © Beth Bergman 1969, 2014.

As Manon in the Saint-Sulpice scene of Massenet's *Manon* with Michele Molese as des Grieux, New York City Opera, dress rehearsal, March 1968. Copyright © Beth Bergman 1969, 2014.

As Giulietta in Offenbach's *Tales of Hoffmann* with Norman Treigle as Dapertutto, New York City Opera, October 1972. Copyright © Beth Bergman 1972, 2014.

As Lucia in Donizetti's *Lucia di Lammermoor with* Robert Hale as
Raimondo, New York City Opera, dress rehearsal, October 1969.
Copyright © Beth Bergman 1969, 2014.

As Marguerite in
Gounod's *Faust*,
New York City
Opera, October 1968.
Copyright © Beth
Bergman 1968.

Beverly Sills and Peter Greenough in Milan, Italy, at the time of her La Scala
debut, 1969. Courtesy of Meredith Greenough.

As Queen Elizabeth I in Donizetti's *Roberto Devereux*, New York City Opera, opening night, October 15, 1970. Copyright © Beth Bergman 1970.

As Mary Stuart in Donizetti's *Maria Stuarda* with Pauline Tinsley as Queen Elizabeth I. Sills delivers the line "vil bastarda" (vile bastard). New York City Opera, March 1972. Copyright © Beth Bergman 1972, 2014.

As Anne Boleyn in Donizetti's *Anna Bolena* with Enrico Di Giuseppe
and Robert Hale, New York City Opera, dress rehearsal, October 1973.
Copyright © Beth Bergman 1973, 2011.

As Violetta in Verdi's *La Traviata,* Metropolitan Opera, January 1976.
Copyright © Beth Bergman 1976, 2014.

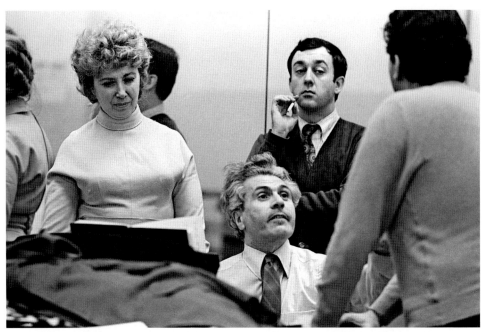

(above) Beverly Sills in rehearsal for *Manon* with Julius Rudel (at the piano), Roland Gagnon, and Plácido Domingo (with his back to the camera), New York City Opera, February 1969. Copyright © Beth Bergman 2015, NYC.

(right) Beverly Sills and Gigi Capobianco after a day of experimenting with Queen Elizabeth's hair and makeup in preparation for *Roberto Devereux,* 1970. Copyright © Beth Bergman 1970, 2014.

Beverly Sills and Tito Capobianco in rehearsal for Rossini's *Turk in Italy*, New York City Opera, 1978. Copyright © Beth Bergman, 2015.

Charles Freeman Stamper (left), Roy C. Dicks (middle), and Taylor Cornish (right) share photos from Stamper's collection with Pete Buchanan (in England) via Skype, June 2011, Hayward, California. Photo by Nancy Guy.

A fan meet-up in New York City, April 2014. Left to right, Pete Buchanan, Roy C. Dicks, Nancy Guy, David Ponder, and Ron Runyon. Attendees not pictured include Richard Anderson, Cynthia Edwards, Kathryn Rider, Daniel James Shigo, and Jerry Vezzuso. Photo by Deborah Barber.

CHAPTER 5

Loving Sills

Many came to love Beverly Sills through her live performances, and many more through her television appearances. They responded not only to her voice but also her persona. Many were inspired by her and continue to share their love for her today via the Internet. In exploring Sills's fandom, numerous individual fans were interviewed and some of their stories are shared here in their own voices.

Opera, and opera singers, have always evoked love from listeners, although music scholars have largely avoided this concept in the interest of maintaining objectivity. However, the passion of opera lovers for the music, drama, spectacle, and especially for the singers of this extravagant art has inspired prose from writers in other scholarly disciplines and across a range of creative forms. Fictionalized accounts, with narrative forms that allow for situating the love for opera within a rich contextual web of the individual fan's life, have sometimes proven the most effective in conveying the profundity of this passion (which approaches the power of a life force for some). For example, Marcia Davenport's *Of Lena Geyer,* a fictional biography of a prima donna, sensitively narrates the attraction of a female admirer for a diva who eventually becomes her lifelong companion.[1] *Mawrdew Czgowchwz,* James McCourt's novel titled after a fictitious prima donna of Eastern European origin, is "a comic tribute" to the unbound admiration, and equally potent jealously and scorn, that surrounds all great divas.[2] The excesses of diva devotees, and how their devotion is vital to their lives, is taken up in Terrence McNally's highly successful stage play *The Lisbon Traviata* (first produced in 1989 with important revivals in 2004 and 2006). The obsession with a singer's voice, and capturing it on tape, is central to Jean-Jacques Beineix's classic film *Diva* (1981). All of these artistic representations are vivid and apt tributes to the power of opera singers to enchant and overwhelm the lives of those who fall under their spells.

The vast majority of writings produced by musicologists on operatic subjects have carefully sidestepped the visceral effect of the singer, and the singer's voice, on listeners. There has been an almost total avoidance of operatic devotion and fandom, with many musicologists treating these as if they were contagions—at the least, irrelevant; at the worst, capable of invalidating the carefully constructed objectivity of studies focused largely on works, composers, and directors. Not surprisingly the most significant academic work on these subjects has come from the fields of English (Koestenbaum 1993; Castle 1995), theater (Abel 1996; Risi 2011a), and sociology (Benzecry 2011).

Two major works that approach the question of operatic fandom from different disciplinary stances are Wayne Koestenbaum's now-classic *The Queen's Throat: Opera, Homosexuality, and the Mystery of Desire* (1993) and Claudio Benzecry's award-winning *The Opera Fanatic: Ethnography of an Obsession* (2011).[3] As a sociologist, Benzecry brings the full arsenal of cultural sociological theories to bear in investigating the passion of dedicated opera fans in Buenos Aires, Argentina. True to his disciplinary training, Benzecry initially seeks an answer to the key question of what drives his consultants' commitment to opera in socioeconomic and educational factors. Employing an ethnographically based research method, he interviews individual fans and spends a good deal of time together with them in the standing-room sections on the upper floors of the famed Colón opera house and on sojourns to opera houses on the outskirts of the capital city. As Benzecry discovered, theories spun out in volumes and volumes of scholarly works dedicated to music consumption are inadequate for understanding the "long-term, passionate commitment of the opera fan" (2011, 5).[4] Even sociologist Pierre Bourdieu's influential theory of taste as a mode of distinction fails to explain the role of opera in the lives of devoted fans (Bourdieu 1984). Instead, the fans under Benzecry's study have developed their sophisticated tastes as forms of personal transcendence and belonging.

In the end, Benzecry finds that a metaphor of love is central to understanding the deep attachments of passionate opera fans. As he applies it, the love metaphor relays the idea that "despite a lack of outside recognition, something we engage affectively with and charge with value becomes a building block of who we are" (2011, 184). Hence, opera is central to the fans' understanding of themselves and their identity.

Although Benzecry investigates the personal circumstances of his consultants, he seems not to have engaged deeply with the details of their emotional attachments to specific elements of operatic performance, such as a star soprano "whose voice is 'magic,'" for example (ibid., 173). In a section titled "Being One with Music," he notes that only a few of his interviewees named specific singers in discussing their love for opera. Given the centrality of attachment to a specific performer discussed in most writings on operatic fandom—and other forms of fandom, too—this seems peculiar. One cannot help but wonder if perhaps Benzecry's sociological research paradigm discouraged him from moving into more explicit personal details with his individual consultants.

Contrasting sharply in nearly every way to Benzecry's book is Koestenbaum's *The Queen's Throat*, now in its second printing (2001). Although Benzecry crafts a detailed study in which he subjects his data to the rigors of social-science inquiry, Koestenbaum is fairly free of disciplinary constraints. *The Queen's Throat* is a poetic elegy in which Koestenbaum foregrounds his own passionate experiences with opera. Sexuality is only a tangential consideration for Benzecry, while the queer positionality of Koestenbaum and his associates, whose stories he also weaves throughout his tome, is absolutely central to Koestenbaum's thesis. He organizes his material as a "scrapbook" of fragments (1993, 29). These fragments are colorful and often poignant vignettes drawn from his own experience and those of other opera lovers, as well as excerpts from literature, history, and film, all of which Koestenbaum frames in support of his deconstruction, and sometimes flippant analysis, of the passion for opera. In many of these, we find profound kernels of truth—insights into the practice of loving opera shared from extremely personal perspectives (as matters of love and intimacy must be).

Two decades or so after the publication of *The Queen's Throat*, I have found many of the feelings and practices of adoration Koestenbaum chronicled still current among the Sills fans I have come to know. In exploring Beverly Sills's appeal for her fans, I reference issues identified by Koestenbaum, and Benzecry's "love metaphor" is extremely productive for interpreting Sills's allure for many of her devotees. I also draw on the body of scholarly writings on the fandom of artists from divergent musical genres and traditions, such as Daniel Cavicchi's work on Bruce Springsteen fans (1998) and Mark Duffett's writings on the Elvis phenomenon (2000, 2001, 2003).

Becoming a Fan

How does it happen? Among the multitude of voices and singers and myriad musical traditions and genres, how does a listener become dedicated to one artist above all others? Koestenbaum writes that "[c]hoosing a diva to love is like inaugurating any erotic arrangement": there is the first encounter when a special someone catches your attention, the sometimes long process of gaining her notice, listening for her voice above the din of a crowded room, and so on (1993, 20). Anna

Moffo possessed Koestenbaum's chosen voice, though he shares his ranked list of nineteen other sopranos and a few "honorary men" whom he admires (ibid.). Like most great love affairs, he came across Moffo by happenstance when he purchased an inexpensive LP set of *Rigoletto*; Moffo was the Gilda. He marks this purchase as a defining moment: "I began to put my life together" (ibid., 19). A single musical utterance reeled him in: "[I]t was Moffo's delayed, dusky, under-the-note attack on the word 'disvelto' in a passage from *Rigoletto*, the way she took a word not in itself meaningful or musically crucial, and marked it with individuality and pathos; I noticed that in the performances of other Gildas, the word 'disvelto' passed unremarkably, unrewarded by emphasis. I knew that when she chose, Moffo had the power to warm up a note from within, and that I had the power to listen for that instant when unspeakable complexities textured a note" (ibid., 21).

Though Koestenbaum writes of the way in which Anna Moffo became his diva as a selection process, it often happens that a listener is struck by a singer's voice instantly. There is no rational choice involved. If there is a process, it is lightning fast, happening undetected by conscious thought. In his work with Bruce Springsteen fans, Cavicchi muses that becoming a fan is not so different from experiencing a religious conversion. The narratives of becoming Springsteen fans, which Cavicchi collected over the course of his fieldwork, were "remarkably similar to those found in the conversion narratives of evangelical Christians in the modern United States" (1998, 43). Cavicchi found that fans usually came to their idols by one of two processes (1998, 43). The first type is similar to that described by Koestenbaum. An individual becomes a fan gradually, either through listening to the performer's music, or by going to concerts, or through the influence of a friend who is already a fan; over a period of time, his or her appreciation for the artist grows. The second type involves an instant transformation that is akin to an epiphany. A fan having experienced this type of conversion often can recall the exact moment when he or she was struck by the epiphany and precisely how he or she felt as the revelation revealed itself.

The stories gathered here typically fall into one of these two conversion models. Three fan narratives illustrate the instant-transformation variety. To demonstrate that the medium through which the listener first encounters the singer does not appear to be a factor, I have chosen a story of a very public conversion, when the listener's first exposure to Sills was in live performance; a case of a young television viewer who became a fan during the course of a single broadcast; and a listener who fell in love with Sills when he first listened to one of her records.

Taylor Cornish was twenty years old and a piano major in college when he first heard Beverly Sills live in recital in September 1970. I was introduced to Cornish via e-mail by Pete Buchanan, a long-standing Sills fan profiled in chapter 6. Buchanan constantly searches the Internet for Sills devotees, and several of

Cornish's YouTube comments had caught his attention. After Cornish and I had exchanged a few e-mails, he told of his first encounter with Sills:

> You know how "wise" we are when we're 20: I was sure opera was a stupid art form, and went to the recital mostly just for the adventure of the 150-mile drive to William Jewell College (and a free pass from classes that day).
>
> The event was sold out and we were sitting on folding chairs placed in front of the first row of auditorium seating. I couldn't have been more than a dozen feet from her. Every piece she sang that night was a revelation to me. Her last group was maybe five Richard Strauss songs including "Breit über mein Haupt" and I just could not keep from crying. Eventually I had my hands clamped over my mouth and was just trying not to move and make any noise because she kept looking at me and I was afraid I was going to throw her off.
>
> Afterwards we all got in line to have her sign our programs. The entire time we waited I could hear peals of laughter coming from the front of the line. She was making everyone laugh as she signed her name. When I finally got to her and it was my turn I just froze—she smiled and gently took my program from my hand and began signing it. Neither of us had said one word. Suddenly I just blurted out, "I haven't cried that hard in years." She looked thoughtful for a moment and then replied, "Well, you know, sometimes I get a little weepy over some of them myself."
>
> And thus began a love affair that lives to this day.
>
> I was lucky enough to see her in most of her signature roles at the NYCO, and as Pamira and Violetta at the Met. I attended both tapings of *Sills and Burnett at the Met* and heard her speak several times after her retirement from the stage and took the opportunity to ask a question (and praise her) each time.
>
> Since that night 40 years ago, opera has become my favorite music (and I am passionate about many forms of music). I am fanatical about lots of singers and musicians, but Beverly Sills is my heart and my favorite artist in any genre. (e-mail, May 28, 2010)

Cornish and I met on several occasions, sometimes in the company of other Sills fans. In September 2012, when we gathered at Freeman Stamper's private Sills museum in Hayward, California, to belatedly mark the fifth anniversary of Sills's death, I asked Cornish to tell his story again, this time before a video camera. Holding up his recital program (which now belongs to Freeman's collection) from that evening forty-two years prior, he began: "So, this is the night that my life changed."

The first time Ron Runyon ever saw Sills was on television when she was costarring in the *Sills and Burnett at the Met* broadcast on Thanksgiving evening in 1976 when he was fifteen years old. Although he enjoyed the show, he admits that he watched to see Carol Burnett. It was not until nearly four years later in

May 1980, when he saw Sills as Norina in Donizetti's *Don Pasquale* broadcast from the Met, that he was enraptured.[5]

I first contacted Runyon in the summer of 2009 when I was searching for Sills's fans who had posted epitaphs in 2007 in the wake of her passing. Runyon's comment that Sills had changed his life, in the www.beverlysillsonline.com "Farewell Guestbook" (hereafter *Guestbook*),[6] naturally piqued my attention:

> Thank you, Beverly. I sadly had never gotten around to my age-long intention of writing to thank you for the beauty and passion you brought to my life. The impression you made upon this young kid changed my world and shaped my artistic and cultural life. The beauty and passion of opera which you introduced me to has given my life its greatest joy, taught me other languages, and taken me to foreign lands to the great opera houses of the world. Never did I not think of you as I entered the historic houses, a world which you opened up to me—La Scala, Staatsoper, La Fenice. Your contribution to your art was a contribution to the lives of so many, and I remain ever indebted for that gift. I will never forget you. Thank you, dear lady.

After reading his entry, I wrote to Runyon directly and asked if he would share more about how Sills had "shaped [his] artistic and cultural life." His reply, of six single-spaced pages, began by mentioning how "opera's musicality" had always struck him, even as a child, such as when he would hear familiar opera tunes used in cartoon sound tracks.

> THEN, it happened, the moment I was converted for life. I was working in a fast-food restaurant at the time, undoubtedly still in my teens, and one day a co-worker commented that Beverly Sills was going to be in an opera on TV that night. I can still hear him telling me, for I remember thinking, ODD that this man would be knowledgeable about Beverly Sills!? "Beverly Sills, yes, I remember her. Gosh, one hears a lot about this woman—just what is she all about?," I wondered. I made a mental note to try to remember to turn the TV on that night and just see for myself what's all the fuss. A few minutes after 8 PM, I was late, but YEAH, let me turn on PBS. As I did, applause had just ended on act 1, scene 1 of *Don Pasquale*. As if on cue, the moment I sat down to watch, it was Beverly's entrance, sitting on a wicker chair, out on Norina's patio, just launching into her opening aria, cigarette in hand, panache and wit on display along with the most gorgeous, shimmering, crystalline voice I'd ever heard. AND, this time it had SUBTITLES on screen so I could follow! By the time she finished her aria, I WAS HOOKED. I was mesmerized, enraptured of her abilities as well as in awe of the art form. To this day, Donizetti remains my favorite composer, whether or not it was love at first sight (hearing) of his work, I do not know, but it's no coincidence that *Anna Bolena* and *Pasquale* (and *LUCIA*) rank in my top five favorite operas. It was Beverly, however, who

"hooked" me. I enjoyed that evening so much and as LUCK would have it, I had the presence of mind to record it on EARLY VHS tape! She was just so convincing in her acting, so responsive musically, and one could SEE her JOY in singing, it was evident. (e-mail, July 27, 2009)

Runyon touched on numerous themes that come up repeatedly in the online epitaphs and in my personal communications with fans—being hooked, mesmerized, or enraptured, feeling an attraction to the joy with which Sills sang, and feeling gratitude to her for making a life-changing impact.

Composing his entry to the *Guestbook* posted at www.beverlysillsonline.com as though he were addressing Sills directly (as did Runyon and many other epitaph authors), David Alan Tidyman also declared that she had changed his life. He wrote, "When I heard you sing 'Breit über Mein Haupt' of Richard Strauss, the sensitivity, love and poetry that you sang with changed my life forever."[7] I contacted Tidyman and he explained that he was first exposed to her as a student in organ performance at North Texas State. He had accompanied an opera singer who gave him Sills's *Bellini and Donizetti Heroines* album. Tidyman explained that he was not interested in opera, but the voice student insisted. David recalled:

I wasn't more than 30 seconds into the first cut and I was totally transformed by the sheer brilliance and clarity of the voice. . . . That started this crazy fan thing that has lasted over the last 30 years. This is like so much of life, the thing that you said you didn't want to do opens the biggest doors. (phone conversation with author, July 17, 2009)

Some of Sills's most dedicated fans did not experience the sudden epiphany-type conversion, but came to adore her over repeated encounters. It was through multiple introductions to Sills that she gradually became a constant in Bill Bond's life. His first exposure came when, as a teenager growing up in Iowa in the mid-1960s, a fellow chorister played her recording of *The Ballad of Baby Doe* for him. Bond marveled at Sills's "Willow Song." From then on, he watched her on a variety of television programs. When he went to college as a music major in 1969, his voice teacher suggested he listen to her *Bellini and Donizetti Heroines* album, after which he set out to collect all of her records. He recounted that he and his fellow music majors, as well as a few faculty members, began a phone tree. Every Sunday, when the week's television listings were published in the newspaper, they would call around so that everyone knew when she would be on. Bond remembers: "She was everywhere! I couldn't get enough. And I wore out my recordings. . . . I followed her all through the rest of her life. I replaced my recordings on LP with CDs but will never let them go because of the wealth of photos from the inserts. And there is rarely a day that goes by I don't listen to her" (e-mail, July 15, 2009).

What Was It about Sills?

In seeking to understand what it was that drew people to Sills, I sought answers through private correspondence with individuals who proclaimed their fondness for her in public forums, either in print media or online. Public proclamations led to private correspondences. What was it exactly that "hooked" Cornish, Runyon, Tidyman, Bond, and countless others? I gathered statements from more than eight hundred people—some written by passionate fans, others by casual admirers. From the vast majority of these, I have only collected single statements. However, I have shared multiple communications with about one hundred Sills admirers (not including her former colleagues) and have had the pleasure of exploring their memories of and feelings toward Sills with more than half of these, some of whom have become a vital part of my own life.

Generalizing about the demographics of Sills fans is no easy task. It is impossible to know how many people self-identify as her fans but have not done so on public websites discovered during this research. In addition, there are no doubt individuals who hold a deep appreciation for Sills's singing, but have never applied the moniker "fan" to the nature of their engagement with her art. It also should be noted that of the more than eight hundred people who have come to my attention during the course of conducting this research, I have only come to know about fifty personally. These are people I contacted after finding their epitaphs particularly touching or detailed, or whose other activities (such as purchases made on eBay or their maintenance of a Sills website) gained my attention. Of these, my knowledge of their lives regarding their socioeconomic backgrounds, educational levels, race and ethnicities, professional histories, and sexual preferences (to name a few factors that may be of interest to academic investigators) is uneven at best, because I chose not to focus on these areas in this study.

Of the people with whom I have had extended contact, the vast majority are Euro-American, although a handful of epitaph writers reference their African American heritages. There are also several members of "The Beverly Sills Crazies!" Facebook group who participate from Asia, Africa, or Europe. Insofar as class and educational backgrounds are concerned, the body of fans I have come to know runs the gamut from highly privileged to humble. Perhaps not insignificant is that I became acquainted with those hailing from more elite circumstances not in Internet environments, but through personal networks. Numerous fans, including myself, are the first members of their families to attend a university or college. Some received no tertiary education, while others have advanced degrees.

Much has been written on opera and homosexuality (e.g., Koestenbaum 1993; Robinson 1994; Castle 1995; Abel 1996). I can only verify this aspect of the fans with whom I have had extended contact. It is fair to say that women and heterosexual men are in the minority. Most of the men self-identify as gay; most of the women as straight. Not being a focus of this study, I did not ask my consultants about sexual orientation, but over time the subject entered our conversations, sometimes in ways as subtle as a partner's name on a Christmas card. With a similar delicacy, the fans profiled in this chapter and the next share details of their personal lives in their own ways as they tell the stories of their engagement with Sills.

In identifying my consultants' attraction to Sills, I refrain from seeking a psychoanalytical explanation such as that employed by Michel Poizat in his investigation of operatic passions (1992). Applying Lacanian theory to a subject such as this is often little more than trading one complex reality (i.e., the fan's passion for a diva) for a contrived complexity (i.e., complex in its jargon, but often reductionist in the final analysis).[8] The application of psychoanalytical theory, whether that of Freud, Lacan, or others, to an ethnographically based study strikes me as fundamentally disrespectful to those whose actions and feelings are being analyzed. I share Cavicchi's observation that far too often fans' understandings of their own actions are "revised according to scholars' ideological concerns—that is, either dismissed as 'false consciousness' or 'pathology' or transformed into 'resistance' or 'rebellion'" (1998, 185). I believe my consultants are self-aware enough to not only have insights into their own passions, but also to be fully capable of articulating these.[9] My approach is therefore similar to that of Cavicchi, who aimed to "engage fandom as it is experienced" (ibid.).

As I studied the vast number of detailed and often touching personal narratives from Sills fans, certain broad themes emerged. Many of these remark on her artistry and are not unlike observations found in published reviews, though typically expressed with greater fervor; other topics are more personal and intimate. While it is beyond the scope of this work to address every detail and nuance, I have parsed five broad qualities that attracted the attention, admiration, and affection of her fans: (1) her voice and musicality; (2) the totality of her operatic performance; (3) the joy with which she sang; (4) her personality characteristics, such as her warmth, determination, and down-to-earth manner; and (5) her standing as an all-American icon. A single person may have been profoundly influenced by one or several of these factors. Likewise, the relative importance of each of these may have changed over the long course of an individual's engagement with Sills; they may even shift from moment to moment. Beyond these five qualities, there is also the frequent heartfelt expression of the general influence, manifested in myriad ways, she had on the lives of individual admirers.

The lifelong attraction to a singer is, not surprisingly, often sparked by the voice itself. Answering why listeners respond viscerally to one voice and not to another deserves multidisciplinary study, which is beyond the scope of this exploration of Sills fandom. Unfortunately, fans, critics, and scholars far too frequently fail to admit, or fairly represent, the subjectivity involved in their own proclivities for certain voices, or even types of voices. In exalting one voice, they denigrate another. Even Roland Barthes's influential essay "The Grain of the Voice" is constructed around a thinly veiled proclamation of personal taste (1977, 178–89). I would like to see future studies of the attraction of listeners to certain voices conducted along the lines of Judith Becker's investigation of the emotional, physiological, and neurological responses to music by "deep listeners" (2004). Becker identifies deep listeners as a subset of music lovers "who experience chills or goosebumps, who cry, or who are otherwise deeply moved when listening to their favorite music" (Penman and Becker 2009, 51). When listening to music they love, deep listeners in secular contexts experience physiological and emotional reactions similar to those of people who become ecstatic or go into trance during certain religious rituals (for example, Pentecostal services, the Balinese Rangda/Barong ceremony, and so on). The question as applied to fan studies is why does one singer strike a measurable reaction in her or his listeners while a different singer does not? Narratives of being in the presence of Sills's voice, such as Taylor Cornish's recollection of hearing her in recital, often point to deep-listening experiences among Sills fans. This study only scratches the surface of this rich topic by necessarily limiting examples to a handful of passionate fans and their reactions to Sills's voice.

Several of my interviewees and correspondents shared their own metaphysical theories on the nature or origin of their affinity for Sills's voice. For example, Freeman Stamper, profiled in chapter 6, owns and curates a private museum of what is likely the largest collection of Sills-related materials in the world. He situates his theory around a "rhythm of life:"

> We all have a rhythm of life which is a vibration feeling running from the top of the head to our toes. That vibration is what causes our response to people and sounds. For me, Beverly Sills' voice marries perfectly my rhythm of life—her vibrato, her range, her Fach. Her speaking voice causes me to feel warm and complete. Her laugh is infectious. I feel at one with the world when I hear her voice. (e-mail, February 8, 2013)

Stamper had never seen an opera before he attended one of Sills's performances of *Lucia di Lammermoor* at Wolf Trap in 1971. He said, "I found her because I had come out gay. And through a quirk, I made some connections that led me to her in a performance that married my rhythm of life" (conversation, October 5, 2009, New York City). During one of our many conversations, he wondered if another soprano had been singing that night, would she have made the same impact on him that Sills did? He believes, however, that "there was just something about Beverly Sills that grabbed me and made me pay attention. I mean, you just couldn't ignore it, you *had* to pay attention" (conversation, September 5, 2012, Hayward, CA).

Gary Browne was not an opera fan before he attended a Sills recital in Syracuse in 1974. He says, though, that when he tells people about his experience that evening, he describes it as the "most wonderful day of his life." He had a chance to hear her live in San Francisco a year or two later. Although he had the good fortune to attend recitals by both Joan Sutherland and Leontyne Price, neither them, nor any other singer, affected him as did Sills. As he observed, "Music and voices are very mysterious. Different voices affect different people differently." When Sills sang, he experienced a strong physical reaction. He recalled that "every note created a physical reaction in my body that I can only describe as body rushes" (e-mail, April 18 and 19, 2013).

The experiences shared by Stamper and Browne resonate strongly with those reported to Benzecry in his work with passionate opera fans in Buenos Aires. Expressing a sensation quite similar to Stamper's "rhythm of life," one fan said: "I feel there is some music that vibrates to the same frequency I do. It happens close to what we call the heart, but it actually does something funny to your breathing too" (2011, 88). Benzecry concludes that his consultants spoke "as if music had taken their body over, occupying the space where the core of the self used to be with such force as to make them forget who they are or at least forget their daily problems" (ibid.). Unfortunately, Benzecry did not mention if fans tied their physical responses to specific singers' voices or to particular operas, scenes, or arias.

Some of my correspondents and interviewees reported that what they appreciated the most in Sills was her total performance. This quality was also the topic of published critiques as well. Writing not long after Sills's Met debut, when her voice was undeniably past its prime, Harold Schonberg gave his summation of Sills's artistry in his article "The Total Theater of Beverly Sills." He wrote:

> Beverly Sills stands for much more than singing. She always has tried for total theater, and that is what sets her apart from so many of her colleagues. She has, in her way, the kind of magnetism that Callas had, and she exerts enormous authority on stage. A gifted actress who has dispensed with all of the old-fashioned gestures, she extends action to her voice. Few opera singers of our time have had her ability to echo by purely vocal means the psychological stresses of the character she happens to be singing. (*New York Times*, April 13, 1975)

Robert Nelson, who lived in New York City from 1962 to 1977, heard Sills live many times. In one of his first wonderfully detailed messages, he shared his analysis of why "she enjoyed such an intimate and devoted response from her audience."

> I would say it was because the experience she delivered to them was so complete. One can regard a singer as gifted in several respects, but in most instances can point to at least one respect in which he or she has a problem; not so with

Sills. She was flawless in technical accomplishment to the point of being absolutely dazzling; the actual sound of the voice was one of great beauty, although
some would take exception, this aspect being perhaps the most subjective; she
always looked sensational on stage, always true to the nature of the character
being portrayed; her command of dramatic thrust was great, employing physical presence, vocal address and deep psychological insight. . . . We will allow
that Sills was not a small woman and was not conventionally beautiful, but she
was perfectly able to project physical delicacy and vulnerability at will, as well
as the impression of great beauty to the point of absolute glamour. (e-mail,
July 23, 2009)

Not surprisingly, fans who witnessed Sills live on the operatic stage comment
on her "total" or "complete" performance; however, fans who came to know her
primarily through sound recordings also note this quality. Joey Hawker, who was
in his early twenties when Sills died, knew her mainly as a "spunky red-haired
broad from PBS" prior to her death. When she passed, he was immediately drawn
to her obituaries and tributes. He downloaded both the *Art of Beverly Sills* and
Beverly Sills and Friends albums from iTunes and was "hooked." When I messaged
Hawker on Facebook and asked for his "Beverly story," he detailed the progres-
sion of his coming to appreciate Sills:

There's plenty to like right off the bat: the gloriously feminine voice with a
timbre like clinking champagne flutes, the superhuman runs, the ornamentation that sounded as if it had been written under an electron microscope—so
intricate and fine was the level of detail and accuracy. For sheer vocal beauty,
the "Breit über mein Haupt" literally stopped me in my tracks the first time
I heard it; I think I had something like sixty-four plays on it by the end of
the week. And then there was the superb Bolena mad scene with that blood-
drenched final note. Good god. It still feels like a punch in the gut every time
I hear it. . . .
   She was no Wagnerian, but Bubbles understood the concept of a *Gesamt-
kunstwerk*. Her roles were just all so exciting and well informed that I have
constantly felt compelled to learn more. And there's always more to learn,
too: the better I learn a text to whatever aria or scena, the more nuance I can
appreciate in what she did dramatically. And I think that suits (or perhaps
even is?) the Sills legacy: Totality. Comprehensiveness. She was superficially
appealing enough to be accessible, but boy, once one is through the door, it
becomes clear very quickly that this was an artist and an intellect who truly
left no stone unturned. (Facebook message, April 15, 2013)

Jay Brennan's story touches on nearly all of the common themes outlined
above. Introduced by a mutual friend who is also a Sills admirer, Brennan and I

met in April 2010. He was in his teens, growing up in New Jersey in a household of modest means, when he experienced his sudden conversion to Sills and opera fandom. Home alone one Saturday afternoon, he was channel surfing when he landed on Sills's *La Traviata* broadcast from Wolf Trap. He recalls:

> It was just the middle of act 1. I remember very clearly, it was right before the "Sempre libera"—right before "Ah forse lui." I don't know why I stopped. But I just did. I stopped, and I was immediately hooked. I watched the whole thing, absolutely fascinated and rapt by the entire thing. And so, after that, I became a huge opera fan, just fell in love with opera, everything to do with opera. I begged my parents, "Let's go into the city, and let's go see things." They never wanted to because, you know, we weren't . . . I guess, they felt opera was for the rich, and we weren't terribly rich.

Inspired by Sills, Brennan began to study music, took private voice lessons, and majored in music and math in college. He continued to study voice in graduate school and sang professionally for twenty years until a blood vessel on one of his vocal cords burst and did not heal properly, thus ending his performing career. To this day, Brennan is taken with Sills's voice. Among the qualities that he adores most is her unique vocal timbre.

> There's something in the way that Sills sings that is so—it is such a unique sound and immediately identifiable. I've never heard another singer—ever—who you could mistake for that sound. . . . There's something in the way she produced her voice; there's a tone, or a clarity, or a ping, that is unmistakably hers. . . .
>
> She was such a consummate actress, she could put so much emotion into the simplest of words or the simplest phrases. The way she can shape a tone, from a shriek of pain down to just the most . . . I think that's what clicked with me with that Wolf Trap *Traviata*—and on all the recordings since then. Because on all of her recordings, you can find moment after moment after moment where she sacrifices a perfectly shaped vowel or a perfect tone to create an emotion. Just the way she can say "si" or the way she sings "Adieu notre petite table." The way she produces the tone carries so much weight. (Brennan interview, April 18, 2010)

Giving through the Total Joy of Singing

Beverly Sills loved to sing. She loved sharing a world of emotion through her voice. She loved the sense of giving and communion she felt as she connected to her audience through her voice, actions, and sheer bodily presence. Her joy of being in the moment swept across the audience; her joy was infectious. In reflecting on what Sills meant to them, contributors to the *Guestbook* frequently mentioned joy, both theirs and hers. An analysis of the entire *Guestbook* text shows that "joy" is one of the most frequently used nouns (outside of standard parts of speech and nouns one would expect to encounter in this context such as "opera," "voice," and "life").

John Carroll of Seattle closed his *Guestbook* entry by citing *Washington Post* critic Paul Hume, who wrote that Sills was "the dazzling irresistible embodiment of the total joy of singing." Carroll told of how he first heard Sills when he checked out her *La Traviata* album from the public library when he was in ninth grade. He became obsessed with hearing and collecting every live recording of hers he could find. In a heartfelt statement, Carroll articulated what it was in Sills that attracted him to her:

> This is so hard to put in words the impact she had on my life: Sills will always be my musical touchstone because for me, more than any other singer, she synthesized all the elements of lyric art—a uniquely beautiful voice, a vital charisma, a refined technique, a thrilling virtuosity, uncanny musicianship, empathy, joy, thoughtfulness, spontaneity, delicacy, taste, style, expressive sense of melody, an innate sense of character, drama, humor, and poetry. There are so many other great singers, great sopranos, great coloraturas—but none match Sills' ability in her prime to make it all come together in an inexplicable divine musical alchemy.

In his *Guestbook* entry, Bill Brunston of Austin, Texas, recalled his single experience of being in Sills's presence. When she came to Jackson, Mississippi, in 1971 to perform *Lucia*, Brunston, a junior high school student at the time, begged to be a supernumerary in the production. He recounted:

> As for her singing, we all literally trembled with the electric thrill of her voice— there is no one in my memory that seemed to be "ordained" to sing opera, as she did—and to be infused with such energetic joy! . . . I don't know how she came about it, but Beverly Sills, even with the enormity of her musical, vocal, and mental gifts (she was always the "sharpest knife in the drawer"), had a desire to give to OTHERS. She did this while she was in our little Mississippi production. This selfless perspective, to me, is her greatest legacy.

Of the 504 *Guestbook* epitaphs (several of which are duplicates), forty-four mentioned the joy Sills brought to them:

> Your infectious joy will forever be missed. Even though we are separated in more ways than one, you will forever be etched deep in my heart. (Asril Ibrahim)

> Thank you "Bubbles" for all the joy and goose bumps you've given me. (Ronald Hake)

Beverly Sills brought opera to the common person through her incredible ability to connect straight to the heart. Bubbles put a new energy and joy to an art form that was becoming distant to the general public. The magnificence of the voice, the gracious humanity of the woman, and the joyful tenderness of her soul will resonate forever. (Teryle Watson)

Henri J. M. Nouwen said, "Joy is the infallible sign of the presence of God." If any proof is needed, just watch Beverly Sills as she sings, just hear her, and be touched by the Divine in her. (Tana Sibilio)

Thank you for letting your light shine. You have brought so much joy to so many. I will always remember you laughing. That's how I know you are an angel—they take themselves lightly! (Martha Magee)

Her joy seemed to come through her love of sharing it with others. Thank you my darling Beverly for brightening up the world. My heart is sad, but my gratitude and love will remain forever. (Barbara Bishop)

Inspiring Lifelong Pursuits

Sills had a tremendous influence on many of her fans—through her singing, the joy that she exuded, her charisma onstage and off, and her strength of character. For some, this included an influence on their career choices; for others, an encounter with her (even if from afar) simply, yet undeniably, lit a new life path. The *Guestbook* includes contributions from singers and musicians whose first spark of interest in becoming performers was ignited by Sills, whether through listening to her recordings or seeing her on television or in live performance. Some went on to have professional careers, while for others, their personal engagement with music simply enriched their lives. Deborah Fennelly wrote that she was fifteen years old when she decided to be a singer during a rehearsal of *La Traviata* she attended with Sills playing Violetta. Sills giving of herself in performance motivated Fennelly to do the same. In her *Guestbook* entry, she wrote:

When I witnessed Sills's final scene that day I forgot myself. Tears welled up and I fell instantly in love with this artist and this art form. All I wanted to do was to sing and move an audience the way she moved me that day. When I graduated from high school I did study voice performance and opera at a conservatory. I never had an extensive career but have been blessed with using my voice to entertain and uplift and sometimes to raise money for worthy causes. To this day whenever and wherever I perform I try to give as much of myself as Beverly Sills did. I am deeply grateful to her for her dedication to her art and to her audience.

Ladd B wrote that Sills's broadcasts from Wolf Trap were a driving force in not only his childhood years, but also his entry into the musical profession.

> What Beverly Sills meant to me as a child into adulthood cannot be condensed here. Those Wolf Trap telecasts were the highlights of my childhood. I played her *Lucia* recording, at age 10, until it skipped miserably. Her visibility in media gave me license to dream. Those dreams came true. Thank you Beverly for what you gave me, an accepting portal into a life as a performer. When other boys were playing baseball I listened to you sing and I believed my dreams could come true. You were not a diva, in the negative sense of the word, you were a human being who brought magic to everything and everyone you touched!

Another young singer who idolized Sills was Gianna Rolandi; she went on to study voice at the prestigious Curtis Institute and have an international career. She made her Metropolitan Opera debut as Sophie in *Der Rosenkavalier* in 1979 and performed with all other major American opera companies as well as in Europe. When I spent an afternoon with Rolandi in Chicago in June 2011, she shared that she would never forget when, as a beginning student at Curtis, she saw Sills on the cover of *Time* magazine as Queen Elizabeth. And then there were Sills's appearances on the *Dinah Shore Show,* the *Merv Griffin Show, The Tonight Show,* and the extended interview on *60 Minutes.* Rolandi mused:

> This was all beyond anything that you can imagine for an opera singer. But that was so exciting to think that, yes, look at the interest that these people have. As a young singer, a young performer, to see what she was doing, and the kind of reaction she was getting from the audience, you just think, Wow! Everybody likes opera. They're all going to come. Wow! We're in a real business. (Rolandi interview, June 26, 2011)

In 1975, even before Rolandi graduated from Curtis, she was hired by the NYCO. The first time she bumped into Sills, Gianna was looking at the timesheet posted on the wall in the company offices in the New York State Theater. When she turned and saw Sills, she was so overcome that she dissolved into tears. Sills graciously acted as though she had not noticed her outburst. Rolandi made her NYCO debut as Olympia and came to be cast in other performances of Sills's most successful roles, including Cleopatra, Elvira, and Lucia. She reported how she felt the first time she was given a costume to wear with "Sills" written on the inside label: "They gave me the costume for Olympia and it said 'Sills' in the back. I was twenty-two years old. I really nearly fainted. You just can't imagine. It's like you're living in some alternate universe or something" (ibid.). Once Sills took over as the company's general director, she mentored and nurtured Gianna. Eventually, Gianna told her how as a child she sang along with her recordings trying to sing the coloratura as quickly as did Sills.

Obviously, admiration and fondness for Sills did not lead all of her fans to lives as professional singers. Her dynamism and greatness was nonetheless inspiring to those whose lives followed different paths. Two days after her passing, William V. Madison posted a tribute to Sills on his blog BILLEVESÉES, in which he shared that Sills was one of the most important teachers in his life. He first saw her in the *Siege of Corinth* on the Met tour to Dallas when he was thirteen years old. There, he found a "voice that sang the things [he] couldn't speak." He went backstage to get her autograph where his awe left him dumbstruck. He had to skip school the next day because he was too excited to say anything but "I met Beverly Sills." As Madison recalls:

> Her music became the soundtrack of my life. I played the mad scene from Lucia every morning before school, firm in the belief that listening to Sills go crazy prevented me from going crazy.[10] When my aunt and uncle died in a plane crash, I played "Addio del passato" all night. Pining for my girlfriend, I played "Ruhe sanft, mein holdes Leben" and "Breit über mein Haupt," and when she spurned me, I played "Ah! Fuyez, douce image" and the last scene of *The Ballad of Baby Doe.* At night, "V'adoro, pupille" sent me gliding into sleep.
>
> But while I was listening, Sills was teaching. She introduced me to a huge chunk of Western culture, which in turn served to introduce me to even more Western culture. There was something in her performances that made me want to find out more, to read the novel that one opera was based on, to hear other works by the same composer, to explore the history and art behind the music. We'll never know how much I owe her, how many wonderful things I'd never have discovered if not for her inspiration. . . .
>
> Birth defects made it impossible for Beverly Sills to pass on these lessons to her own children. But Sills did pass on her mother's lessons to other people's children, and she always made an effort to reach out to young audiences: I am merely one product of that outreach, one satisfied alumnus of the Silverman School of Culture. I even had the benefit of a graduate education, because when I first moved to New York, I'd see Mrs. Silverman at almost every opera, ballet, concert, and play I attended. It was as if she were overseeing my mastery of the studies her daughter had launched. (http://billmadison.blogspot .com/2007/07/beverly-sills.html, accessed October 18, 2007)

Joseph Malloy also took Sills as his teacher. Posting to the *Guestbook* from his home in Istanbul, Turkey, Malloy told of how he saw Sills perform many times in New York. It all started when an "adventurous" high school teacher took one of his classes to Lincoln Center to see a Sills performance with the NYCO. He concluded his epitaph:

> [H]er influence led me to explore and experience the arts, and through it, so much about life. I consider her my great teacher, she opened a world to me

that surpassed opera, it gave me a wonderful window to the world. . . . Thank you, Beverly Sills, you changed the world's view of opera, and what it means to be an artist that lives in the real world. And, thanks again, for changing the world for me.

Ethnomusicologist as Opera Fan

Although I conducted the research for this study following the norms in my field, there is no question that, similar to the fans interviewed, I also was transformed when I attended a Sills's recital many years ago. The following is my story:

Beverly Sills inspired me to learn about and reach for a world beyond my shrinking industrial hometown. A year after she died, on a visit back to Ohio, I told one of my high school friends that I was embarking on a Sills research project. She immediately recalled how I had reacted to Sills's recital back in 1977, saying, "Your feet didn't touch the ground for a year." Her vivid memory of my post-recital euphoria was reaffirming. I had forgotten something of the intensity of Sills's effect on me.

Now, as I piece it all together, I remember that after her visit, I purchased a subscription to *Opera News* and to the *New Yorker,* which provided a window into Beverly Sills's distant hometown. Seeking further encounters with more "larger-than-life" greatness, I found ways to travel outside of northwestern Ohio to hear great orchestras, such as the Cleveland Orchestra, the Chicago Symphony, and the New York Philharmonic. I even made it to the Met tour in Cleveland while still in high school. Sills set me on this path. Encountering someone of her magnitude (her charisma, her strength, her brilliant artistry) made an indelible impression. Deepening that impression by listening to her recordings on a daily basis, I was inspired—she opened up a new world. I fell in love with opera, thanks to Sills. Years later this would translate into a passion for Chinese opera, the subject of my PhD dissertation and first book. My encounter with Sills live was of a similar magnitude to that which Taylor Cornish described as the night his life changed. For me, however, as the years passed, the intensity faded as my memory of the event was overtaken by new experiences.

Her passing brought it all back in a jumble of thoughts and emotions. I had barely listened to her recordings during the previous twenty-five years. The day she died, I owned only one of her recordings, a compilation CD I had purchased in a secondhand shop. Her death left me perplexed. I felt as though a long-forgotten part of me was suddenly awakened. I was compelled to remember and reconcile this estranged aspect of myself. Several months later, I told one of my former graduate students, Alexander Khalil, over dinner that I was at a complete loss for understanding how I could feel so deeply for someone I did not know. Always one to think holistically, Khalil looked at me with an intensity that signaled he was imparting an important truth. He said, as though it was obvious, "But you did know her." He explained that she shared herself through her singing. I had heard her joy, pain, humor, anguish, and beauty. I had engaged with her intimately, even if from afar.

My feelings of almost having known Sills were not unique. In January 2008, I called Sills's close friend and publicist Edgar Vincent to ask for an interview. He sounded irritated as he replied that he was frequently contacted regarding Sills. He said her personality was such that people felt as if she were their sister. Evidence of this feeling of closeness is clear in many *Guestbook* entries.

Crossing Divides

One aspect of Sills fandom not yet explicitly addressed here was her success in crossing class divides. Through her presence in mainstream print and television media, people in the United States who had little or no access to opera, either due to physical distance from performing arts centers or to socioeconomic barriers, gained exposure to it because of Sills. For some, after an introduction to the art through Sills, opera became a meaningful part of their lives. Certainly one of the most poignant *Guestbook* entries came from Lindsey Wilhite, who wrote from Kalamazoo, Michigan:

> I remember vividly the first time I heard Beverly Sills. I consider myself an opera buff personified having fallen in love with opera at the age of eight. Opera was my salvation, growing up in the projects of Benton Harbor, Michigan; it was the world of music in general and opera in particular that gave me the courage to continue life and to try to accomplish something with the life I was given. Beverly Sills, along with all the other greats of this singularly difficult art form, was and will always be for me a source of solace in a world that is not always filled with happiness. I have heard live all the current great sopranos past and present and not a single one could equal Beverly Sills and the ease with which she sang in her prime. . . . She sang the way most of us talk, with an effortlessness that was incredible and, to top it all off, with a sensitivity to lyrics that went straight to the soul.

In his *Guestbook* entry, Tim Kee remembered watching Beverly Sills on television when he was young. For Kee, who grew up and still lives in a small town in southern Illinois, Beverly Sills "WAS opera." Shortly before her death, he saw her guest appearance on *The View*. Seeing her again "brought back so many memories. . . . She is that old friend who melted the years away." When I wrote to him, he elaborated:

> We were definitely not "Opera" people. But Beverly was not typical. She was able to laugh at herself and have fun. One thinks of opera divas as high

class. Beverly was able to appeal to everyone. . . . I remember the shows that Beverly did with Carol Burnett. . . . It was a rarity to see someone from the field of opera appear in slapstick comedic shows, but Beverly did. It was the fun of seeing someone from such a lofty place in society come down to the level of us, the common folk. THAT is what I was feeling when she passed. Beverly Sills made the opera accessible to everyone. . . . It was for the "stuffed shirts" until she brought it into my family's blue-collar household. . . . When she passed it was like losing a piece of my childhood that I really didn't realize was so important to me until it was taken away." (e-mail, July 28, 2009)

An anonymous *Guestbook* contributor from Philadelphia credited Sills with bringing

> this art form to people who either did not have the financial means to go to an opera house or would never think of going to an opera house in the first place. She made opera accessible to all not only because of her great artistry, but also because she was not what many people would stereotype as a "diva." She was the people's "diva" . . . human, funny, down to earth, and made in America.

Dedra Kaye DeHart, whose only exposure to Sills was through the mainstream media, posted her epitaph to the *New York Times* Cityroom Blog on July 5 (hence the reference to fireworks).[11]

> I never met her, never heard her sing live; being from a rural area in the middle of nowhere Illinois, there's no way. I could barely even watch her on PBS cause the channel only came in if you stood a certain way and the wind blew from the south, but I will always remember my favorite episode of *The Muppets* when Beverly Sills came to visit. Hers was the first autobiography I read, the first inspiration I had for my dyed red hair, and always a delight if she was going to be performing on television whether it be singing or giving an interview. It was nice to find out that someone you admired was really just as nice in real life as they were on television. Wish more people would follow her lead with their attitudes in their careers and lives. The fireworks are all for you Bubbles.

In response to my Facebook message in which I asked DeHart to share more about her impressions of Sills, she explained that opera lovers were scarce in her small town of about one thousand residents. She described herself as "an odd duck" because she appreciates "highbrow music" whereas no one else in her family can stand it. Although she does not consider herself an opera fanatic, she enjoys certain singers, including Sills.

Sills's success in crossing the elite-mass, highbrow-middlebrow cultural divides made her vulnerable to attack from certain quarters. Writings published after her passing spotlighted how her broad popularity and accessibility threatened her

standing as a legitimate bearer of the operatic tradition. The announcement by
the New York Public Library for the Performing Arts in fall 2009, reporting that
it had purchased Sills's personal scores at her estate sale (held October 7, 2009),
unwittingly hinted at this sentiment as it represented her scores as evidence that,
despite her broad appeal, she was once a serious, dedicated opera singer.

> In numerous interviews, talk shows, and autobiographies, Sills revealed herself
> as a cheerful and ebullient personality. But her scores reveal a different side
> of her. They show that she was a hard-working and dedicated performer. A
> number of her scores are marked (some in great detail), indicating her great
> commitment to singing with a striking attention to detail.[12]

Further evidence is found in Ira Siff's *Opera News* article "Pentimento," with
its reference to the traces of an earlier painting hidden beneath layers of paint
on a canvas. As Siff observed, Beverly Sills's vast accomplishments, including
the administrative offices she held and her ubiquitous presence on television,
"[threaten] to bury her greatest accomplishment, and the one that brought her
all the others—her singing" (2007, 30). Siff is positive and sincere in his effort
to peel back the layers of history, which obscured Sills's artistic legacy for some.

However, an obituary published in the British magazine *Opera* by Sills's long-
standing foe, critic Peter Davis, was mean-spirited in its survey of Sills's career,
especially when touching on her popular appeal (2007). Davis's obituary is largely
a repetition of similarly worded attacks he peppered throughout his writings over
more than three decades. In his essay "Beverly Sills: Media Heroine or Genuine
Superstar?" published in the *New York Times,* Davis attributed Sills's fame among
"people who have never set foot inside an opera house" to three elements: "Sills
herself, through her talent and tenacity; her fans, by their loyalty and blind devotion; and the media, stimulated by a Johnny-come-lately eagerness to exploit a
drama-laden success story regardless of the musical facts" (1975). Sills's fame
both inside and outside of the opera house angered Davis, who referred to her
as a "self-absorbed media heroine" (1985, 79), a "calculating media darling" (1997,
496), and a "media creature named Supersills" (2000). Reflecting on Sills's career,
Davis opined that it became difficult "to recall that once upon a time she was
a great singer and a magical stage presence. She lost it all much too soon, in
part because unwise repertory choices overtaxed her voice, but also because she
decided that being a media heroine was more important than serving music as
a singer" (Davis 1987, 94). Davis also habitually demeaned her fans (2007, 1997,
1976, 1975) out of what seems to have been his frustration that "[e]ven as her
vocal powers waned . . . Sills's fame and influential position in America continued undiminished" (1997, 496). In a brief review of Sills's recording of Bellini's *I
Capuleti e I Montecchi,* which was recorded relatively late in her career, he takes a

swipe at her fans: "Fans of this soprano have never overly concerned themselves with the current shredded state of her vocal equipment, and apparently remain contented with what's left: a shrewd dramatic presence and a keen musical sensibility" (1976).[13] Similarly condescending attitudes toward Sills fans continue to be voiced in public forums. A particularly telling example appeared in July 2009 on the opera blog Parterre Box when, in a heated discussion of the CD release of Sills's *Norma,* two participants hurled the slur "Sillsbillies"—with its obvious reference to "Hillbillies"—at Sills supporters.[14]

The contempt of Davis and others for Sills's popularity with listeners who might never have set foot in an opera house if not for her resonates with the ideals of the "sacralization of culture," which began to take hold in mid-nineteenth-century America (and elsewhere). The result of the sacralization project was that average, nonelite citizens were distanced from what we now term "classical" music, serious drama (such as Shakespeare), and other of the fine arts.[15] Turn-of-the-century critic W. J. Henderson of the *New York Times* voiced the sacralization ideal well when he wrote that opera was "too important, too exalted an art form to present itself to an uninformed, eclectic audience, many of whom cared more for the performers than the art being performed" (quoted in Levine 1988, 103).[16]

Tied up with sacralization was the ascendency of the concept of the "work" of art—the notion that performers are mere servants to composers' intentions and their musical masterpieces. This resonates well with Davis's criticism that Sills failed in her role as a servant to music when she allowed herself to become a "media heroine." In her study of opera in London between 1780 and 1880, Jennifer Hall-Witt traces how during this period there was a significant shift from opera being viewed as event-oriented to work-oriented. The event-oriented approach takes the "singers as more important than the composer, seeing the arias as the most important feature of the opera" (2007, 44). Musicologist Martha Feldman points out that according to the traditional eighteenth-century view, "the very identity of an opera rested on performers and performative occasions," not on the composer's work, as later became the case (1995, 470). Singers generally held the greatest power (and commanded the largest salaries) in opera's creative arena. Their singing, which included a good deal of improvisation, "could weave magic spells on distracted audiences, reflexively intertwining the arts of 'cantare' and 'incantare,' singing and enchanting" (ibid., 469). Reformists and critics sought to replace this dynamic, event-oriented perspective with a work-oriented view by diminishing the singers' creative input, which in turn bolstered the composers' authority. The idea was that performers and the audience must "revere the music, drama, and the composer's creative genius" (Hall-Witt 2007, 10). This ideology also took hold in the United States. For instance, Boston critic John Sullivan Dwight, who was active in the mid- to late 1800s, asserted that art should remain spiritual and pure and ideally "never becomes secondary to the performer or to the audience" (quoted in Levine 1988, 120). Dwight went so far as to write that "it would be better if the performer were invisible" (quoted in Levine 1988, 121).

Echoes of this attitude still ring today and were certainly in full force at the height of Sills's popularity. Part and parcel of this sentiment is an unmistakable element of fan bashing because fans are typically more invested in the performance than the work. That is, the fans of singers are inclined to take the work as a vehicle for the performance, not as an unchanging monument. Alan M. Kriegsman's review of Sills's *Lucia* performance from Wolf Trap provides an example of how fans are subject to ridicule due to their taking an event-oriented rather than work-oriented attitude. He found the evening's performance of *Lucia di Lammermoor* unremarkable, certainly not "memorable," but he noted that his "was not at all the sentiment of the overflow crowd, which found cause for unbridled jubilation. They's come to hear Beverly Sills do her stuff, and they lapped it up, though from the way the show stopped at her entrance, one had the feeling the fans were so primed for cheers it didn't matter much how Sills sang" (*Washington Post*, July 23, 1971).

In an adept yet concise overview of Sills's singing career written for the *New Yorker* on the occasion of her farewell gala in 1980, Andrew Porter cautioned that in evaluating her legacy, Sills's future biographer "must weigh the role of the modern 'media,'" with its ability "to inflate the popular reputation of, say, a Pavarotti out of all proportion to his artistry." Porter went on to say that he did not believe that the publicity, such as the *Newsweek* and *Time* covers, "harmed Sills's artistry. She is too scrupulous a musician." However, he wondered if it may have affected her repertory choices. Perhaps it encouraged her to place "too much emphasis on the bright, merry heroines, set too many Merry Widows, Regimental Daughters, and Rosinas scampering across the country at the expense of tragic heroines."[17] Most important for this discussion, he suggested that her prevalence in the media might "account for a carping note found in many of her reviews: a corrective to unthinking, 'unhearing' popular adulation" (Porter 1980, 179).

Through her crossing of the high/low cultural divide, Sills inspired listeners who might never have had the chance or inclination to explore new worlds of artistic appreciation and musical engagement. Because the sacralization of culture ideal (a legacy of the nineteenth century) still holds currency, Sills's broad stardom continues to make her the occasional target of elitist scorn.

For the Love of Sills

Opera Fanatic author Claudio Benzecry develops and applies his notion of the "love-for" metaphor as part of his effort to rescue the passion that fans feel for opera from sociology's reductionist theories of taste. The *love* he points to "is nothing other than the intense personalized investment fans charge opera with" (2011, 178). While he focuses on a general love for opera, this chapter has explored how the love for a single singer finds expression in the words and deeds of passionate fans. As documented in this and chapter 6, Beverly Sills is a still-significant focus of concentration for some fans in terms of both their mental and emotional energies. For others, her place in their lives is not as central, yet she has been a positive force throughout their lives.

With only a few exceptions, the fans whose stories are shared here are in their late forties or older, with a large cluster in their fifties and sixties. This is not surprising because the height of Sills's fame in the 1970s coincided with these fans' formative years. Following the love metaphor, Sills became a building block in their personal narratives and a touchstone for positive, pleasurable experiences both past and present. Part of this pleasure comes from transcending the commonplace through engaging with her voice.

And yet the question remains, what was it about Sills that gave her the power to launch these listeners on their transcendent travels or to inspire their lifelong pursuits? In the end, there remains the central, often unnamed quality that draws us in. Scholars are only now beginning to take love in all of its many guises (including familial, romantic, religious, or, as here, "passion for") as subjects of their work without translating it into other concepts (such as care, reproduction, Self-Other relationships, or distinctions, and so on). Without resorting to the rationalizing and necessarily diluting effect of translation, we are freed to ask questions such as "what does it mean to do something in the name of love?" (Morrison, Johnston, and Longhurst 2013, 508) or how does love operate as a force in building communities or in the building of one's life?

The stories of Sills in the lives of her fans provide many examples of the fruit that love and dedication bear. Not only does it shape the trajectories of individual's lives, but especially in the digital age as fans have found each other, love for Sills has brought her admirers together in a community rich in the sense of belonging to something greater than themselves.

CHAPTER 6

Sills in the Lives of Her Fans

As a means of illustrating Beverly Sills's presence in the lives of specific individuals, profiles of seven fans are presented here. Five of these seven came to my attention through their online posts displaying admiration for the singer. This small sampling includes those who shared a close friendship with Sills, those who only met her backstage after performances, and those who exchanged letters with her. These fans were chosen to profile because of their descriptions of the significant influence Beverly Sills made in their lives.

The Ames Sisters

The story of Alison and Katrine "Cage" Ames's youthful devotion to Sills provides a vivid window into the world of Sills fandom in the late 1960s and the 1970s. Their experience illustrates the reciprocity of goodwill that Sills shared with her admirers. Sills—through the inspiration she animated and the connections formed in her company—played a vital role in shaping the trajectory of both of the Ames sisters' professional lives.

In going through the Beverly Sills scrapbooks housed in the Library of Congress (LOC), I came upon Alison Ames's essay, "Beverly Sills Is a Good High: The Story of My Friend the Opera Star," in an alumnae issue of the *Hollins College Bulletin* published in November 1971 (LOC scrapbook no. 16). Little did I know when I contacted the Hollins alumnae office for assistance in contacting her that Alison was once one of the world's most highly regarded classical music executive producers. Luckily, Alison responded to my request and several days after I found her essay, we were sitting together in the Alice Tully Hall café at Lincoln Center. In getting to know Alison and her sister Katrine, I discovered a type of fan that I had not previously encountered. In both her 1971 essay and our 2010 conversation, Alison distinguished herself from what she termed the "lifelong groupie" type of fan: "I had never been a backstage type or star-follower and was quite innocent of the whole frenetic pace kept up by the True Fan" (*Hollins College Bulletin*). For four or five years, she was an eager Sills fan, never missing a Sills performance in New York, but eventually her musical interests broadened. And, by then, she and Sills already shared a genuine friendship. Sills sparked a passion for opera and music that in part launched Alison on her highly successful career. Alison's experience as a Sills fan "bridged the divide between being a groupie and being paid in a legitimate job" (A. Ames interview, December 9, 2010).

It all began when Hubert Saal's 1967 essay, "The True Story of Beverly Sills," piqued Alison's interest in Sills. Saal's essay compelled her to travel to New York from her home in Rhode Island to buy tickets to all of the operas he mentioned in his *New York Times Magazine* profile of Sills. Recalling her first time hearing Sills in performance, Alison said: "It was her joy in making music—when you first meet Cleopatra, she's singing 'Non disperar.' This was my introduction to opera. I had heard other operas, but they didn't do much for me." When asked if she had been struck right away, she replied, "I was knocked down like a bowling pin" (ibid.).

Alison continued to attend Sills's performances, though it was not until May 1969, when Sills was signing autographs at a record store, that Alison mustered the courage to speak to her. Alison boldly asked Sills if she could have a backstage pass so that she could greet her after her upcoming performance with the Boston Symphony at Tanglewood. Sills replied, "Sure, but why do you want Tanglewood on it? I'll leave it blank so you can use it wherever you want" (*Hollins College Bulletin*). To Alison's surprise, Sills remembered her when they met again. Alison says that once, out of the blue, she received a note from Sills encouraging her to visit her backstage. Sills wrote that she liked seeing Alison's and her sister's "cute mugs at the performances." She eventually invited Alison and Katrine, who quickly joined her sister in Sills fandom, to visit her backstage *before* performances. Unlike most opera singers who prefer an environment congenial to introspection and private vocalization before a performance, Sills held court in her dressing room, laughing and talking until five minutes before curtain.[1]

Alison and Katrine enjoyed frequent backstage visits and road trips as they and their friends followed Sills to various performance venues along the East Coast and as far away as San Diego and San Francisco. Katrine even flew to London on the occasion of Sills's Covent Garden debut. On one of their most ambitious trips, they and three other fans rented a car and drove from New York to

Chicago and back in one weekend to hear Sills and Tatiana Troyanos sing *Norma* at Ravinia with James Levine conducting the Chicago Symphony. To economize, they packed their own food and slept on a friend's floor in Chicago. In her *Hollins College Bulletin* essay, Alison wrote that in two years she heard Sills sing more than seventy times—almost half of the diva's performances during that period.

The scene after a performance usually involved hundreds of fans lining up to greet Sills, who would stand for an hour and a half signing autographs while she came down from the performance high. During her time as a Beverly Sills groupie, Alison frequently saw many of the same folks, mostly young gay men, hanging around backstage. She and Katrine gave the regulars nicknames such as PF-1 and PF-2 (i.e., professional fan number 1 and number 2). The Ames sisters have remained lifelong friends with some of these fans,[2] several of whom, like Alison and Katrine, found professional careers in fields related to music.

As did other devotees, on their backstage visits the sisters usually presented Sills with tokens of their affection such as photographs, flowers, or their own creative works. Sills especially appreciated the acrostic and double-acrostic poems Katrine composed for her. Certainly the most enduring of Alison's creations was the "Beverly Sills is a Good High" lapel button, which is now a vintage collector's item among Sills fans. Alison sold more than five hundred of the buttons and donated all of the proceeds to the NYCO.

After one performance, Katrine and Alison met Hubert Saal in the New York State Theater elevator on their way to the dressing-room area. Unaware of their relationship with Sills, Saal generously offered to introduce the young women to the star. When Sills greeted them with, "Oh, it's the Ames sisters," Saal was mystified. Through this meeting and their follow-up letters to Saal, the sisters came to know the influential *Newsweek* music critic. Once when they met him at his office, he suggested that Katrine, an aspiring journalist, come to work at the magazine. She explained that she had already sent a letter of inquiry and no one would see her. He immediately got up from his desk, went around the corner, and said to Olga Barbi (a formidable *Newsweek* institution), "You have to see this girl." Barbi interviewed her, and Katrine was hired about a week later. She worked for *Newsweek* for twenty-six years and eventually took over Saal's position, though at that point there was no longer a dedicated music critic. In her role as a senior editor, she wrote on a wide variety of arts topics, of which music was just one. She left *Newsweek* in 1996 when she believed the magazine had surrendered serious journalism and the coverage of high arts in favor of pop-culture subjects. Katrine became features director at Condé Nast's *House and Garden* until the magazine closed in 2008. She has also worked as a freelance journalist; her writing has appeared in the *New York Times*, *Opera News*, the magazine *Antiques*, *Real Simple*, and other publications. Katrine was a frequent contributor to National Public Radio's *Performance Today* program. She served as a major contributor to *James*

Levine: Forty Years at the Metropolitan Opera (Milwaukee, WI: Amadeus Press, 2011), a project for which she interviewed more than fifty Metropolitan Opera artists.

Sills inspired Alison to seek a life in the recording industry. Of Sills's influence, Alison said, "I have a great deal to be grateful to her about because I didn't remain a groupie for the rest of my life, but I certainly got a lot out of the foundation and turned it into something more professional" (A. Ames interview, December 9, 2010). Her first position was as a secretary in the Deutsche Grammophon (DG) office in New York. She later moved to Germany, where she was hired by DG's head office in Hamburg. After a little more than three years, she returned to New York as DG's label head in the United States, a powerful and prestigious position in the classical-recording industry. Through this work, she was able to arrange for the rerelease of Sills's first full-length opera recording, *The Ballad of Baby Doe*, on the DG label. Alison stepped down as label head after nine years and moved into the company's A and R (Artists and Repertoire) department as an executive producer for artists including Leonard Bernstein,[3] the Emerson Quartet, and André Previn. In 1995, Alison took a position with Angel Records as the vice president of EMI Classics. She continued to work in related areas until she retired in 2010.

What began as a star-fan relationship between the Ames sisters and Beverly Sills evolved into a personal friendship. Alison and Katrine became close to Sills's family, and sometimes traveled on family vacations. They remained part of one another's lives for the rest of Sills's days. As a final tribute to her friend of more than three decades, Katrine composed (in one sitting without need for checking dates or sources) Sills's obituary published in *Newsweek*. She concluded by recalling the simple folk song, taught to Sills by Miss Liebling, with which she always ended her recitals: "'Time has come for me to leave you,' she sang. 'You'll be forever in my heart.' And you in ours, Beverly" (Ames 2007, 12).

David Ponder

Lip-synched drag performances to the music of operatic divas are certainly not unheard of. In fact, several of the Sills fans I have come to know have spent hours of their leisure time publicly and privately lip-synching to Sills recordings. What is rare, however, is a devotee who sings his crossed-dressed performances in falsetto. For nearly three decades, David Ponder expressed his deep devotion to Sills through singing in drag.[4] He made his first drag appearance using the stage name "Beverly Trills" at the age of twenty-three. Although he had never sung in public, let alone in falsetto two octaves above his normal range, he was cajoled into appearing in an April Fools' Day benefit concert at the University of Iowa, where he was a first-year graduate student in piano performance. Wearing a red wig and a dab of nose putty, he modeled his appearance after Sills. To his surprise, he stole the show. This success prompted him to continue performing as Beverly Trills at charity events. As Ponder evolved as a drag performer, he changed his stage name to Davina Pons, Dragmatic Soprano, because his aim was to pay tribute to Sills rather than imitate her. With his new stage persona, though still donning a red coiffure, he incorporated influences from other singers including Maria Callas, with Sills remaining about 50 percent of the mix.

For the next two and a half decades, he performed hundreds of times in piano bars and cabaret settings, and dozens of times on concert stages, occasionally with symphony orchestra accompaniment. In 2004, Davina Pons released her CD titled *The Art of Can Belto,* which sold approximately one thousand copies. Analyzing the reasons for Davina Pons's career successes, Mark Panos, writing for *QVegas Magazine,* opined it "cannot be mere stage presence alone, although that is certainly a factor, insofar as the not-so-diminutive diva towers just shy of a statuesque seven feet in heels. The real drawing power of this Amazon indisputably lies in her sublime sound. . . . Pons approaches legendary artistry with a firmly controlled technique and a sensitive emotional interpretation of nearly everything she essays" (Panos 2005, 56).

Ponder retired Davina Pons in July 2008 when he reached the age at which both Sills and Callas gave their last performances. Several weeks before his final appearance, he wrote: "It is bittersweet, but I'm looking forward to a life without diets and high heels! Every girl's dream!!" (e-mail, June 30, 2008). He ended his drag career singing Puccini's "Vissi d'arte" before a crowd of two thousand at the Gay and Lesbian Association of Choruses festival in Miami, Florida.

It was his heartfelt *Guestbook* epitaph—which he posted on September 18, 2007, from Baltimore after returning home from attending the Metropolitan Opera's tribute for Sills—that originally compelled me to contact him. He wrote:

As a teenage boy the first thing I would do when the *TV Guide* came in the mail was to check it for appearances of my favorite gal. I wanted to grow up and marry Beverly. Of course, there were some rather big hurdles such as her husband Peter and the age difference. I had to settle for just buying all her records and CDs.

It's been a very sad summer for me and I've listened to her singing every day since her passing. I only met her briefly three times (actually 2.5 since one was just sign language when I told her "I loved and adored her" before she hosted a fourth of July concert from Washington, DC) and I had just drafted a letter to send her just a few short weeks before she died. Beverly was always so busy, I didn't want to bother her with my silly babblings. . . . There is a beautiful song by Korngold, "Marietta's Lied." The last line translates something like this: "If some day you must leave me, trust that we'll meet in heaven." If there is such a place and they let me in, it will be Beverly that I'll look for first and thank her for making my life so much richer. Thank you Beverly, I love you, rest in peace.

Over the years, I learned more about Ponder and the reasons for his devotion to Sills. Recently, he shared an essay that he penned for a creative self-therapy class in which he candidly recounted how Sills came to play a formative role in his life.

> Being now solidly middle-aged I find it remarkable, looking back, to see how much influence someone that I didn't personally know had on my life. The profound gravitational pull Beverly Sills exerted on my life's orbit has been undeniably powerful in a number of ways and over a long period of time.
>
> I had a very unhappy childhood and could have been the poster child for "A Child Left Behind." My father was physically abusive, frequently beating me for things I did or didn't do. These beatings . . . happened steadily for years and eventually became fistfights when I grew big enough to fight back. I think at some level my father was trying to beat the gay out of me, and Jesus into me.
>
> While my mother was not as physically abusive as my father, she was, however, verbally abusive and regularly reminded me that I was dumb. . . . I was also bullied and taunted in school for being a sissy and dumb. . . . I had constant fantasies from an early age of running away from home, killing myself, or killing my father. . . . It's probably a good thing that I didn't have access to a gun.
>
> There were some forces that came together when I was an early adolescent (13–14) that began to turn around my unhappy situation. A great-aunt realized I needed some "intervention." Neola began to have me work on her and her husband's farm over the weekends. Mondays I would be back to school and back to my fucked-up home life. Neola was the first person to realize I was bright and she frequently told me what a handsome young man I was. This positive reinforcement was a new experience and I wasn't quite sure I believed it.
>
> About the same time, I became fascinated with a bubbly red-headed woman that began appearing on television. Beverly Sills was my first exposure to operatic singing and to classical music, in general. . . . Art music and Sills were exotic and fascinating for me. She made me fall in love with classical music and with her. Beverly Sills was funny, gracious, and so honest about the difficulties in her life. How could I not have a huge crush on her? She also taught me to keep trying and not to give up on my dreams. (e-mail, October 6, 2013)

Ponder also wrote of another turning point in his life. When his friend badgered him into joining the school orchestra, he acquiesced. His interest in classical music had been piqued by Sills's television appearances. He took up the viola and progressed rapidly. The orchestra director became the first teacher not to consider Ponder as below average; in fact, he listed him as gifted and talented.

By his senior year, he was recognized as the top player in the orchestra. He went on to earn both bachelor's and master's degrees in piano performance as well as a master's degree in harp performance.[5] He concluded his personal narrative with this summary of Sills's role in his life:

> Sills often mentioned being influenced by her mother who said that the goal of every day should be to improve and make someone else's life a little better. I truly believe that I might have ended up in jail if a few key people hadn't come into my life at the right time. Beverly was one of those people and I'm sure that is part of why I was so heartbroken when she died. She was not only a great singer, and a major influence on my musical life, but her beautiful voice calmed the beast and anger in me. (e-mail, October 6, 2013)

Edward Specht

In fall 2007, while experiencing my own reaction to Sills's passing, I read Ed Specht's simple, plaintive posting under a YouTube video of Sills's "Spargi d'amaro" from *Lucia di Lammermoor*: "My heart is breaking . . . July 2, 2007 . . . the darkest day of my life" (ellipses in original). I wrote to him, but when I did not receive a reply, I searched for his name and discovered his blog where I learned that he shared a friendship with Sills for more than thirty years. I contacted him through his blog and quickly received a reply: "I am in the process of gathering, sorting, and remembering 37 years of notes, gifts, fax messages, Christmas cards, and loving moments I shared with a great and noble lady" (e-mail, October 8, 2007). Specht was hoping to write a book focusing on Sills's interactions with her fans; unfortunately, poor health prior to his death in August 2011 put an end to his aspiration.

Specht first heard Sills in a recital at the Claremont Colleges' Bridges Auditorium in November 1970 when he was seventeen years old. During the next decade, he saw her numerous times in his home county of San Diego performing with the San Diego Opera, but he also traveled around the country to hear her in New York, Boston, Fort Worth, Salt Lake City, and San Francisco, among other destinations. From the very first encounter at Claremont, Specht made a point to greet her backstage. He also sent her fan mail. As she typically did, she replied. Their frequent written communication continued up to the end of her life.

His collection of the many letters, cards, and faxes that crossed between them now belongs to Freeman Stamper's private museum in Hayward, California. Their correspondence documents a relationship that grew increasingly close over the decades. By the 1990s, both Sills and her husband Peter (who frequently wrote to fans when travel prevented her from doing so) shared details of their family travels, health issues, the rare grouse regarding a colleague, and other personal news. In 2006, Beverly discovered that Specht was seriously ill and hospitalized when her repeated attempts to fax him failed (faxing was their key method for fast communication—Sills did not take to computers and e-mail). She wrote: "Please take care of yourself and get well immediately, that's an order! . . . Remember! Get well at once. We need you around and healthy. Lots of love from your devoted and loving friends, Muffy and Bev with hugs & XXX" (card postmarked June 17, 2006). Her last note to Specht thanking him for his birthday gift—and written a little over a month prior to her death—read: "Ed dear, The berries were almost as sweet as the thought of you. Love XX Beverly."

Many of Sills's correspondences are notes thanking him for his generous gifts. Over the years, Specht sent the Greenough family bushels of fresh California produce, especially avocados and strawberries, as well as flowers, chocolates, and his sister's caramel corn, which he expressed via UPS to wherever they instructed him—either their New York City apartment, their home on Martha's Vineyard, or their place in upstate New York. In a note from the early 2000s written on stationery imprinted "Metropolitan Opera, Beverly Sills, Chairman of the Board," Sills thanked him for a shipment of goodies, even though she had just ordered two weeks of food from Jenny Craig. Sills's struggles with weight gain, particularly after her retirement from singing, are well documented. Specht also suffered from morbid obesity in his last decades. Their love of food was mutual.

Specht idolized Sills. In one of his first messages to me, he wrote: "If there ever was a 'perfect' person, she embodied it." Though it was her voice and stage presence that initially attracted him, there were other factors that strengthened his dedication to Sills. First was simply her kindness and generosity. As he sent her gifts, she sent him personal correspondence and items such as autographed posters. For Specht, whose parents had high school educations and "very little classical knowledge," the attention lavished on him by Sills, a world-famous opera star, was precious and uplifting. In reporting on his vigil at her star on the Hollywood Walk of Fame on the first anniversary of her passing, Specht wrote: "In time, I have no doubt Beverly will be recognized as one of the truly gifted people of this period. Not simply for her obvious singing ability, but for her complete immersion of being a genuine 'human' and in the way she interacted with the 'great' as well as the 'small' of the world" (www.beverlysillsonline.com/walkoffame2008 .htm, accessed July 10, 2008). Second was their shared interest in the philosophy of Christian Science. Sills's unrelentingly positive attitude and cheeriness stemmed in no small part from her mother's instilling of Christian Science beliefs. Specht was a devout Christian Scientist. Sills's attitude and actions, including her significant charitable work, particularly with the March of Dimes, made her an ideal role model–cum-idol. Third, Specht felt a connection to Sills that transcended the bounds of the mundane world.[6]

Ed Specht celebrated Sills's career and memorialized his relationship with her in a collection of memorabilia that occupied a wing he added to his home in Carlsbad, California.[7] Specht and his collection were featured in several local newspapers in the late 1970s, including an *Oceanside Blade-Tribune* article published in anticipation of an upcoming appearance by Sills with the San Diego Opera. The article, "World's Only Beverly Sills Gallery in Carlsbad," reported that the gallery included seventy-nine autographed items, including letters, programs, album covers, and posters, displayed in elaborate and expensive frames (April 17, 1979). In addition, he had more than two hundred additional signed mementos on hand. The article quoted him as saying, "When Beverly heard about my collection and the gallery, she urged me to continue the project." Specht saw his collection as having educational value and welcomed passersby to stop and learn more about Sills; he even loaned part of his collection for display at the Carlsbad City Library, hoping to draw the interest of young people to classical music.

Specht worked for many years as an administrator of a care facility for the elderly in Los Angeles before moving with his sister and mother to California's central coast region to open a private senior-care facility. Not long after the 2008 financial crisis, the business failed and they moved to Bellevue, Washington. He lovingly packed and shipped his Sills collection with each move. When finances dictated another move in 2010, this time to Montana, Specht's poor health, and the expense, made it impossible for him to package and move his collection. Fortunately, he had met Freeman Stamper while visiting Sills's star on the Hollywood Walk of Fame in 2009, and they remained in touch. Specht was aware of Stamper's aim to build the largest collection of Sills items in the world and offered him his entire collection, if Stamper would pay for the packing and shipping. His concern was in keeping his entire collection together and safe. Maintaining consistency with his view as recorded in 1979 in the *Oceanside Blade-Tribune*, he expressed his hope that eventually the items would be viewed by many people. In his message to Stamper, he wrote that Sills was with him; he no longer needed to be surrounded by the recordings or mementos that documented her career and her part in his life.

> Times are a'changing and seem to be a bit rough but we know all things work together for good and we will not be left comfortless. I turn to our girl often in memory and hear, without aid of recordings, her angelic voice supporting and cheering me on. The founder of our church once said, "If a friend be with us, why need we memorials of that friend?" I am mentally at the point where Beverly lives and sings in my thoughts and I would consider it a great blessing for you to have these individual treasures I have loved and cherished for so many years. (e-mail from Ed Specht to Freeman Stamper, January 6, 2010)

About a year after Specht's passing, Roy Dicks, Taylor Cornish, and I gathered at Stamper's museum where we opened his eleven large boxes and surveyed the remnants of Ed's life with Beverly Sills. He had framed or laminated many of the letters and cards from the Greenoughs, often along with the envelopes. There were copies of all of her commercial LP and CD releases—in some cases, as many as five or more still-sealed copies of single LPs as well as complete opera sets. In addition to many signed programs, he had also saved newspaper clippings, mostly from San Diego newspapers, and magazine articles and covers featuring Sills. Complementing these mass-produced items, his collection included photographs—some snapshots (sometimes of the two of them together or of Sills with other fans), some professional photographs of Sills. Specht had established a relationship with one of Sills's photographers and managed to acquire shots that were never publically released. He also owned several oil portraits of the singer. Among the rare items of memorabilia was the cover of the 1974 San Diego phonebook that sported Sills in a scene from the San Diego Opera production of *Daughter of the Regiment*.

Specht's collection began with the autographed program from his first encounter with Sills when he was a teenager; it grew steadily until she penned her last personal note to him shortly before her death thirty-seven years later. With his memories of Sills securely a part of his being, Specht entrusted his collection to Freeman Stamper without fear of losing his sense of self or his communion with his memories.

Charles Freeman Stamper

The voices of only three singers make Freeman Stamper tingle: Marilyn Horne, Tatiana Troyanos, and Beverly Sills (phone conversation, July 16, 2008). Of these, only Sills marries his rhythm of life. Stamper's first experience seeing a full-length opera was Sills's *Lucia di Lammermoor* in 1971 at Wolf Trap where he later saw her *La Traviata* and *Daughter of the Regiment*. Living in Washington, DC, from the late 1960s through 1977, Stamper also heard Sills at the Kennedy Center in recital and in *Roberto Devereux*. He moved to San Francisco in 1977 and there saw Sills perform *I Puritani* twice in what were her final performances with the company. Besides her voice, Stamper also has a tremendous appreciation for the thoughtful manner in which Sills treated him the several times he greeted her after performances. He recalled that following her Kennedy Center recital, there were people crowding the green room hoping to share a moment with her; some obviously knew her. When Stamper presented Sills with an album to autograph, she first signed on the front. Then she realized it would soon wear off due to the glossy cover material; she said she had better sign the back. Even with the large crowd clamoring for her attention, she took the time to consider the situation and ensure that she presented him with an enduring autograph. A few years later, Stamper designed a T-shirt that read "I love B.S.*" on the back and "*Beverly Sills" on the front. When he took it for her to autograph after her final San Francisco *I Puritani* performance, she said, "Thank heavens for the asterisks." Stamper was touched that "she took time to spend with little ole me" (phone conversation, July 16, 2008).

In 1999, Stamper made the decision to build his Beverly Sills collection. At the time of writing, it has grown to be what is likely the largest accumulation of Sills-related materials in the world, numbering more than four thousand separate items.[8] He admits to having an "obsessive desire" to collect and decided to fuse his Sills fandom with his desire to collect. Although he collected for almost ten years prior to her passing, he never wrote to Sills to inform her of his collection because he did not want her to fear that he was a stalker.[9]

In an article on record collecting, Kevin Moist writes that a collector's deepest desire is to "bring meaning and coherence to a chaotic world by preserving and organizing some small corner of it" (2008, 99). Even before embarking on amassing his Sills collection, Stamper had long been bringing order to the world—or at least to corners of it to which he felt a connection. For instance, he became an avid participant in the gay square-dancing community and in 1984, produced a membership directory for the Western Star Dancers club, one of the organizations central to the formation of the International Association of Gay Square Dance Clubs (IAGSDC), as well as a travel guide that listed the locations of clubs across the country.

Although he grew up poor in a tiny town in Louisiana, at the insistence of a caring high school English teacher, Frances Morris, Stamper went to college where he earned a BS in secretarial science. With the military draft looming, he enlisted and entered military school to study stenography. After training, he was assigned to work at the office of the secretary of defense in the Pentagon, where he worked (even earning the highest noncombat award, the Joint Service Commendation medal) until his three-year term ended. Over the years, Stamper has done well financially. He endowed a scholarship named for his teacher Frances Morris at his alma mater, the University of Louisiana–Monroe (ULM). His sense of loyalty to the university, which provided him with his first opportunity to explore the world beyond his "strict Southern Baptist household where dancing and other creative expressions were taboo" (Staples 1998, 3), led Stamper to make arrangements to have his collection shifted to the ULM campus when he can no longer care for it.

When his collecting intensified in the late 1990s, eBay became one of the most important resources in his constant pursuit of Sills-related items. In fact, in July 2008, Stamper and I were introduced by eBay seller Diana Price, daughter of John Price, who operated the Musicarnival outside of Cleveland where Sills sang in the mid- to late 1950s. Stamper checks eBay several times a day, and as of June

2013, he has devoted more than $175,000 to his Sills collection. In 2011, he moved his collection to a mobile home next to his home in Hayward, California, and named the entire enterprise "The Assoluta Beverly Sills Museum and Research Library." The more than seven hundred books, eleven hundred magazines, and other materials are easily accessible to researchers, although visitations must be arranged privately.

Stamper's collecting practices differ significantly from those of Ed Specht. Whereas Specht's gallery was largely a tribute to his personal relationship with Sills, Stamper's collection knows few limits. He says the chronological scope is "Beverly Sills cradle to grave." Materials include personal items formerly owned by Sills, remnants of her artistic career, and every possible manifestation of and reference to her in American popular culture. The collection's breadth may make it valuable to scholars researching other topics in mid- to late twentieth-century culture because, in some respects, it is something of a time capsule. In terms of printed materials, any book that mentions Sills, no matter how briefly, is subject to inclusion. He also has an enormous collection of magazines, including such disparate titles as *Opera News* and *Good Housekeeping*. While he would prefer to own copies of complete newspapers that include Sills references, he limits himself to clippings.

Of special importance for this study is Stamper's collection of Sills's performance programs. He and Roy Dicks, profiled next, coordinated their purchasing of programs after I introduced them in 2008. The combination of their holdings forms the basis for the Sills performance annals, available via Dicks's website: http://www.beverlysillsonline.com/annals.htm.

Of Sills commercial recordings, Stamper aims to own each album in every possible manifestation: eight-track tape, reel-to-reel tape, cassette tape, LP (in American and foreign pressings), and CD. In addition to commercial releases of sound and video recordings, he has purchased every bootleg LP he has found. Rare artifacts include 16-mm film clips of public-service announcements that Sills recorded to fund-raise for the New York City Opera and other arts organizations, and as part of her charitable work for the March of Dimes. All items in outdated formats are professionally converted to contemporary formats such as DVD. Other rarities include video recordings of her appearances on popular televisions programs such as *The Tonight Show* and audio recordings where the video has not survived, such as Dinah Shore's programs.

Stamper's voracious appetite for all things Sills has led him to acquire some of her personal belongings in addition to artifacts that document her career. For instance, he purchased several pieces of jewelry sold by Sills's daughter Meredith "Muffy" Greenough through a jewelry estate firm. He also won one of her Judith Leiber minaudières along with miscellaneous accessories at the estate auction held at Doyle New York in October 2009. One of his proudest purchases from the Doyle auction is the winged metal helmet that she wore as a Valkyrie in her 1953 appearance at the San Francisco Opera.[10]

The collection includes numerous novelty items that attest to Sills's pervasive presence in American public culture during the 1970s. A tube of Aida Grey lipstick in the shade "Beverly Sills" provides such an example. First introduced in the late 1970s, the shade is still being produced and is available for purchase on Aida Grey's website. Other curious consumer items include: several skeins of wool yarn in a variegated mix of colors named "Beverly Sills"; a silk scarf, which looks to be a Hermès design and bears Sills's autograph; and a line of costume jewelry, also signed by Sills. The museum displays various porcelain commemorative plates and three Boehm porcelain figurines of Sills as Manon; many other relics created in celebration of Sills's fame are filed away. On the grounds, Stamper has planted a bed of the tall bearded "Beverly Sills" irises. This coral/pink-colored hybrid iris was created and registered in 1979 at the height of Sills's fame.

Stamper's collection is an expression of one fan's devotion to Sills, who provided him with a subject worthy of his desire to collect and organize. However, beyond that, his efforts have made a significant contribution to the documenting of Sills's activities as an artist, a fund-raiser, and an administrator. Furthermore, with his samples of her personal correspondence, such as letters to Ed Specht, we gain a broader understanding not only of her life history (especially in the years following the publication of her second autobiography), but also of the manner in which she conducted personal relationships. Through his determination to possess nearly every Sills-related item he discovers, we can track Sills's presence not only in multiple forms of media, but also in the weft and warp of mid- to late twentieth-century American public culture.

Roy C. Dicks

Roy Dicks first became intrigued with opera while still in junior high school, even saving his money to purchase opera records, thanks to the Metropolitan Opera's weekly Saturday afternoon radio broadcasts and the encouragement of his aria-singing uncle. As a university student majoring in English and drama, he found himself in a circle of friends who were also opera fans. One evening he experienced an instant transformation to Sills fandom when a friend played Sills's recording of *The Ballad of Baby Doe*. Dicks checked the album out of the library many times until he could afford his own copy, all the while wondering "how someone of such obvious talents wasn't already world-famous" (Dicks 2004, 687). Although the *Giulio Cesare* album was released about a year after Dicks first heard the *Baby Doe* recording, it was two more years before her next release, the first recital album. From the very start, he felt invested in Sills's standing in the operatic world. He recalls that with "each new release I felt a peculiar surge of pride, as though, through my constancy, I had willed her career into being" (ibid., 688). Even though Sills held an important place in his life from the time he heard her Baby Doe, he never wrote to her. He attended a number of her performances and was thrilled to greet her backstage, to have his photo taken with her, and to get her autograph. However, he never wanted to impose himself upon her. Over more than four decades, his dedication to Sills has never waned and in recent years has manifested itself in the creation and upkeep of a website dedicated to the preservation and documentation of her artistic legacy: www.beverlysillsonline.com.

In fact, the research required for this book would have been significantly more difficult were it not for Dicks's decades of meticulous and loving documentation of Beverly Sills's singing career. Dicks is the driving force behind the beverlysillsonline.com website. The site's pièce de résistance as far as my work is concerned is his compilation of Sills's performance annals. Another resource, which proved vital for this study, is the site's "Farewell Guestbook" (hereafter *Guestbook*) where Sills's fans posted their memories of Sills following her passing. Dicks's aptly chosen e-mail handle is "infoman." He is meticulous, thorough, and relentless in his research, which is not surprising given that he holds a master's degree in library science from the University of North Carolina–Chapel Hill and worked for twenty-seven years as a professional reference librarian in the Wake County Public Library in Raleigh, North Carolina. Over the years, he has also acted, directed, and sung in choirs. Dicks is a member of the Music Critics Association of North America and has worked as a freelance writer of performance reviews, interviews, and feature articles on classical music, opera, dance, and theater for several newspapers in the Raleigh area since the late 1970s.

Just as my research has drawn on his accumulation of knowledge and data, Dicks has benefited from the labor of other Sills fans. In fact, the earliest form of his performance annals was based on work done by dedicated Sills fan Emo Furfori. In 2005, while browsing the Internet for Sills references, Dicks came across the Yahoo Group "Sills Thrills." He joined the group and discovered one of its main features was a fledgling file of performance annals. Dicks contacted Furfori, the group's moderator, and they became friends through their trading of noncommercial recordings. In the end, he asked Furfori if he could take over the performance annals and make them the centerpiece of the website that he and another Sills fan, Larry Strachan, were planning. Furfori was pleased since the format of the Yahoo Group was very limited in comparison to the website's potential for including music and video. Furfori shares Dicks's aspirations to not only document the logistics of Sills's career, but also to keep the memory of her artistic accomplishments alive.

Dicks joined forces with Freeman Stamper in 2008. They share their program holdings and coordinate their acquisitions of new items. Unlike Stamper's rather omnivorous approach to collecting, Dicks gathers materials and data with a laser focus. He is determined to preserve Sills's artistic legacy by tying together the myriad threads she spun as she blazed through her career. At the most basic level, this has meant documenting what and where she sang and when. The closest Sills came to preserving a record of her extremely dense schedule are the scrapbooks assembled by her family members, especially her husband. However, the news clippings and programs contained in the scrapbooks fall short of forming a complete record of all of her many appearances. Dicks has spent many years searching through newspaper databases and magazines, such as *TV Guide,* in his quest to create a complete and accurate record of Sills's appearances. As of June 2013, he has verified and recorded more than 1,350 performances.

Through connections formed in opera discussion groups and trading communities, Dicks has attempted to acquire all the live bootleg recordings of Sills in circulation. With more than 170 separate opera performances and more than sixty different recitals and concerts, ranging from 1937 to her retirement, Dicks's collection of Sills's recordings appears to be the most comprehensive in one location. These recordings have been essential in his building of the annals. His collection has been strengthened by the activities of other collector-fans (MacLeod 2004, 121), especially those of John Carroll. Carroll and Dicks first met in 1998 through their postings to the online opera discussion group Opera-L. Carroll had been collecting private Sills recordings well before the advent of digital media and the Internet, as he mentioned in his *Guestbook* entry:

> For about 20 years I was obsessed with hearing and collecting every live recording I could find. Long before the Internet I used to write away to pirate recording dealers who had small classified ads in the back of *Stereo Review,* and then pore over endless lists looking for any glimmer in the cast listings of those five letters: S I L L S.

In 2001, Carroll posted his discography of Sills commercial and private recordings to Opera-L and invited list members to send him corrections and additions. Dicks recalls:

> This was thrilling to me because it was the first attempt to identify all the Sills recorded performances. I eagerly checked my audio holdings against his and sent him a list of corrections and additions. That led inevitably to our setting up trades, as we each had things the other didn't. John contributed quite a lot to my live Sills collection and a number of his items are still in my collection, having not been replaced by any other source. Actually, I owe as much to John as I do Emo for supplying so much of what became the full annals. (e-mail, June 13, 2013)

Like many great artists, Sills lived for her moments on stage, moving from performance to performance giving everything she had, while leaving the documentation and preservation of her legacy largely to dedicated admirers for whom the task is a labor of love. A community of collector-fans has formed and evolved over the years in a mutual effort to document, celebrate, and memorialize Sills's artistic career.

In her study of video collecting, Kim Bjarkman writes of the complexities involved in communities organized around collecting on subjects of common interest. According to her study, these communities are hierarchical, with "the collecting cognoscenti at the fandom's hub" (2004, 229). Through his many years of building his collection of Sills materials by trading, negotiating, or purchasing, Dicks has established himself as one of the central authorities on many aspects of Sills's performing career. In the spirit of cooperation that Dicks and his collaborators foster and inspire, the Sills fan community, represented most recently in "The Beverly Sills Crazies!" Facebook group (discussed later in this chapter), does not seem to suffer from the divisive internal factions, friction, or flaming that Bjarkman suggests are endemic to such fandom "microcosms" (ibid., 228). Generally, within the "Crazies!" group there is a feeling of excitement and wonder as newly discovered photos or audio recordings surface and are shared. When new information comes to light, it is often subject to many comments as group members ask and answer questions. From time to time, a participant comments that the feeling of collegiality and camaraderie among the "Crazies!" is uncommon for such groups; invariably, someone else responds that Sills would be proud. No doubt she would.

Pete Buchanan

Pete Buchanan must surely rank among Sills's most passionate and devoted admirers. I first contacted him through YouTube's messaging service, where he goes by the handle "Petelovesbevsills," several months after Sills's death when I noticed his effusive comments on her videos. Buchanan's activities on YouTube, Facebook, and other sites exemplify the high degree of participatory culture and pleasures that the rise of new media technologies have afforded fandom (Penrod 2010, 141).[11]

Buchanan is a central figure in the world of Sills fandom due in no small part to his creation and moderation of the "The Beverly Sills Crazies!" Facebook group, but he became a Sills fan decades before the dawning of the digital age. In one of his earliest messages to me, he explained that Neil, his partner of more than forty years (and a devoted Joan Sutherland fan), was very fond of Sills and tried to get him interested in her. Buchanan recalled, "When I first heard Beverly, I hated opera and her in that order" (e-mail, September 23, 2007) because he was not pleased to share Neil's attention with Sills (or any other opera singer). About a year later, home alone with the flu, he listened to Sills's *Lucia,* following along with the libretto. By the opera's end, he was, as he put it, "an opera and Beverly Sills convert" (e-mail, October 13, 2007). About four years following his conversion, with Neil's encouragement, Buchanan "plucked up the courage" and sent a fan letter. He explained:

> She replied in the form of a postcard, which we framed with other photos and postcards that she sent to me.
> I wrote again and she replied on her own stationery and that was the beginning of our relationship. Peter [Greenough] was such a star, he would write to me if Beverly was out of town and what struck me most was the fact that they didn't have secretaries typing these letters. Where they both found the time to reply I'll never know but I am profoundly grateful that they did. They made a hick from Johannesburg such a happy man!!!! (e-mail, February 21, 2010)

During the following year, he wrote to Beverly several times; in return, he received three letters and a postcard from Beverly, two letters from Peter Greenough, and a Christmas card from their daughter Muffy.

Even with his contact with Sills and her family, Buchanan felt isolated as a passionate fan in Johannesburg, South Africa, where his parents emigrated from England following World War II. References to Sills were rare in the local media, and due to the high cost of foreign subscriptions, Buchanan had to go to the public library to read about her in *Newsweek, Time,* and *Opera News.* His need to possess all things Sills was so great that it drove him to tear pages out of library copies, which he brought home and added to his "Pete Adores Beverly Sills" scrapbooks: "How I never got caught I do not know but I just felt no one could love Beverly as much as I did!" (e-mail, September 23, 2007). Furthermore, Sills's album releases arrived in South Africa many months after they hit the shelves in the United States and came to Johannesburg even later than Cape Town. In expressing his frustration about having to wait to hear Sills's new releases, Buchanan recounted:

> There were two record shops in Johannesburg that stocked Beverly's recordings. One of them, called Recordia, had prissy queens in the Opera Department and THEY used to get quite tweezer lipped when I went into raptures over Beloved Beverly. Needless to say I bought very little there but Neil got all his Sutherland latest releases from them.
> The other shop, Hillbrow Record Library, was run by a man called Lenny, who loved Beverly. I used to visit his shop with Neil every single Saturday. One Saturday we went browsing and found the American Operatic top 10 bestsellers list pasted on a wall above the opera recordings. Oh my god, I looked at it and there was my beloved Beverly's *Concert* album in No. 1, *Anna Bolena* in 3rd, and *Tales of Hoffmann* in 5th positions! Three out of ten were MY Beverly's

recordings. They hadn't even arrived in South Africa and weren't expected until 5 months later. . . .

Neil had to go to Cape Town on business about 1 month later. (He had bought his first Beverly Sills recording while he lived in Cape Town years before, from a record shop there whose owner was a complete Sills nutter!) While he was there he visited the Sills nutter, who HAD all three recordings! . . . When he got home he told me he had bought me a tiny little something from the Cape and to close my eyes, which I did. When he said to open them, he had arranged the three recordings on our bed! I naturally had a good, deep weep! What a thoughtful, loving and kind thing to have done for me! I was elevated to cloud nine and didn't come down for many weeks. The luxury of THREE Sills recordings was too sublime for words! . . .

I am very happy to report that nothing's changed, I still weep and get very, very emotional when a new Sills item comes into my life! (ibid.)

It is hard to imagine someone's fandom being more dramatically influenced by new media than that of Pete Buchanan. Since 2011, he has created new objects of fandom for his enjoyment and that of other Sills admirers (Sandvoss 2005, 30). He has gone from feeling isolated in South Africa (with few other Sills fans with whom he could share his enthusiasm for Sills, little news of developments in Sills's career, no access to private recordings, and significant delays in hearing new commercial releases), to being the founder of the lively "The Beverly Sills Crazies!" Facebook group and producing Sills videos for posting on his own YouTube channel.

Buchanan was not exposed to the Internet until 2005 when he and Neil moved to England following the collapse of the company for which they worked in South Africa. With Buchanan in his mid-fifties and Neil in his late sixties, they were drawn to their ancestral homeland where the hopes of finding employment were brighter. Initially, he turned to the public library as a resource in finding news of Beverly Sills. He recalled the afternoon when using a public computer he came upon Roy Dicks and Larry Strachan's Sills website:

When I discovered the beverlysillsonline site, I was sitting in the library (we could not afford a computer). I tuned in to it thinking it would just have excerpts of Bev's recordings. Well, Nancy, I have to tell you that I put on the headphones and pressed a *La Bohème* duet with James McCracken and Bev singing on the site, heard Bev singing Puccini for the first time ever, and burst into tears in front of everyone in the library!!!!!!! . . . I told Neil about the site and his response was "to hell with the money, we buy a computer tomorrow" and that's what happened!!! (e-mail, November 22, 2007)

Once equipped with a home computer, Buchanan began to make frequent Internet searches for references to Sills; to hunt for photos, videos, and general news; and to search for other passionate fans. He joined Facebook in late 2007, and in mid-2011, created a forum for discussions and sharing of digital content. He founded "The Beverly Sills Crazies!" as a "closed group"[12] to ensure that all members are "genuine Bev lovers" (e-mail, June 14, 2013). He already had sixteen such Facebook friends, including me, and we became the initial members. All potential inductees must be approved by Buchanan, the group administrator. Some people have found the group's listing through an Internet search and have contacted Pete for admission. So far, he has only refused a handful of requests. He turned away one candidate "for listing just about every soprano present and past as being his 'passion'"; he rejected several others for not responding to his "request of details of their interest in Bev" (e-mail, June 14, 2013). Buchanan searches YouTube for "passionate comments," and when he discovers candidates, he invites them to join the "Crazies!" group. He has also extended invitations to roughly sixty contributors to the *Guestbook*. The size of the group fluctuates; in early 2015, the number was 163 members.

Although Buchanan joined YouTube in 2006, it was not until May 2011 that he began creating and uploading his own videos. He composes most of these by combining recordings of arias from live performances with Sills photos from his collection. He has amassed a collection of live recordings through tireless reaching out to Sills admirers, including Roy Dicks, Larry Strachan, and others. As of March 2015, Buchanan has created seventy-seven videos, which collectively have received more than 57,000 views.

Connecting before and after the Rise of Social Media

These seven profiles demonstrate some of the ways in which Beverly Sills became entwined in the lives of her admirers and how some of her admirers have also come to know one another. In the case of the Ames sisters, their fandom came at a crucial stage in their personal development. The passion for opera—and musical performance, generally—that Sills stoked, as well as the connections the sisters formed as a result of their relationship with her, set them on fruitful career trajectories. Their fandom for Beverly Sills, the opera star, morphed into a friendship with Beverly Sills, the woman. The fan behaviors of their youth did not persist into middle age. If not for Alison's 1971 *Hollins College Bulletin* essay, I might never have discovered them—neither have an Internet presence that identifies them as Sills fans. The other five came to my attention through their online activities: Ed Specht and Pete Buchanan through YouTube, Freeman Stamper through eBay, Roy Dicks through his beverlysillsonline.com website, and David Ponder through the *Guestbook*.

The role that social media has played in connecting fans, and the subsequent building of strong affinity groups, cannot be overstated. With the exception of those based in New York, where her frequent performances allowed for friendships to be formed among her backstage greeters, most fans had few outlets for sharing their thoughts and feelings about Sills prior to the connections afforded by the Internet. When asked how he met Sills fans before the digital age, Dicks replied:

> As for meeting Sills fans before the Internet, I didn't really connect with anyone other than people I met locally at parties or at the opera. I had a few friends who were Sills fans (but not fanatically so—they liked her among a number of other singers) and I wasn't particularly seeking any out. . . .
>
> While I was certainly on the lookout for any live Sills material I could come across (catalogs advertised in the back of music magazines and trips to NYC to go to several underground private-label stores), it really wasn't until the CD era in the mid-1980s that offerings of live performances began being easily available (Ed Rosen, chief among those offering such items). But I did that collecting basically in isolation until around 1996, when the Internet started taking off and I joined Opera-L. Then there were many people who identified as fans with whom I could correspond or just read their comments. That of course led to people like John Carroll and others with whom I began to trade performances and information. (e-mail, June 18, 2013)

In the 1990s, through opera discussion lists and trading sites (which were significantly enabled by the CD format), Sills fans began to find one another and share resources. The rise of social-networking sites allowed for even greater opportunities for identifying and connecting with like-minded fans. With the launching of the "The Beverly Sills Crazies!" Facebook group, fans now gather regularly to share photos, sound recordings, and videos; to relay information; or to share revelations made while listening to her sing. On New Year's Eve 2013, Ron Runyon launched a thread of thanks in the "Crazies!" group, which drew a chorus of comments echoing his sentiment, all of which expressed gratitude for the friendship and camaraderie shared by this community of Sills fans.

> Thank you for the pleasure of your company, the sharing of both your insights and intelligence in this world of Opera for which we share mirrored passion—and of course our shared affection for Beverly. It is such a pleasure to escape here, however briefly, from the reality of the day, to be reminded of the beauty and joy of our cherished art form, and all those who create, live and make possible our enjoyment of it. But most importantly, it has accomplished its intent, core and heart—it brings us together.

CHAPTER 7

Experiencing Magic

What was Beverly Sills like in live operatic performance? How did her audience experience her in moments sometimes referred to by the elusive expression *magic*?

Sills used the word *magic* in assessing her own career. Having retired from singing for more than six years, and nearing the end of her term as general director of the New York City Opera, Sills mused on her life as a performer in her 1987 autobiography: "I can't finally analyze what I did or why people liked what I did. All that fits into the category of unnameable magic" (1987, 347). This chapter is a gesture toward identifying the quality in Sills's performance that she and others experienced as being beyond the realm of the quotidian, as being transcendent and uniquely powerful—as magical. Examples include specific moments in Sills's performances; these are complemented with mentions of similar phenomena from the work of other artists. In exploring the magical quality of performance, I draw data from numerous and diverse sources (including written materials such as performance reviews, magazine articles, and book chapters) dating from Sills's years on the stage, items published after her retirement (including her second autobiography and her former costars' memoirs), and all manner of materials posted on the Internet (from YouTube comments to personal blog postings to electronic copies of obituaries from major print publications). These are supplemented by published and unpublished interviews with Sills and with interviews I conducted with her former colleagues as well as with people who attended her operatic performances in New York and elsewhere. Certain common themes have emerged from this large body of data that are facets of the quality or phenomenon experienced as *magic*. I take *magic,* then, as an overarching concept whose components I aim to parse and scrutinize.

My introduction to the idea of Beverly Sills being magical in performance came during my first Sills pilgrimage. In the weeks following her death, the Metropolitan Opera announced a "Tribute to Beverly Sills" memorializing her life and career. I felt compelled to attend. Once at Lincoln Center, I felt as though I were in an enchanted place. Much of Sills's life had been spent on the grounds of the complex, yet I had never been inside either the Metropolitan Opera nor the New York State Theater. Waiting in line in the early morning of September 16, 2007, for tickets to the tribute, which would be staged later, in the early evening, I engaged in conversations that turned out to be the first interviews for this book, although at the time, this was strictly a personal journey. However, I spent the six hours in line outside the Met learning as much as I could about Sills. What I heard that day chatting with people who had seen her perform many times no doubt influenced the trajectory of my research and the questions that I would come to ask of the Sills material.

The first person I engaged in conversation was a sixty-year-old passionate opera fan who grew up in Brooklyn. Though Joan Sutherland was her favorite singer on account of her phenomenal instrument, Sills was her favorite singing actress. As she looked over the line that continued to lengthen behind us, she said: "I'm really amazed there are people here who never saw her live and we're all on this line together. What I find so fantastic is that what Sills had crossed the television, crossed the airwaves, crossed the pit. And we all got it." She commented that she had no idea who would be performing for the tribute; she had come to pay her respects to Sills, not to be entertained. She guessed, though, that Plácido Domingo would sing, if his schedule permitted, because he "grew up with her at the New York City Opera." Recalling their performances in *Roberto Devereux* and *Manon,* she said, "Plácido and she were magical on stage together. It was like nothing imaginable."[1] This was my first face-to-face encounter with someone who was recalling her experiences seeing Sills live as she sought to convey what made those moments special. There can be an uncommon intensity involved in the transmissions of such memories. Her choice of the word *magical* to describe Sills in performance alerted me to listen for similar depictions. I continued to think about her assessment that Sills possessed a special quality that reached across distance and through mediation.

Next I struck up a conversation with a retired music teacher in her late seventies who introduced herself as Rita Greenstein. She used to take the train in from Long Island to see Sills perform and witnessed Sills in every role she performed in New York. She and her grandson, who were at the very front of the ticket line, must have arrived by five o'clock in the morning to ensure seats at the event. We engaged in conversation twice. The first time, she reported that when Sills was on stage, you could not take your eyes off her. Wanting to document more of her memories, I recorded our second conversation.

> The first time I really remember seeing Beverly Sills was the first performance of *Julius Caesar,* and I had the privilege of being there. One thing I remember about *all* of her Cleopatra performances was her in this gorgeous pink dress, and how she came out from the back of the stage. As she walked out, she just took over the stage; she swirled in. She just glorified opera, glorified the stage, and glorified everything wonderful about music. She *was* the stage. I saw her four times as Cleopatra and every performance was the same. She just glowed. And she made everything about her glow. . . .
>
> Everything that she did had this marvelous, spectacular touch that made it special. Her three queens were unbelievable. No matter what she did, she was that person. She changed. She was never Beverly Sills. She was always one of the queens, or she was Baby Doe. Whatever she did, she was just incredible.

In this excerpt, Greenstein touched on three themes that, in the coming years, I would hear echoed again and again by Sills's former colleagues, audience members, and critics: Sills's command of the stage,[2] her complete embodiment of the characters that she portrayed, and the sense that she seemed to emit light.

In framing this discussion of the elements in Sills's performance sometimes referred to as inexplicable or "unnameable," this chapter draws upon the work of performance studies scholars, particularly Jane Goodall, Jill Dolan, and Erika Fischer-Lichte. Whereas they each theorize these elements differently and apply their own chosen terminologies, I employ *magic* as the umbrella term under which to recount the extraordinary in Sills's performance.

Situating Magic

As I have explored the scholarly literature for writings that expound upon the power of a performer's electrifying presence to render feelings of communion, transcendence, or mesmerism, I have found the word *magic* is indeed employed. However, it is typically used as an effusive marker denoting a fantastic moment in a performance without further elaboration.[3] Rather than unpacking *magic,* some scholars create new terminology—such as "utopian performatives" (Dolan 2005) or "moments of enchantment" (Fischer-Lichte 2008)—around which they spin theories of the extraordinary in performance. For example, in her inspiring book *Utopia in Performance: Finding Hope at the Theater,* Jill Dolan uses the word *magic* sixteen times yet does not include it in the index. Other related concepts such as *charisma* (which appears six times in the text), *communitas,* and *presence* are indexed. The exclusion of *magic* as a defined concept worthy of indexing is peculiar given that Dolan makes reference to the theater as a "magic place" (2005, 4), to the "magic of theatricality" (ibid., 96), and to a "captivating magic through the power of the performers' presence" (ibid., 31). Dolan also writes of "moments when people sense themselves in sync with the group in a common sentiment of wonder, magic, and possibility" (ibid., 102) and "moments of magic and communion in performance" (ibid., 55). In *The Transformative Power of Performance*, Erika Fischer-Lichte employs *magic* or *magical* at least eleven times. As with Dolan, the term is absent from the index even though she writes of the "'magic' of presence," which, as she claims, "lies in the performer's particular ability to generate energy so that it can be sensed by the spectators as it circulates in space and affects, even tinges, them (Fischer-Lichte 2008, 98). Fischer-Lichte also makes an intriguing reference to audience members being struck by an actor's presence "as by lightning—a stream of magic" (ibid., 96). Jane Goodall takes a daring approach in her remarkable book *Stage Presence,* in which the word *magic* appears more than thirty times, as she aims "not to demystify presence, but to discover how this mysterious attribute has been articulated and what kinds of imagery surround it" (2008, 7). As she traces references to this special quality across mainly Western writings, she delineates and explores the history of related concepts, such as mesmerism, which are sometimes components of presence.

Central to the theoretical aim of Dolan's book is her concept of "utopian performatives," which she describes as "small but profound moments in which performance calls the attention of the audience in a way that lifts everyone slightly above the present, into a hopeful feeling of what the world might be like if every moment of our lives were as emotionally voluminous, generous, aesthetically striking, and intersubjectively intense" (2005, 5). Dolan cites music and dance critic John Rockwell's review of Anne Bogart's production of *bobrauschenbergamerica* as an illustration of how a utopian performative is experienced. Rockwell wrote: "Mesmerizing moments are what those of us addicted to performance live for. Suddenly and unexpectedly we are lifted from our normal detached contemplation into another place, where time stops and our breath catches and we can hardly believe that those responsible for this pleasure can sustain it for another second" (quoted in ibid., 8). The notion of utopian performative is useful as it directs our attention to those instances when magic is at its strongest, when the artist and her or his audience are mutually enveloped in an extraordinary moment.

Although a good deal of Dolan's book explicates how utopian performatives are experienced by performers and audience members alike, much of her theory is devoted to attributing purpose beyond the immediate sensation or transcendence they elicit. These fleeting moments have the power to influence the lives of those who experience them. For Dolan, this influence is capable of inspiring positive social and political change. She asserts that "[u]topian performatives persuade us that beyond this 'now' of material oppression and unequal power relations lives a future that might be different, one whose potential we can feel as we're seared by the promise of a present that gestures toward a better later" (ibid., 7). Dolan makes clear her motivation for envisioning the efficacy of utopian performatives in this way. As she explained, she wrote her book in the aftermath of the September 11 attacks at a time when "progressive citizens of the United States have plenty about which to be cynical" (ibid., 3). She pointed to the Bush administration using the "calculated politics of fear to keep the citizenry passive" while demanding the "uncritical acceptance of diminished privacy and nationalist racism" (ibid., 3). The toxicity of this milieu was only compounded by an already deeply cynical postmodernism with its abandoning of the possibility of "the transcendence of meaning and truth for a far more cynical relativity" (ibid., 20–21). In short, Dolan designates the theater as a site of hope, a refuge from the cynicism of the post-9/11 world, where she herself had so often been overcome by a feeling of utopia during energized moments when everything clicked. As she says, part of her argument, "in trumpeting the progressive potential of utopian performatives in performance, is that reanimating humanism and seeing, through performance, more effective models of more radical democracy might reinvigorate a dissipated Left" (ibid., 21).

No doubt the discouraging milieu in which Dolan developed her concept of utopian performatives was critical in influencing her identification of sociopolitical change as the target for the efficacy of these moments of wonder. Evidence from the Sills material suggests, however, that utopian performatives spark other possibilities as well. These mesmerizing moments do indeed have the power to create change and to affect the lives of those who experience them. However, their potency lies in allowing individuals to visualize the world that they *personally* need to envision. Faced with the phenomenal artistry that makes such moments possible, and caught up in the feeling of interconnectedness, spirits are raised and hope abounds. Such moments inspire the desire for the positive, for greatness. However, the hopeful future that each person envisions is not limited to (or may in no way include) greater social justice or a thriving liberal democracy. Inspiration strikes in a personal direction according to an individual's life narrative. Some may be inspired to gather their energies in pursuit of their own aspirations, or to reach for a brighter future, without a specific notion of what this will entail.

The stories of fans, including those of William Madison and Joseph Malloy introduced in chapter 5, who had their lifelong pursuits launched by encountering Sills in performance, attest to this. Whatever touched thirteen-year-old William Madison the evening that he saw Sills perform in 1975 fueled his quest for learning for many years: "We'll never know how much I owe her, how many wonderful things I'd never have discovered if not for her inspiration" (http://billmadison. blogspot.com/2007/07/beverly-sills.html, accessed October 18, 2007). Joseph Malloy, who saw Sills perform many times when he was a high school student, closed his epitaph by thanking Sills for changing his world. Sills left a long trail of young people, including myself, whose brushes with utopian performatives in her performances set in motion lifelong reverberations. Perhaps the young, filled with youthful optimism, are especially able to act on visions of possibility inspired by utopian performatives? A similar example from beyond the world of Sills fandom comes from Robert Gottlieb, former editor of the *New Yorker,* who attributes witnessing a single ballet performance with inspiring the course of his life. In an interview on *Charlie Rose,* Gottlieb recounted: "The first really *thrilling* moment in my dance life was when I was seventeen and went to the New York City Center. And there, the company that became the New York City Ballet later that year, did Balanchine's great work called *Symphony in C* to a symphony by the young Bizet. And, watching that unfold, changed my life . . . it steered me in the direction of dance" (originally aired on PBS on October 21, 2010).

Of course, it is not only the young whose lives are influenced by an experience with utopian performatives. Sills's vocal coach and occasional accompanist, Roland Gagnon, witnessed Sills in performance many times. Speaking of audience members' reactions, he said, "She has a kind of magic. . . . She entrances people. She changes things" (Scheader 1985, 55–57). In a personal note to Sills, Jonas Salk (the American physician and epidemiologist who developed the first effective polio vaccine) mused on the effect Sills had on her audience during one of her last performances at the San Diego Opera in October 1980:

Dear Beverly
You were transcendent on Sunday
and you took all of us with you.
When I'm in your presence I keep looking
at you and into you
to see the magic with my eyes.
I know it's there, but only by the effect
it has on those touched by your presence.
A wondrous mystery.
Affectionately, Jonas[4]

The notion of utopian performatives identified and theorized by Jill Dolan—and experienced by William Madison, Joseph Malloy, and countless others—goes to the heart of the magical experience that overtakes an audience when, as Ian McEwan puts it, performers "together touch something sweeter than they've ever found before in rehearsals or performance, beyond the merely collaborative or technically proficient, when their expression becomes as easy and graceful as friendship or love. This is when they give us a glimpse of what we might be, or our best selves, and of an impossible world in which you give everything you have to others, but lose nothing of yourself" (cited in Dolan 2005, xiii). This is the magic identified by Jonas Salk, Roland Gagnon, and so many others.

Communitas and Flow/Silence and Breathlessness

At the height of the magical experience, audience members are mesmerized, almost afraid to draw breath for fear of breaking the spell the performer has created through her or his dazzling singing and/or electrifying stage presence. Jane Goodall writes of the "compelling power often referred to as 'mesmeric,'" through which performers "convert a mass of individuals into a highly charged unity; they erase the everyday thoughts and mundane reactions of their audiences by transporting them to another plane of feeling" (2008, 87). The notion of an audience of individuals morphing into a "highly charged unity" is suggestive of *communitas,* a phenomenon most famously theorized by anthropologist Victor Turner.

Inspired by his observation of rites of passage among the Ndembu of Zambia, Turner suggested that communitas is "very frequently associated with mystical power and to be regarded as a charism or grace sent by the deities or ancestors" (1969, 137–38). Through ritual, practitioners hope to create the conditions that will "cause the deities or ancestors to bring this charism of communitas among them" (ibid., 138). Turner argues that in complex industrialized societies, attempts to invoke communitas are still found in the liturgies of churches, among other settings. Although the "numinous supernatural character of archaic ritual" (Turner 1985, 297) has been significantly reduced, the theater—"a detached, still almost-sacred liminal space" (ibid.)—is "one of the many inheritors of that great multifaceted system of preindustrial ritual" (ibid., 295). Victor Turner's partner, anthropologist Edith Turner, expanded his work by exploring communitas as it appears in numerous contemporary contexts, including festivals and work situations, and in disasters, revolution, and music. She considers music a "fail-safe bearer of communitas" due to its being the "most ephemeral" of genres (Turner 2012, 43).

> It is as if music by its very limitation—sound—provides a clean path to spirituality, and allows the spirit language to enter it easily. Sometimes music is not merely the vehicle of the spirit, a means or channel. At certain moments music *is* the spirit; it incorporates all one's consciousness at these times, and spirit is right there. In those moments, one hears the spirit playing in the music like

a fountain, as in Sibelius's *Finlandia*. Again, this kind of religious experience, music, may change one's life. (ibid., 49)

Performance studies scholars have productively employed the notion of communitas in their work. Jill Dolan, for example, uses it to describe "moments in a theater event or a ritual in which audiences or participants feel themselves become part of the whole in an organic, nearly spiritual way; spectators' individuality becomes finely attuned to those around them, and a cohesive if fleeting feeling of belonging to the group bathes the audience" (Dolan 2005, 11). Characteristic of communitas as experienced in the theater is a silence that descends over the audience as its members become aware of and part of an atmosphere of inter-subjectivity. Whether it is experienced by tribesman in their rites, practitioners of Judeo-Christian rituals, or an opera audience in rapt attention, in communitas individuals find "a transformative experience that goes to the root of each person's being and finds in that root something profoundly communal and shared" (Turner 1969, 138).

Sills spoke of her experiences before audiences whose silence communicated a heightened sense of focus and attention. This *silence in the silence* signals a kind of congealing that takes place when an artist joins her performing colleagues and audience to her, and her audience members to one another, in a moment of palpable communitas. As Tito Capobianco shared in our interview, Sills was often at her very best on opening nights when she would marshal every ounce of her considerable energy to meet the challenges presented by such occasions. Recalling her premiere performance of *I Puritani* Sills wrote: "On opening night, when I made my entrance atop those stairs, a total hush fell over the audience. *Nobody* coughed. It was the kind of silence every singer dreams about" (1987, 255). In the silence that denotes the audience is "hanging on every note" (ibid., 166), the singer is filled with a sense of power as her energies are interlocked with those of the audience. One of Sills's most profound experiences with this sensation came the night of her debut as Cleopatra. Of that evening, Sills reported: "I must say that I experienced an enormous sense of power that I had never felt before so that I was even able to do things vocally that I hadn't even anticipated doing."[5] Sills's experience as Cleopatra resonates with another key characteristic of communitas as identified by Turner, who wrote that "communitas has something 'magical' about it. Subjectively there is in it the feeling of endless power" (1969, 139).

New York–based voice teacher Marlena Kleinman Malas, wife of bass-baritone Spiro Malas, was in the audience for the *Giulio Cesare* premiere. Asked how it felt, she replied, "I couldn't breathe. I think the audience just couldn't breathe. I mean, it was so stunningly beautiful, nobody dared to make a sound or take a breath or just break the moment. You couldn't hear a sound in the house when she finished singing. It was just amazing, just amazing" (M. Malas interview,

October 9, 2009). Writing for the *New York Times Magazine,* Hubert Saal also commented on audience's cohesion, as evidenced by their "collective breath."

> Instead of a dying fall in her second aria, "Piangero," she floated one pianissimo after another as fragile and clear as silvery bubbles. From then on, each time she appeared, the astonished audience seemed to draw a deeper collective breath of anticipation and all evening long she made hungry where most she satisfied (1967a, 58, 60).

Sills described a similar moment when she engaged her audience in rapt silence during her long-awaited Metropolitan Opera debut.

> Our opening night was magical. Roland had been right about the "Dal soggiorno." When I began singing it, that wonderful hush from the audience was there again. Schippers was the kind of conductor that sopranos dream about; when I hooked on to a high D pianissimo, Tommy just let me sit on it until I'd had enough. When I came off the high D, the audience *sighed.* It was an incredibly exhilarating moment. There were times in my career—and that was one of them—when I felt like a trapeze artist doing dangerous somersaults without a net underneath. When you execute those somersaults flawlessly, the audience feels the same sense of triumph the performer does. Moments like that are memorable and damned exciting. (Sills 1987, 189)

Through the vital intersubjectivity present in such moments, the performer energizes the audience; the eager audience lifts and sustains the performer. This intensity has been termed *flow* by psychologist Mihaly Csikszentmihalyi. The notion of flow has been applied productively to the studies of ritual, the performing arts, and athletics. "Flow denotes the holistic sensation present when we act with total involvement" (Csikszentmihalyi and MacAloon cited in Turner 1982, 55).

Essential for flow to occur is a balance between the person's skills and the demands of the task. With mastery of the required skills, worry and fear dissipate. Speaking of her Cleopatra debut, Sills commented during her 2002 interview on *Charlie Rose* that "there wasn't a hurdle in that score" for her. In the moment of performance, with the audience virtually mesmerized, the sense of power she felt propelled her to "do things vocally" that even she had not imagined doing prior to attaining this heightened state. On the eve of her retirement, Sills said, "I've come to the conclusion that this whole profession is based on whether you can perform a somersault in midair without a net underneath you. I think my Cleopatra attracted so much attention because I was taking so many chances" (Livingstone 1979, 92). Even in situations where the execution of the task is truly life-threatening—such as in rock climbing, for example—"the moment 'flow' begins and the activity is entered," the pleasures of flow "outweigh the sense of dangers and problems" (Turner 1982, 57). While not life-threatening, singing a high D pianissimo in "Dal soggiorno" was risky; hence, Sills's reference to feeling like a trapeze artist without a net.

Many of Sills's former colleagues have reported to me at length (and with terrific intensity) on Sills's total engagement in the performative moment. She almost seemed to have an on/off switch. Once she was in the moment, she was there completely; her transformation to *on* was instantaneous. She was renowned for joking around, engaging in small talk, and even for sitting just offstage filling in crossword puzzles prior to her stage entrances.[6] But, as Charles Wendelken-Wilson told me, when she heard her music coming up, she would fall into character. Photographer Beth Bergman, who saw Sills perform and rehearse countless times from every possible vantage point (from the wings, the catwalk above the stage, from the orchestra pit, and so on), paints a vivid picture of how Sills would "snap" instantly and completely into character:

> She warmed up vocally before a performance, but when she was set she'd socialize with everyone, chat, laugh . . . and then—snap—she'd be in character and on stage. I think it's *Devereux* that has the jazzy overture. She'd dance to that in the wings, and then in a split second she'd step onto the stage as regal Queen Elizabeth. In some operas the star is preset on stage, in place. In most operas, the star makes an entrance. Comic, tragic, everything in between, she'd be herself, the jolly human being, and then—snap—she'd be the opera role person. I saw this many times: Bubbles morphs into opera character. (e-mail, November 23, 2009)

On the stage, she very rarely dropped character (as is not uncommon, especially when singers turn their backs to the audience).[7] On the subject of her total engagement and its effect on his own performance, Robert Hale said:

> She was always *so* in character. I love to react and to bring drama to my singing as well as beauty to my work. But it was more likely to happen with a person like her, who was so good and honest in her presentation. When she looked at you, she looked at you in your eyes. I loved the eye contact. Then the drama builds and you can see what's going on in a person, and their reactions.[8] Wow! It's a dynamic building of emotions. I would say it was this higher level of concentrated drama. Beverly brought that with her presence on stage and it was great to play opposite of her because you would never find her anywhere but in character. Never. Never out of the character. (interview, August 17, 2010)

To illustrate the intensity of Sills in the moment, both Dominic Cossa and Robert Hale told of their experiences performing with Sills in Gounod's *Faust* and in *Lucia di Lammermoor*. Cossa played Valentin, the ill-fated brother of Sills's character Marguerite, in Frank Corsaro's production of *Faust*. Cossa described how he and others would stand in the wings watching Sills's gut-wrenching execution of the opera's final scene, acting out how he and those around him (and no doubt the audience, too) drew in and held their collective breath at a key moment when Marguerite tragically regains her sanity.

Corsaro had Marguerite—who has suffered a major psychological break and is in prison for murdering her child—pantomime playing with and then drowning her baby. In his controversial staging of the last scene, in which Marguerite typically finds redemption as her soul rises to heaven, Corsaro had her walk to her execution compos mentis. As she ascends a staircase to meet the headsman, the burlap cloth—which she had used to swaddle a bundle of hay as her surrogate newborn—begins to unfold. As the pieces of hay fall to the ground, Marguerite regains her sanity—only to go to her death fully lucid. In the flash that brought her character back to reality, Sills communicated Marguerite's horror and then acceptance of her fate. Of Sills's Marguerite, director Frank Corsaro wrote: "Beverly Sills was particularly amazing, revealing depths of feeling hidden beneath those conventional attitudes. She managed to humanize this much-abused heroine. Hers remains one of the most subtle and beautiful performances I've witnessed in the opera house" (Corsaro 1978, 83).

Robert Hale made his role debut as Mephistopheles in the Corsaro production and expressed gratitude for having had the chance to perform the work with her because she dropped it from her repertoire shortly thereafter. Commenting on Sills's performance of the "Jewel song" in an earlier, happier scene for Marguerite, Hale commented on how Sills's energy flowed into the audience: "She could effervesce. You would see all this joy and power and love and happiness just flowing out over the audience. You couldn't help but love her." (interview, August 17, 2010)

In *Lucia di Lammermoor*, Cossa played Lucia's desperate brother Enrico in the first performances of Tito Capobianco's 1969 production. In the first scene of act 2, Enrico implores Lucia to marry the wealthy Lord Arturo Bucklaw to save their family's crumbling financial estate. He even produces a forged letter proving to her that her beloved Sir Edgardo of Ravenswood has been unfaithful. Lucia resists, but Enrico is unrelenting. Capobianco staged a portion of the scene with Lucia's back to the audience while Enrico cruelly threatens her. Cossa recounted his experience with Sills as Enrico terrorizes her character Lucia:

> "If you betray me, this will be on your head. I'll be a ghost who will haunt you
> for the rest of your days." Enrico is browbeating her unmercifully but her back
> is to the audience. Now, a lot of sopranos would use that time to think about

what they're going to sing next. The audience can't see their faces so they're doing their own thing.

The audience couldn't see her face, but I could. The look of sheer terror on her face would put me on a whole different level as a performer. I never forgot that. She wasn't doing it for me, she was in the *moment*. She was acting in the moment; that was important to her. And she was able to pull it off. Probably it even translated to her back for the audience. (Cossa interview, December 3, 2010)

In the role of Raimondo Bidebent, a duplicitous chaplain, Robert Hale performed *Lucia* more than thirty times with Sills. He shared a similar view of how Sills's total involvement lifted the intensity level for everyone involved.

As a colleague, being on stage with Beverly, her powerful presence radiated such strength of character and presence of the moment, of the action, that it absolutely encompassed all of us. Everybody on stage was caught up in that moment because of her great involvement and her *power* to portray....

The energy level was raised because of her presence on the stage and that doesn't necessarily happen when you sing with a Pavarotti or a Sutherland. Joan Sutherland was a wonderful singer and I love her. She's a great person. You can't say anything about her singing. It was phenomenal. It was a bigger voice than Beverly's, but what she didn't have, what Beverly had, was that magic quality. Which I, frankly, would rather have than the great, glorious pear-shaped sounds. I'd rather be *moved* by somebody that didn't possess such a great voice. I've always been that way. And I have sacrificed my voice often for the moment. Forget bel canto [i.e., "singing beautifully"]; if you're in character then, believe me, it develops a presence on stage.... You yourself get involved and if you're involved, they're involved. They're looking at you. That's what she could do *so* powerfully. She just raised the level of any performance that she was in. She would raise the level of everyone. (interview, August 17, 2010)

Another dimension of flow is the merging of action and awareness. Here, the person becomes one with the activity; her actions flow as if they are automatic (Csikszentmihalyi 1990, 62–63). Turner notes that in this moment, the past and the future must be given up—"only *now* matters" (1982, 56). While in normal life, we often interrupt ourselves with questions of doubt and evaluation, "in flow there is no need to reflect, because the action carries us forward as if by magic" (Csikszentmihalyi 1990, 54). Leonard Bernstein's experience conducting exemplifies this aspect of the flow state. He once shared: "I honestly don't realize what I'm doing on the podium. When I'm conducting, nothing else exists but the music and the players" (Harris 1956, 52).

During her 2002 appearance on *Charlie Rose*, more than two decades after her retirement from singing, Sills detailed what was likely one of the most profound flow experiences of her entire career. Rose asked if there was one performance she cherished above all others. With a sparkle in her eye, she immediately replied that there was: the opening night of *Roberto Devereux*. She also claimed it was the only perfect performance she ever sang. She swore she was never able to do it again. However, as mentioned in chapter 4, a bootleg recording from that evening documents that she lost her footing with her intonation in one of her first phrases. From an entirely objective standpoint, the performance was not perfect, even though these vocal problems were minor and largely limited to a few seconds of instability (and the rest of the performance is truly extraordinary). Furthermore, fan and music writer Katrine Ames, who saw nearly every Sills East Coast performance of *Roberto Devereux*, disagreed with Sills's perception that the premiere was her best performance in the role. Ames said that the premiere was indeed extraordinary; however, she believes Sills continually improved in the role because her characterization grew increasingly rich (K. Ames interview, December 27, 2010). Bringing a new role to the stage in live performance presents one of the greatest challenges for a singing actress. I believe that the exceptional difficulty of the role of Queen Elizabeth demanded a level of engagement and sheer mental and physical strength from Sills that allowed, or even forced, her to reach a flow state of greater intensity than any other roles of her career. Hence, Sills experienced the performance as the most perfect she ever gave. Further analysis of what other factors may have contributed to her perception follows in an excerpt from the Charlie Rose interview.

ROSE: Is there one performance, for you, that more than any one performance, one evening, on an opera stage, that you cherish more than all others?

SILLS: Yes. It was the opening night of *Roberto Devereux,* when I played Queen Elizabeth. It was the only perfect performance I ever sang in my life; and I was never able to do it again.

ROSE: Why was it perfect?

SILLS: Everything I set out to do, I did. Every note that I wanted to sing in a particular way, to get something across—worked. Every gesture I made . . . was where it should have been, and I was never able to do it again. It was one of those nights that it didn't—it was just for me. I can remember everything about that performance. . . .

The *Devereux* was such a challenge for me. There were fifty-five pounds of costume. I was sixty-something years old on the stage. And I was twenty-five years younger than that at the time I did it. The score was so difficult. I cannot describe to you how difficult it is to sing Queen Elizabeth. There is no score that I've ever attempted that was that much of a challenge. And I thought, you know, I'll do the very best I can. I thought 85, 90 percent, if I can get what I wanted. And—

ROSE: You got 100.

SILLS: It just poured out of me. I never did it again!

ROSE: And you—

SILLS: God, I was so frustrated with that woman, I could've killed her. But, you know—it was—I remember I took a high D pianissimo and it just lasted and lasted. I don't know where the breath came from. I remember listening to myself, and thought, "Drop it, kid, drop it! Don't—don't prolong it any. . . ." It just poured out of me. Never could do that again! . . .

I couldn't wait to get on the stage to start it. That was the first thing. I mean, my voice—I wasn't even thinking of my singing, I wasn't thinking of anything. All I could think of was to get on that stage, and do this woman. By the time I got to the final mad scene, I was on another planet. I really sort of took on this woman's body. I mean, I—it was a weird, weird feeling, but what was so incredible, to me, was I felt I could do anything with my voice I wanted to, and that just doesn't happen a lot. Never to me, never happened again.[9]

Sills touches on several cornerstones of flow in her description of this performance. First, she acted with total involvement. Second, her skills were matched to the task: "I could do anything with my voice I wanted to" and "Every gesture I made . . . was where it should have been." As an example of what Sills was remembering, a close listening to a bootleg recording of the performance reveals her "Vivi, ingrato" (Live, ungrateful man) near the opera's end to be an essay in artful singing and musicianship. Her aria takes on the form of one long floated line that she shapes and ornaments with a myriad of delicate inflections, each subtlety communicating Elizabeth's disappointment and enduring love for the man who has betrayed her. Her singing flows as though she has no need to breathe; it simply pours out of her in an expansive, delicately controlled line that finally ends with an effortless, crystalline high D. Third, neither before nor during the performance did Sills experience anxiety or fear, just an eagerness to be in the moment: "All I could think of was to get on that stage, and do this woman." Fourth, she seamlessly merged her actions and awareness. In fact, this merging occurred to an extraordinary degree, with Sills describing something akin to an out-of-body experience. She remembers listening to herself sing and not knowing where her breath was coming from. It "just poured out" of her, or *flowed*, to borrow Csikszentmihalyi's term. Lastly, she mentions the "weird, weird feeling" of "sort of" taking on the body of Queen Elizabeth; with this, she suggests possession. By the final scene, she was "on another planet." Sills's intensity of feeling for Queen Elizabeth never waned, even though the vocal demands of the role forced her to drop it from her repertoire in 1975. At the age of seventy-one, Sills quipped, "If God gave me back my voice, say, for just three hours . . . I'd say: Get me the old queen's costume. Quick!" (*San Francisco Chronicle*, December 17, 2000).

During our interview, I asked Tito and Gigi Capobianco if Sills ever talked with them about feeling as if she were watching herself perform. Gigi confirmed that she had. When asked if this is something a performer aims to achieve and if it is unusual, she replied, "Well, sure! It's like you are a puppet of yourself." Tito added, "Yes, this is when you become an artist, when you become a puppet of yourself. You control how you look, how you project. . . . Some people are the exception to the rule, because God gives to them some intuition, the ability to be a puppet of themselves." This wasn't the only instance when Tito mentioned a celestial influence. Later in our interview, he pronounced that miracles only happen in two settings: "In the church and on stage. And that is magic. That is magic" (interview, July 28, 2010).

One further dimension of flow as theorized by Csikszentmihalyi, and of critical relevance to Sills, is that while in the flow state, "one is able to forget all the unpleasant aspects of life. This feature of flow is an important by-product of the fact that enjoyable activities require a complete focusing of attention on the task at hand—thus leaving no room in the mind for irrelevant information" (Csikszentmihalyi 1990, 58). In numerous interviews and in her own writings, Sills commented on how she could not wait to get on stage. These were her three or so hours of escape from her own troubles. The situation with her children was a nearly constant emotional presence for her; performance supplied her with a temporary haven from her unrelenting sadness. In the performative moment, Sills was free to experience unfettered emotion with an intensity of feeling that she did not often permit herself in her own life. In the 1969 *Newsweek* cover story, Sills was quoted as saying: "I can't tell you what a good time I have onstage. Everything sparkles. I glow. I love being about to sing well, to have it just pour out of me. I'm happy onstage, I'm greedy for those three hours. They're hours of pure joy" (Saal 1969, 75).

Shortly after her death, the Capobiancos published a eulogy in which they commented on this aspect of Sills's life and performing career:

> She found solace from her wrenching personal and family sorrows by los-
> ing herself in the passionate sensuality of Violetta, Thaïs, Manon, the ill-fated
> intrigues of the three Donizetti Queens, the superb Norma, the unparalleled
> dementia of Lucia, the charming frivolity of the Merry Widow, Adele, and
> Queen Shemakha, the tragic mother in Borgia, the vocal flowing of Cleopa-
> tra, Ginevra, as well as Elvira. In this way she created, for a few hours—a very
> few hours—her own little world with her only great joy: singing. That was her
> only true joy.[10]

Katrine Ames also related the intensity of Sills's performance directly to her dire need for a reprieve from her reality. Performance was a kind of abandonment for Sills. For Ames, Sills's complete intellectual and emotional commitment to her performance was a gift not only to Sills's audience, but also to herself. Sills completely surrendered to her character, to the music, and to everything else; everyone had a truly remarkable experience as a result. "Music saved her from going nuts from all the sadness she had and the great tragedy in her life," Ames opined (K. Ames interview, December 27, 2010).

As Victor Turner observed, "To flow is to be as happy as a human can be" (1982, 58). Sills found her happiness in the flow state. Naturally, the audience senses it when a performer achieves flow because he or she becomes part of the intersubjective field that engages all those present. This intense intersubjectivity was at the core of Sills's creation of the magical experience.

Presence and Mesmerism

Even when a singer possesses extraordinary vocal and acting technique, vocal and physical beauty, and fine musicianship, there is no guarantee that she will also possess that difficult-to-describe, special quality "experienced as uniquely powerful, perhaps even transcendent or magical" (Goodall 2008, 17). In seeking to address the fundamental question "What is it that makes a performer compelling to watch?" Jane Goodall looks to stage presence (2008, 17). Her exploration of presence provides a useful framework for addressing this quality in Sills's performance. *Presence* is frequently alluded to by a variety of metaphors, including *magnetism, attraction, electricity,* and *radiance*; all of these contribute to conceptualizing its dynamics. Presence also has a strong relationship to genius (ibid., 18). Goodall argues that far from being ineffable or untellable as is typically claimed, "the notion of presence has inspired some of the most memorable passages in the literature on performance" (ibid., 7). In her detailed historical survey of writings describing exceptional performers (mostly in Western traditions, including opera and ballet), Goodall concludes that "[s]omething beyond the natural" is evoked (ibid., 2). Where "stage presence is concerned there is no getting away from the strange and the uncanny" (ibid., 11). In short, Goodall asserts: "Presence is a coalescence of energy, mystery, and discipline," with all three of the qualities operating in differing balances in every exceptional performer (ibid., 19).

Historically, presence has been largely conceived in the West as following two models. The first, to which *discipline* belongs, stems from the figure of the dignitary, the classically educated nobleman who, through his speech, manners, and bearing, is viewed as having gravitas or presence. In theatrical practice, this form of presence belongs to the realm of training and technical prowess. The second, to which *energy* and *mystery* belong, involves "magnetism and mesmerism, a sense of inner power being radiated outwards" (ibid., 8). Legendary performers possess both forms in varying proportions.

Many of Sills's former colleagues made a point of stressing that Sills was extremely hardworking and disciplined. She was always impeccably prepared for rehearsals; she not only knew her parts, but those of the other singers as well. Speaking of the early rehearsal stages of *Anna Bolena,* Robert Hale (who played King Henry VIII to Sills's Anne Boleyn) recalled that Sills set a very high standard by always being extremely well prepared.

> We were all trying to do our best, but her presence elevated everyone. It challenged you to reach up like she was, to reach up in those levels. She was an example in her discipline and her approach to music; she was so serious. And yet, she could laugh and joke, but she was not joking about being prepared—never. With her, it was a religion. . . . I think she was one of the greatest influences in all my life during those early years in the New York City Opera when I was forming my whole stage presence, and how to approach a role, and how to study, and how to become real onstage. (Hale interview, August 17, 2010)

Sills rarely lost her temper except when her collaborators were ill prepared. Charles Wendelken-Wilson recalled gleefully: "If somebody came to rehearsal and goofed off, she could stand there and throw a good fit as well as any other prima donna that you've ever seen. But, if everybody was working, she could put up with mistakes; she could put up with people who were just plain slow" (interview, August 1, 2008).

Charles Wadsworth, Sills's primary recital accompanist from January 1970 through to the closing number of her farewell gala in October 1980, commented: "She was so enormously prepared. And brilliant. I don't know what her IQ was, but it must have just been off the charts" (interview, April 19, 2010).[11] As an illustration of her extraordinary intelligence and diligence, he mentioned how she would sometimes use their time flying to concert destinations to learn her new roles.[12] He recounted how once, when she was just beginning to work on the three Donizetti queens, she boarded the plane with a score. At the end of their three- or four-hour flight, she said, "Well, I've got the first act now." By this, she meant that she knew it in terms of the words and the music. Wadsworth commented, "It was just an incredible accomplishment. I don't think I had ever been with any singer who could accomplish that sort of feat" (interview, April 19, 2010).

In the realm of acting, much of Sills's development came from her intensive work with the Capobiancos, although other directors, including Sarah Caldwell and Frank Corsaro, also had an influence. Tito Capobianco said that once they made it through the rough patch that marked their first encounter, Sills always asked him to give her more. She was forever eager to further her characters' development and to strengthen her communication of their feelings. "She was hungry," Gigi Capobianco said. Sills worked tirelessly with both the

Capobiancos, especially on the physical aspects of acting with Gigi, a former ballerina.

In her role as a photographer at both the New York City Opera and the Metropolitan Opera, Beth Bergman closely observed nearly every major opera singer in the world during the past four decades. She astutely tied discipline and integrity to magic in performance in writing about Sills: "She was herself, brilliant, well prepared, vocally secure, historically informed, and with a huge sense of humor. One can say she was magical and she was, but it was the result of hard work, respect for her body and her voice, respect for the music, respect for the audience. What she did was the truth and that's why it was magical. I have been fortunate to have observed many performers with this kind of integrity and it is always magical" (e-mail, November 23, 2009).

An artist with a mesmeric presence is one who has holding power; she draws the attention and imagination of the audience to her (Goodall 2008, 127). Part of Sills's ability to mesmerize her audience stemmed from her total inhabiting of her character. In one of his first messages, fan Taylor Cornish relayed his experience of being spellbound by Sills's Elvira in *I Puritani*.

> Her realistic acting style was one key, I feel, to her brilliance in creating roles. But if something was stylized, it was there to serve a dramatic purpose as well. Case in point: when she sang Elvira's mad scene in *I Puritani* that begins with the exquisite, "Qui la voce," she entered at least ten feet above the stage floor at the top of a steep ramp that extended straight forward and down toward the front of the stage. She held both arms in the air over her head, attractively arranged as a dancer would in a simple symmetrical arabesque. She held them there for the entire aria as she slowly descended the ramp, singing passionately, of course, but staring straight ahead, or perhaps looking at nothing, appearing unaware of her surroundings. She never stopped moving—but walked so slowly in her full-skirted gown that she almost appeared to float forward—and she reached the end of the ramp and stepped onto the stage floor at precisely the moment the aria ended. I don't know how it sounds to you reading these words, Nancy, but the effect—coupled with her gorgeous legato line and her astounding breath control (she sang the entire aria much more slowly than others dare to)—was absolutely mesmerizing. She didn't appear to breathe and it seemed to me that no one in the audience did either; we were all in such rapt attention. It's a cliché to say it like this, but it was one of those transcendent "time stood still" moments. I remember I didn't move a muscle. I almost felt I couldn't. I was spellbound. As I mentioned, the aria ended as she stepped off the ramp. Then as other characters interacted with her she came to her senses intermittently, and appeared distressed and unwell in a more conventionally acted way, but it made dramatic sense since it was the very interaction with those other

characters that brought her tentatively out of her delirium. When the scene was over she had created a unique portrait of heartbreakingly delicate femininity and madness "simply" through her vocalism, her otherworldly expression, the placement of her arms, and her almost imperceptible movement toward us as she sang. It was musical and theatrical magic.[13] (e-mail, May 9, 2010)

Cornish speaks to one of the recurring themes of this chapter: breathlessness as Sills seemingly takes hold of her audience. Everyone feels it and no one wants to rupture the connection; hence, they are held breathless.

In his heartfelt posting to the *Guestbook*, Joseph Malloy, who saw Sills in nearly every role she performed in New York during the 1970s, recalled one performance that stood out for him. Malloy felt hypnotized, as though time had stopped, as Sills's deranged character swept across the stage:

[M]y biggest memory of her on stage was and always will be as Lucia. I remember one performance (had I seen it 5, 10 or 15 times?) when I had the experience of time standing still during the Mad Scene, of being hypnotized—how she moved and flowed around the stage like a 19-year-old 90-pound ballerina, and sang and ran the arpeggios and trills—and all the time convincing us that she was indeed insane. They say there are peak moments in life, when time indeed stands still, that you will always be able to recall. I think of that moment from time to time, and very often over the past few days.

Cornish's and Malloy's recollections of time standing still recall Victor Turner's explication of communitas as almost always being thought of as a "timeless condition, an eternal now, as 'a moment in and out of time'" (1974, 238).

In his obituary for the *Baltimore Sun* published on July 4, 2007, Tim Smith reported on an equally powerful experience seeing Sills in live performance as Queen Elizabeth. Before witnessing her at Wolf Trap, Smith was not yet a passionate opera fan. Sills's extraordinarily strong presence as Elizabeth reached out over the Wolf Trap lawn.

I owe a lot to this artist. Although I had partially opened up my ears to opera, it wasn't until one night, sitting on the grass in the low-price section of Wolf Trap in Virginia, that the power of the art form really hit me, converted me totally. That was the night I saw Sills portray Elizabeth I in Donizetti's *Roberto Devereux*.

She was mesmerizing, even at a great distance from the stage. She inhabited the role. And she made every note an integral part of the character. The intensity of her tone—a thing of fine silver, with a glint of steel—had a rare and penetrating magic....

As for the recordings, I don't think microphones were up to the task of capturing all of Beverly Sills, the complete picture, the whole package of talent.

The voice, with its fast vibrato, could take on a strident edge in the studio, and that no doubt fueled the critical carping. At other times, the sheer force of the singer seems to have been simply too much for some listeners; what they heard on disc or experienced in opera houses was more Sills than they could handle.

The rest of us could never get enough of this endearing artist. And whatever shortcomings there may have been in her singing, at any point in her career, they were easily turned insignificant by the many virtues of her innate musicianship, her deep expressiveness, her spirited presence.

Smith makes the important observation that Sills's intensity was simply too much for some audience members (and even for some who listened to her recordings). Katrine Ames observed, "I never felt that Sills put a curtain between herself and the audience. It was just here I am; here we go. And it was kind of like being invited along on a ride" (K. Ames interview, December 27, 2010). Not everyone could bear the immediacy of the soul baring that Sills enacted before her audience; the intensity of her feelings went beyond some people's comfort zones.

Goodall writes that all mesmeric performers, including Maria Callas and Edith Piaf, have detractors. Some people are simply not bound by their spell and remain "coldly aware only of unreliable technique, overused mannerisms, bizarre emotive registers" (Goodall 2008, 86–87). This represents one of the great divides of reception, one that is not limited to operatic performance. On one end of the spectrum are listeners who wish to be drawn in and swept away by a mesmeric performer; on the other end are those who guard against surrendering to such abandonment, often seeking to expose magnetism as fraud. The divide extends to performers. Some, like Sills, are willing and able to lose themselves in their characters and to surrender to the moment, while others—particularly those who place their greatest concentration on delivering a pristine (vocal) performance—maintain a certain coolness and distance.

The notion of "perfect musical performance" versus "perfect performance of music" as advanced by music philosopher Lydia Goehr speaks to a facet of this seeming polarity. Goehr sees attitudes toward musical performance as two ends of a spectrum: On the "perfect musical performance" end, "value resides in the creative acts of individuals *who give meaning to music in the very moment of each act of performing*" (Goehr 1995–96, 15; emphasis added). On the "perfect performance of music" end, the emphasis is on the performance of a *work*, which the performer must render with the greatest transparency possible. "Performances are regarded as subservient in purpose to the work" and "subordinate in value to the work" (ibid., 7). Sills's artistic orientation, at least since the birth of her children, was in sympathy with the "perfect musical performance" end of this spectrum. Her aim was to give a total performance, one that would envelop and even hypnotize her audience. In their obituary for Sills, the Capobiancos wrote that she "created singing/acting interpretations that were endless magic, human, and visceral. Her hypnotizing performing can only be compared to the greatest in the history of Opera." When asked to elaborate, Gigi Capobianco said that Sills often would say that she was going to hypnotize her audience. "And she could!" Gigi exclaimed. Tito Capobianco added that Sills was happy to go on the stage and appear before three thousand people: "Many people use the word *communion*; there is a magnetic feeling. When such an artist appears on the stage, you cannot take your eyes off of them. It is a magnetic thing. People are born with that. The seed is inside. Sometimes you discover you have it, and sometimes somebody else—the director—teaches you to discover that you have it. Nobody can create that magnet. God gives you the seed. You are an artist or not? We don't create artists. We mold them" (Capobianco interview, July 28, 2010).

Charisma, Energy, and Light

Sills possessed both presence and charisma.[14] Goodall distinguishes an important difference between these two qualities, arguing that charisma must be viewed over time "as a heightened life force that animates a whole career and fuels the trajectory of a sustained mission in the world" (2008, 46). Presence, however, "is an expression of life force in the moment, so that the moment itself is transformed in a way that has an impact on all who witness it. Its very transience is a factor in its uncanny potency" (ibid.). She additionally observes that those with charisma frequently also have stage presence; they can "turn it on" when needed. However, the reverse is not always true. Not all actors with stage presence are charismatic in their ordinary lives.

Over the course of interactions with people who spent time with Sills, I heard numerous accounts of her uncommonly vibrant energy. In striving to describe the energy that surrounded Beverly, a retired NYCO staff member began by asking if I were familiar with Reiki (a spiritual healing practice developed in early twentieth-century Japan that involves the transference of universal energy). She said that even with your back to the door, you could feel when Sills entered a room. Voice teacher and former member of the NYCO chorus Daniel Shigo put it simply: "The air vibrated differently around Sills."[15] Another longtime associate of Sills, who wishes to remain anonymous, mentioned how when walking down a busy Manhattan street with Sills, people's attention would be drawn to her. However, if Sills was not feeling well or needed privacy, she would pass by unnoticed. Entertainer Carol Burnett, who became Sills's close lifelong friend after they worked together on their *Sills and Burnett at the Met* program, said,

"It's a cliché … but when Beverly's around, the room lights up. She's the most incredible woman I've ever met" (Chase 1976, 70). In writing of Sills's charisma and presence, psychologist Beth Hart commented that she had it whether she was "performing, raising money, or asking people to buckle up in a New York taxi. It is in her voice, her manner—in her being. It fills a stage; it fills a room" (Hart 2004, 625). No doubt Sills's enormous charisma was a significant factor in her attaining star status among average Americans whose primary contact with her was mainly through television programs.

Sills's extraordinary energy—which radiated as charisma in her regular life and as stage presence in performance—was sometimes experienced by those who encountered her as a form of light or brilliance. The *Guestbook* provides a fine sampling of how people from varied backgrounds who encountered Sills under a variety of conditions, such as in live performance or in televised appearances, commented on this quality:

[Her] smile is really like a light and I'm sure it was always a sincere and spontaneous smile. (Alesio, Rome, Italy)

I am left feeling an unmistakable sadness that this brilliant light has gone out. (Heather Glynn, Los Angeles)

I have bragged that I never would have found my voice nor my calling nor had the life I have had without Beverly giving me a push and a start and showing me her light. (Kristine, Erie, Colorado)

She was a bright light in an otherwise dim world. (Scott Eaton, Auburndale, Florida)

We have lost a bright, effervescent light. Beverly was a joy! (Carol Rudy, Lakewood, Washington)

Her musicianship, her attitude toward life and her spirit was a light in a dark world. (Mary, New Jersey)

As a young soprano, Ms. Sills was my hero, my shining light, someone who inspired me to work hard at my art and sing my best. (Rene Strohecker Thompson, North Los Vegas, Nevada)

Beverly Sills had nothing to prove and therefore no axe to grind. No big ego. She simply allowed her light to shine, and she did it with grace and character. (Martha Magee, New York City)

A light unto the world. An angel, who graced this earth for but a moment, has now returned to heaven. She will be sorely missed. (Scott Widitor, Beverly Hills, California)

Hers was a life well lived and as a human being, not just a singer, she is very much an inspiring light. Part of my youth has died with her. (James Black, Rye, East Sussex, UK)

Truly a bright light from here to heaven. (Kathryn Reid George, Terre Haute, Indiana)

AH! The light we have lost!! I fell in love with Beverly Sills the first time I heard her sing. (Marsha Dempsey, Forest Grove, Oregon)

In the early days of our correspondence, longtime Sills fan Robert Nelson went role by role as he shared detailed memories of seeing Sills in performance. When he came to *Manon,* he brought up the subject of light. Nelson recounted: "Most memorable, probably, was the Cours-la-Reine scene of Act III. Sills here projected a figure of such brilliance that the intense lighting playing on her somehow seemed outdone by the light emanating from her. It was a staggering display on her part, one that made the viewer seek a repeat to verify its magnificence—which made this offering a hot ticket indeed" (e-mail, August 4, 2009). I was delighted to hear this description given the numerous references to light previously encountered in the *Guestbook* epitaphs. The topic has remained a continuing thread throughout our years of correspondence. Nelson made it clear that just as Sills was able to light up the stage, she could also adjust her level of radiance as necessary: "To answer your question about her luminosity when not singing: I found her able to cede the focus of audience attention to where it belonged at any given moment. She seemed fully able to turn this light thing off at will, to allow another singer his or her share of attention. Maybe we all have an inner light, but not all of us have the ability to shine it outward at will. . . . Along with you, I guess I will settle for 'presence' as a suitable label for this phenomenon, whatever its source may be" (e-mail, August 9, 2009).

Sills's ability to concentrate her "inner light" so as to give the perception of luminescence (or "glow," to use her word) worked to concentrate her audience's rapt attention even when she was standing completely still and silent. Nelson also commented that her luminosity became animated when she engaged in rapid-fire pyrotechnics: "With the emergence of Sills as Cleopatra, the performance moved to a new level. She fired off the coloratura with simply amazing confidence and accuracy, and simultaneously brought to life a calculating and genuinely sexy and appealing character. The discussion about light that we've had applies here too; she tossed out roulades and trills and such so vividly that one seemed to see rays of light emanating from her" (e-mail, August 7, 2009).

Writing for the *New York Times,* Donal Henahan indirectly called attention to Sills's luminosity by commenting on her lighting up the stage in a performance of *I Puritani* in fall 1975: "The production was Tito Capobianco's appropriately dark and puritanical conception, but Miss Sills personally lighted it up every time she came into view as the virginal Elvira, and set fires of enthusiasm every time she opened her throat. . . . As a singing actress and simply as a presence she radiates so much life and intelligence that a stageful of her perfectly respectable colleagues will sometimes resemble a statuary garden by comparison" (August 30, 1975).

Sills was keenly aware of her ability to "glow" and recognized this quality in other performers. In 1985, when asked what she looked for in a singer in her role as general director of the New York City Opera, she replied: "A kind of magic, a presence. You can spot it when somebody walks on stage. My mother once described it as 'somebody who doesn't have to be lit.' They bring their own light with them" (Sweeney 1985).

Across theatrical history there are stories of other actors and actresses who lit up the stage. A famous example is English actor Edmund Kean (active in the early nineteenth century) who cast such brilliant light that his performances were said to irradiate with flashes (Kershaw 2007, 280). Gesturing toward this phenomenon, Polish theater director Jerzy Grotowski metaphorically equates art with light: "Art is a ripening, an evolution, an uplifting which enables us to emerge from darkness into a blaze of light" (2002, 256). What is the source of the energy that manifests itself as radiant light and draws the audience's attention like moths to flame? Does the performer "vampirically" draw energy from her or his audience or is she or he the "source of super-concentrated power seeking release into empty vessels" (Goodall 2008, 121)? From whichever side of the footlights the energy originates, there is no doubt that once the artist locks into her or his audience (or audience into the "open" performer), there is "a circuit between the energetic polarities of performer and spectator" that "brings the present moment into sharp relief, opening the channels of receptivity for the unexpected and the unprecedented" (ibid.).

Writing in the late 1990s, Freddie Rokem commented that the notion of "energy" is simply a concept "floating around 'out there'" and has yet to be examined systematically as a key concept for the theory of theater and performance (2003, 292). In his book *Theatre Ecology,* Baz Kershaw keenly observes that in his more than forty years in the theater he has rarely encountered a performing colleague who does not speak about energy. Even though shaping energy is "crucial to performance," Kershaw found that there is no entry for "energy" in the main English-language theater encyclopedias or dictionaries, nor is it a key concept in the history of dramatic theory, "although there are a number of terms—such as action, emotion, magnitude—that obviously point to it" (Kershaw 2007, 284).[16] Scholars are only beginning to openly explore and theorize energy—and other intense and magical aspects of performance—as manifested by luminosity or presence.

Beverly Sills in the performative moment represents a case study in presence and energy flow that is made all the richer due to the many perspectives or entry points (that is, the recollections of her former colleagues, her audience members, and Sills's own understanding of her experiences) from which we can document how these moments were experienced and assess their long-term influence. The testimonies of audience members and performing colleagues alike evidence that the transformative power of great performance is not just a momentary, quickly dissipating "flash in the pan," but continues to resonate and sustain throughout the course of individual lives.

Communication

The components of Sills's performative magic all worked toward one key goal—communication. As Sills entered deeply into the drama and took on her characters' personae completely, she communicated their thoughts and feelings through the total expression of her voice and body. In her tribute essay published on Sills's seventy-fifth birthday, Beth Hart commented that Sills was always a communicator with an inexplicably personal touch. From "the moment she came onstage, she embraced an audience, won it over, and took it with her on a memorable journey" (2004, 624). Hart saw Sills perform many times because one of her relatives who worked at the NYCO made certain she had tickets to all of the singer's performances. She recalled seeing Sills live for the first time when at the age of twelve she attended a performance of *The Ballad of Baby Doe*. Hart felt Sills seemed to look directly at her as though happy that Hart had come to the performance. Years later, reflecting on the deep, welcoming impression that Sills made, Hart mused that with Sills, something leaped across the footlights, "a contagious something" that drew people into her world and made them feel that they were the occasion for her joy (ibid.).

Sills's gift for communicating directly and personally was not only limited to the operatic stage, but also extended to her recital and concert performances and even sound recordings. At the end of my interview with accompanist Charles Wadsworth, I asked my customary closing question: "What do you think is the most important thing that we remember about Beverly Sills? What's the most important thing for the historical record?" He replied without hesitation:

> The *enormous* power of communication. In my lifetime of being involved with a huge number of gifted singers, it was the most extraordinary I'd experienced. Hers was a total, knowledgeable, intellectual approach to the music, which tied in completely to the final result that came directly from the heart. And it was so powerful. The projection was like that of very few artists that I've ever known. The fact that she could project directly from her own emotions and heart set

her apart really from most performers that were out there in front of the public. She spoke through the fact of the heart being so directly connected to those vocal chords. The resonance, the intelligence, and the projection was enormous over the footlights—just full blast. Rare. (Wadsworth interview, April 19, 2010)

In considering what accounted for Sills's extraordinary ability to connect to her listeners, this research points to two factors: her musicianship and her personal need to connect. Sills possessed a virtuosic vocal technique and rock-solid musicianship. Many people interviewed for this study commented that when Sills performed, they could lose sight of the fact that she was singing. The strength of her technique allowed her to produce even fiendishly difficult vocal lines with seeming ease. With her musical lines securely in her voice and body, she was free to involve herself completely in the drama, energetically connecting with her performing colleagues and with her audience. With the effortlessness of speech, she inflected her lines with meaning and emotion that bridged her and her listeners' hearts. Only in the final few years of her career did the ease of her vocal delivery diminish.[17] Gigi Capobianco said: "She knew the notes were going to be there. She never had to think about notes. And when she felt that it wasn't the same, she quit. She stopped singing" (interview, July 28, 2010).

Sills inability to commune with her severely autistic and developmentally disabled son[18] coupled with the impossibility of using her voice to communicate with her deaf daughter combined to create a fierce desire to communicate, to feel the affirmation of human connection, to touch those for whom she sang. Sills needed to love and to be loved.[19] She thrived on this connection, even when the bond was across a huge auditorium with thousands of listeners. Her need and extraordinary ability to connect formed the basis for the magic in Sills's performance.

CHAPTER 8

Listening for After-Vibrations

What remains as a testament to Beverly Sills's artistry? What sources record her voice, body, energy, and impact in performance? Sound and video recordings provide documentation, but even these do not entirely capture an event. While no single recording can completely recall a performance, a combination of resources—including the memories of those who were present—potentially bring us closer to knowing how a performance was executed, and even experienced, than we often regard as possible. This chapter briefly overviews the evidence of Sills's artistry as preserved in recordings of both commercial and bootleg origins. Broadening the scope further, a variety of sources are employed in exploring what elements of a performance event might be recovered in addition to those typically captured by professionally shot video. These elements go beyond "the work," and even its execution, to include audience reaction and performer intention. In some cases, they evidence the efficacy of the communicative link between the artist and her audience and document that a performance may continue to have meaning in the lives of those who witnessed it, even decades beyond its moment of initial sounding. This is explored by reconstructing some of the ways in which Beverly Sills embodied and enacted Donizetti's *Anna Bolena*, one of Sills's Tudor queens for which we have no video record.

Sound Recordings: Studio and Bootleg

The corpus of Sills's commercially released albums leaves an uneven and incomplete document of her creative work. The majority of her studio recordings were made after she started singing Queen Elizabeth in *Roberto Devereux,* the role that more than any other pushed her vocal equipment beyond its healthy, natural limits. Thus, as early as the *I Puritani* and *Norma* recordings (and some would argue even earlier), both made in August 1973, we hear the beginnings of the wobble that would increase in prominence during the following years. Other factors also combined to limit the impact of Sills's recorded legacy. First, her voice did not record particularly well. The shimmer and coloration heard in the house during live performances was sometimes lost in the recording process. Stripped of its sheen, and with the natural brightness laid bare, her voice could take on a strident quality. Voice teacher Gerald Martin Moore shared that recording engineers have mentioned that Sills's sound was hard to capture (e-mail, September 7, 2013). They explained that microphones tend to emphasize the high harmonics of certain voices, thus making them sound steelier on record than in the opera house or concert hall where the acoustics tends to dissipate the slight edge that the microphone picks up.[1] Moore added that one way "some producers tried to disguise the harshness was by adding that awful 'bathroomy' acoustic used on the Sills' *Plaisir d'Amour* disc, and to a lesser extent, her *Music of Victor Herbert* album" (ibid.). That her earliest recordings (with the exception of the 1967 recording of *Giulio Cesare*) were made on second-rate labels, such as Westminster/ABC Audio Treasury, exacerbated the challenges of capturing Sills's voice on vinyl. All but one of her recordings on the far-superior Angel label were produced after her cancer surgery in late 1974. Second, the studio-recording process, in which arias and scenes are recorded out of sequence and sometimes in multiple takes, presents a particular challenge to an artist such as Sills, who was overwhelmingly at her best in live performance. As explored in chapter 7, Sills thrived on the intersubjectivity between herself and her audience and on the interaction—which burned the hottest in staged performance—with her performing colleagues. She also thrived on the challenge of being in the performative moment with all of its pressures and perils. Sills commented in an interview for *Stereo Review* that she liked to go home after a performance "emotionally exhausted," yet when she returned from a recording session all that was tired were her feet (Stevenson 1970, 84). The studio recording did not lend itself to the abandonment and intensity of live performance she favored.

Fortunately, the sound recordings documenting Sills's artistic career extend beyond those created under studio conditions. By the mid-1960s, "the tape underground," as Conrad Osborne termed it in his *High Fidelity* article, was in full swing (1966). Recording and trading in bootlegs of radio broadcasts preceded the efforts of the daring recordists who set up their tape recorders in theaters and concert halls. Osborne commented that the "joys and risks" of this "On-The-Front-Lines school of recording" were open to anyone who could afford the rather expensive recording equipment and who was "willing to run the risk of smuggling it to his seat location and then down the hall to the restroom at intermission to change the reels." Writing in 1966, he noted that making in-house recordings did not pose "any significant legal risk," but did subject the recordist to being "discovered and ejected from the hall" (Osborne 1966, 45–46). Copyright laws would soon up the risk, but only rarely slowed the traffic in the trading and selling (which crossed international borders) of the precious commodity of live opera recordings. An entire cottage industry sprung up around the recordings, including small-scale producers of album pressings. As a result, some of these recordings are well preserved because they were not transmitted through generations of analog tape dubbings, but on LP records.

These privately recorded and transmitted sound recordings of live performances—made either in the opera house or recorded from radio broadcasts—capture Sills in her true element. Not only do they document her in roles never commercially recorded, such as Marguerite and Lucrezia Borgia, but they also preserve an aural record of Sills's at her dramatic best. Furthermore, these recordings—often made with the microphone tucked in the bootlegger's clothing as he sat among the other attendees—document real-time audience response including not only applause, but also sighs, gasps, and even verbal comments, both whispered and shouted. Thus, the rich body of operatic bootleg recordings preserve sounding residue of experiential moments and feelings that are typically surrendered as lost ephemera.

Clemens Risi has explored the utility of such recordings in monitoring audience members' bodily engagement with singers "in co-presence or co-vibration" in his article "The Diva's Fans: Opera and Bodily Participation" (Risi 2011a, 50). In listening to a YouTube recording of Natalie Dessay's *Lucia di Lammermoor,* Risi found convincing evidence of the listener's "active perception of a singer's voice in performance" and even his bodily synchronization with the singer (ibid., 49). Risi's close listening reveals that the fan, whose breathing can be heard in the bootleg YouTube video, becomes breathless as he engages physically with Dessay's "vocal high-wire act" (ibid., 52). He breathes normally (at a rate of one breath every three seconds) at the aria's opening. As the vocal part becomes more difficult, the fan's breathing becomes louder. Finally, in anticipation of Dessay's culminating high E-flat, he holds his breath for twelve full seconds. The corpus of Sills's bootleg recordings also retains evidence of her audience's physical and emotional engagement with her performances.

As for the ethical concerns surrounding bootlegs, it seems that many of the artists themselves did not object to the recordings. While no one enjoys a cracked high note preserved for all time, many of the artists I interviewed admitted to listening to and owning bootlegs of their own performances. Some recordists presented Sills with their recordings as gifts, which she gladly accepted. In fact, when Sills's daughter was consolidating her possessions in 2012, she gave me a number of her mother's albums. Mixed in with her studio recordings and a couple of other unusual items such as her Christmas album released in a very small pressing in 1955 were several bootleg albums. One of these still included a note to Sills from one of her closest friends, who also recorded and sold some of her finest bootlegs. His note urged Sills to begin on side C of the *Coq d'Or* set, where she would find her "Hymn to the Sun." When asked directly how she felt about being recorded "in house," Sills once responded that if it were not for the bootlegs there would be no document whatsoever of a good deal of her career.[2] Thanks to the efforts of bootleggers, there are more than three hundred recordings of Sills live in circulation; newly discovered recordings still surface from time to time.[3]

Video Recordings

The video record of Sills in fully staged, live operatic performance is rather paltry, due in no small part to the timing of her career with the development of video technology. The first broadcast from an opera house in the United States was ABC's televised simulcast of the Metropolitan Opera's opening night in November 1948. To cope with low light levels (as opposed to the high light levels in television studios), ABC added infrared lighting, which was visible only to the cameras, but also generated a good deal of heat. The Met did live broadcasts of its next two opening nights as well as cinema transmissions in 1952 and 1954, but that was it for broadcasts from the house until the historic 1977 *La Bohème* with Renata Scotto and Luciano Pavarotti. Sills's first live broadcast came from the New York State Theater during the more than twenty-year gap between Met simulcasts. In 1971, a breakthrough in camera technology developed by the United States Air Force made the New York City Opera's broadcast of *Coq d'Or* the first anywhere in the world to be shot under existing performance lighting. The picture quality was less than ideal, however. Bootlegs of this performance still circulate, but the graininess of the original broadcast has been made more severe by multiple generations of analog copying.[4]

The best-quality broadcast recordings of Sills in live operatic performance all came from Wolf Trap. All three are commercially available on DVD from Video Artists International: *The Daughter of the Regiment, Roberto Devereux,* and *La Traviata.* The setup at Wolf Trap made it possible to employ television lighting, hence the superior quality of the videography of these recordings. Though a delightful performance, a comparison of her July 1974 *The Daughter of the Regiment* (in English) from Wolf Trap with her 1969 concert performance of *La Fille du Régiment* (i.e., the original French version of *The Daughter of the Regiment*) from Carnegie Hall (preserved on a bootleg sound recording that is now sold commercially)[5] reveals a significant decline in Sills's voice. The vibrato in 1974 is almost uniformly wider—breaking into a full-blown wobble at times—although her coloratura is still beautifully precise and the voice very flexible.

Roberto Devereux followed in 1975 and *La Traviata* in 1976. Sills played Queen Elizabeth thirty-eight times between her role debut in October 1970 and her two Wolf Trap *Devereux* performances in July 1975. These were the last of her career and her only performances of Queen Elizabeth following her hysterectomy. The most demanding of all her roles, Elizabeth drained Sills physically, vocally, and emotionally even when she was perfectly strong and healthy. Following the cutting of her abdominal muscles, she never fully regained her breath control or stamina. Therefore, our only video record of Sills live in the role she considered to be the greatest achievement of her career finds her undeniably past her vocal prime. A specific example can be seen in the final high D at the end of her "Vivi ingrato." A close viewing reveals that she dropped the note shortly after hitting it. Her chest collapses and she sits back in her throne—clearly, she has ceased singing, yet the sound continues. The video's producers patched in the final high D from a recording of the previous evening's performance. One might assume that Sills chose to perform *Roberto Devereux* for the videotaping at Wolf Trap because she recognized it as perhaps her last—albeit late—opportunity to preserve her historically important characterization.

Despite the shortcomings, this video allows us to see Sills's exceptional acting ability in a challenging dramatic role. Her talent for seamlessly and organically integrating physical movements, including facial expressions, with the musical flow is particularly rare for a singer of European opera.[6] Part of this ability stems from Sills's extraordinary attention to detail—from the movement of her hands and fingers, to eye expressions, to body gestures, and, of course, to her imparting of meaning in her musical line through subtle nuancing of vocal expressions. She no doubt developed and fine-tuned the control of her body in motion through her years of intensive and intimate collaborations with the Capobiancos, especially with Gigi Capobianco, given her acute attention to onstage corporeality. As Elizabeth, she executes a wide range of emotions, from the queen's last feelings of amorous affection, to her blazing anger, and, finally, to her heartbreaking resignation and loss. This broadcast video is a priceless document because it records Sills in a role for which she felt a special affinity and to which she, and her colleagues, devoted years to develop.

The Wolf Trap *La Traviata* filming captures Sills in one of her most frequently performed and touching roles. Little known, however, is that this performance took place during a period in which Sills was struggling with major health issues. In preparing for the performance, she only asked that director Tito Capobianco allow her to rest every twenty minutes or so. This, as well as many other events in her personal life—sometimes involving her own physical health—demonstrates Sills's unrelenting determination to move forward despite significant adversity.

Sills starred in two broadcasts from the New York State Theater, both of which were released in VHS format on the Bel Canto label. Unfortunately, neither has been rereleased in digital form. The first was a November 1976 performance of Sarah Caldwell's satirical production of *Il Barbiere di Siviglia*. In his review for *The Metropolitan Opera Guide to Opera on Video*, London Green commented on the video's capturing of Sills's relationship with her audience in this comic opera: "Beverly Sills is an engaging mistress of the audience, and the videotape is most valuable for preserving that aspect of her style, muted even on her 'actual performance' audio records. In 'Una voce' she decorates outrageously and plays her cadenzas to the audience. 'Here I am,' she implies with a wink, 'a prima donna with a sense of humor, and I am going to entertain you. This is Rosina. Isn't she amazing, and aren't we having fun?'" (Green 1997, 284). Writing for the English publication *Records and Recording*, Peter Rosenwald observed: "It was an exhilarating broadcast. Sills was radiant and gave off a special glow which managed to convey its magic through the difficult medium of television and bring warmth to viewers: a rare feat" (Rosenwald 1977, 16).

The October 1977 broadcast of *Manon* gave Sills a last opportunity to leave a video document of one of her signature roles. Although it had been more than two decades since she first brought *Manon* to the stage in Baltimore, and nearly nine years since this Capobianco production made its premiere, this performance finds her in remarkably fresh voice, especially when compared to her singing of Italian repertoire around the same period. Gerald Martin Moore offers the insightful theory that in returning to *Manon* after a break of more than four years, Sills called upon muscle memory for her vocal production that she developed years earlier under the watchful tutelage of Estelle Liebling (e-mail, March 22, 2013). As Sills told him in his 2006 interview, Liebling was strongly opposed to her moving into heavier repertoire such as *Roberto Devereux* and refused to work with Sills on it. Rather than seeking another voice teacher,[7] Sills devised her own "new, 'more open-throated' way of singing" (Moore 2006, 1422). If Moore's theory is correct, for the 1977 *Manon*, Sills drew upon her body's memory of her earlier, well-founded vocal technique; thus with this video we hear a relatively fresh-sounding Sills, complete with her agility, "high-soprano range extension," and signature "girlish, floating quality capable of fullness and color" (Osborne 1997, 129).

Sills appeared in four additional broadcasts of live performances of complete operas. These, however, were never made available for purchase. They have been preserved and transmitted through bootlegging networks. The first is Tito

Capobianco's visually stunning San Diego Opera production of Lehar's operetta *The Merry Widow*. The performance took place in October 1977, just a month before the *Manon* broadcast. As with the *Barbiere* video, Sills's playful interaction with her stage colleagues and audience is on full display. This video captures her intense feminine sensual allure about which many critics commented throughout her singing career. Her ability to focus the audience's attention, even when the stage is filled with other performers, is illustrated well in the opening scene of act 2. Capobianco's staging, as well as her costuming and especially the lighting, work to enhance the effect. The curtain opens on a festive garden party; the stage is filled with dancers donning black or neutral-colored costumes. Sills sashays to the front of center stage in a peach-colored gown, then turns her back to the audience. She continues to sway her hips for a few phrases; then stands fairly still until she turns to sing her aria "Vilja." Even with her back to the camera, and through a now slightly grainy image, she is stunning with her hourglass figure on full display. The sight of her draws the viewers' unwavering attention, even though the stage is filled with dancers executing a finely choreographed number.

Sills's final broadcast with the New York City Opera from Lincoln Center was in an English-language production of Rossini's *Turk in Italy*. Filmed in October 1978, Sills is an ebullient stage presence, but her voice is in poor condition. As is obvious from her intermission interview, she was suffering from a severe cold. This alone, however, does not account for her wide, slow vibrato and strident, if not harsh, vocal timbre. Her last appearance in a live broadcast from Lincoln Center hailed from the stage of the Metropolitan Opera in January 1979. As with the *Turk in Italy*, Sills's vocal estate is unquestionably in its twilight. Yet her stage presence, extraordinary musicianship, and "amazing vocal fireworks" (to quote Renée Fleming during the 2007 PBS broadcast mentioned next) remain striking, as evidenced by the life-changing impact her performance had on a young Ron Runyon, and no doubt others, as discussed in chapter 5. Furthermore, in late 2007, PBS's *Great Performances* held a contest in which viewers chose their top fifteen favorite moments from thirty years of televised performances from the Metropolitan Opera. The winning segments were broadcast in a program titled *Great Moments at the Met: Viewer's Choice,* in which Sills's aria "Quel guardo il cavaliere" from *Don Pasquale* was in tenth place.[8] Hostess Renée Fleming quoted one of the voter's comments in her introduction to Sills's aria: "Beverly's joy in singing is contagious. She made *us* part of her love for her art form."

Sills's last known video broadcast is of *Il Barbiere di Siviglia* performed with the NYCO on tour in May 1980 at the Cervantes International Festival in Guanajuato, Mexico. Two bootlegs with differing genealogies have recently emerged in the United States. One is of very poor quality with the image and sound out of sync, while the other is in fairly good condition with the main flaw being a number of tape pulls and dropouts. Sills is in good voice considering that she is just shy of six months from giving her final performance. She avoids singing some of the high notes she would have taken in previous years, incorporates several lines from the mezzo-soprano version of the opera, and has recomposed her cadenzas to avoid the upper reaches of her range while shortening the length of some phrases in order to accommodate her diminished breath capacity.

Like so many aspects of Sills's career, one cannot help but wish that the timing had been different. Much of it came too late—her commercial sound recordings, her Met debut, her rise to fame and recognition. Filming technology developed too slowly to capture her in her vocal prime. Sadly, we only have a few isolated excerpts of her Cleopatra; there are two extant videos of her singing "Da tempeste il legno infranto" in television studios. The *Roberto Devereux* is quite late and we have nothing of her *Maria Stuarda* or *Anna Bolena,* to name only a few of her finest dramatic roles. Of her *Lucia,* there is an excerpt from the mad scene filmed in England for a BBC special.[9] However, she is alone in the performance space with no other characters with whom to interact. Because she thrived on engaging with her colleagues and audience, she is something of a fish out of water in this segment. Furthermore, in preparing the scene for filming, she was given no directorial assistance (Capobianco interview, July 28, 2010). Therefore, we are left with only a faint shadow of Sills's truly mad Lucia. With the exception of the *Manon, La Traviata,* and *Roberto Devereux* recordings, all of her filmed full-length operatic performances are of her "cream puff" roles; that is, the roles performed at the end of her career when her loss of stamina and diminished breath control—following the 1974 cancer surgery—coupled with her general vocal decline, curbed her ability to perform the dramatic and emotionally demanding roles she loved best.

Still other videos of Sills singing complete operas exist, but these are either in concert version or filmed in a studio. For instance, her remarkable Zerbinetta in the first US performance of the 1912 version of Strauss's *Ariadne auf Naxos* with Erich Leinsdorf and the Boston Symphony is available from Video Artists International. Performed in January 1969, Sills is in fine voice, although she did not attempt the two high F-sharps in Strauss's score, which were beyond her range. The *Boston Herald* wrote of Sills's performance as "beautiful work" and described her aria "Grossmaechtiger Prinzessin" as spine tingling (January 4, 1967). Sills also performed Hindemith's one-act "sketch with music" *Hin und Zurück* (There and back) with Sarah Caldwell conducting in a July 1965 studio taping. The recording of this ironic tragicomedy was released in 2011 on the Kultur label as part of a three-disc set titled *Aaron Copland: Music in the 20's.* Many other brief video recordings, such as her 1969 appearance on *The Ed Sullivan Show* and her 1979 performance with the Indianapolis Symphony, are in circulation, either commercially or in versions with bootleg origins.

Tracing the Details of Performance

All live performances are unrepeatable and ephemeral, of course. Even when video-recorded, the visceral sensations and the energy flows in the auditorium belong to the moment. What, then, can we recover of the lived experience generated within the confines of the performance time and space?

Even the briefest survey of musicological scholarship on opera shows that the vast majority of studies are devoted to issues surrounding "the work" (that is, the composer's intended creation as documented primarily in scores and manuscripts) or to questions regarding the transition of a work's score and text to the stage through musical and theatrical interpretation. Clemens Risi rightly observes that in most cases "the unique, actual performance is not considered a worthy object of analysis" (Risi 2011b, 283). Audience response is even less of a concern, except in studies of reception history, where reaction typically serves as a gauge for the success of the work, not of the performance. Carolyn Abbate argues persuasively that musicology's retreat to the work, the dissection of its technical features, and the interpretation of its meaning "reflects the wish *not* to be transported" by its performance (2004, 505–6). Turning away from performance, and toward the work, stems from a desire to domesticate the experience, lest one (and indeed, the entire musicological endeavor) be taken as unscientific or overly subjective. This attitude no doubt lies at the root of the scorn cast upon fans and their passionate engagement with music through its performance. Yet it is precisely the details of the performance—the exquisite moments brought to life by singers through their voices and embodied presence—that touch listeners most deeply, that create in the passionate opera fan an almost insatiable desire for a repeat experience.

In placing the moment of performance at the center of this investigation, I am responding partially to Carolyn Abbate's questioning of what it would mean to write about "opera live and unfolding in time and not an operatic work" (2004, 505).[10] However, Abbate calls for taking "a material, present event" and "not a recording, even of a live performance" as the "object of absorption" (ibid., 506). This is not possible in Sills's case because the material acoustic and theatrical events are long past. However, as argued in the following, they are not lost.

Sills performed her last *Anna Bolena* in 1975. Attendance at a live performance, which Abbate forwards as a requirement for true "drastic" engagement, was never an option for me as a teen in the Midwest. However, I believe that drastic residue, or "after-vibrations," remains long after the last note has been sung. Here, I seek to recover fragments of this residue in no small part through what Abbate terms "music's necropolis" (that is, "recordings and scores and graphic musical examples"); the necropolis I visit, however, still rings with the audible sounds of breaths drawn, gasps, sighs, and bodies in motion (2004, 510).

In further response to Abbate's suggestion that only the actual live performance may serve as the "object of absorption," I turn to Jill Dolan, who also struggles with the question of writing about performance as it unfolds live. Dolan points out that as she scribbles notes in the darkened theater, "utopian performatives" inevitably force her to stop transcribing her "experience of the present to some sort of imagined future." She writes that "in those moments, I sit bolt upright, caught in the density of a communal epiphany that I need to experience now, that gathers its power through the impossibility of doing it justice in any subsequent moment" (2005, 14). Dolan articulates well the conundrum inherent in Abbate's proposition. The most engaging instances in a performance demand that they be fully experienced *in the moment*. Yet not all is lost once the performance ends.

At the root of the anxiety over the impossibility of capturing the moment—in the moment—lies what Rebecca Schneider terms the "archive logic in modernity," according to which, documents are valued over events (2011, 100). Following this logic, the "archivable" (such as written materials and sound recordings) holds authority over lived experience and embodied memories. Both Dolan and Abbate, among others, recognize the impossibility of fully capturing the most powerful performative moments and sensations in archivable documents. However, they also do not fully trust their own memories to preserve an adequate record of an event. Hence, we find Dolan frustrated as she gives up scribbling notes on her program during a show and Abbate wondering what would become of musicology if it set its sights on "actual performances" (2004, 504). However, as explored in the following, certain sources do allow for the recovery of something of transfixing instances or utopian performatives. One vital resource is precisely the kind eschewed by archival logic: the experiential memories of those in copresence and covibration at the moment of their unfolding. Experiential memory, as opposed to factual memory, can be understood as the difference between a person remembering *herself* (and how she felt) watching an opera versus remembering *that* she saw the opera (Yang 2013, 20).

The attempt to (re)capture events that are by their very nature ephemeral poses obvious challenges; however, these challenges have led to a variety of sources that until recently have been rarely tapped by opera scholars. The available sources make Sills's interpretation and performance of *Anna Bolena* a good test case for recovering aspects of a performance (and a production) that was not recorded on film.[11] Furthermore, these sources offer the possibility of documenting elements unlikely to have been captured by professionally shot video, even if it were available. Essential to this recovery effort are bootleg audio recordings made in the theater during live performances. At the time of writing, six such recordings circulate among collectors and fans. These are of the following performances: October 3, 1973; October 7, 1973; October 10, 1973; October 18, 1973; March 10,

1974; April 25, 1974; and March 7, 1975.[12] This text draws examples primarily from the recording of the production's premiere on October 3, 1973. There are four reasons for the focus on this performance. First, the bootlegger's microphone was placed so that it captured audience reaction, including sighs, gasps, and verbal comments, better than any of the other recordings. Second, this recording best captures the sounds of physical movement on the stage. Third, as noted, Sills was typically most intense at a production's premiere. Fourth, Sills's interpretation of her characters, even within the same production, evolved from performance to performance. This is heard in minor variations in embellishments, but for those who witnessed multiple performances, it could also be seen in shifts in gestures and dramatic timing. As suggested by fan and interviewee Thom Billadeau, who saw Sills on stage hundreds of times, the notes Sills wrote in her personal scores most closely reflect her interpretation of *Anna Bolena* at the time of her role debut rather than her portrayal as developed in subsequent performances (e-mail, December 18, 2011).

In addition to the bootleg recordings, a copy of Sills's heavily annotated personal score is central to this investigation.[13] Other vital sources include written and verbal accounts of the production in both preparation and performance, as well as still photos taken of the live performance by New York City Opera's house photographer Beth Bergman.[14] I also draw on the experiential memories of those who witnessed Sills as Anna Bolena. These varied sources allow us to know in specific instances what Sills intended, to hear what she did in performance, and, in several cases, to hear her audience's reaction. Attention is drawn to the singer's intentionality, to the musical and dramatic "consequences of the mise-en-scène" (Levin 2007, 7), and to the audience's experience of Sills's performance both in and out of real time. This exploration seeks to recover not only aspects of Sills's characterization and performance as well as the production's structure and form, but also, perhaps most important, something of "the ineffable emotion it provoke[d] in its moment of presence" (Dolan 2005, 9).

Sills's commercial recording of *Anna Bolena* may be considered as a foil, which, when contrasted with recordings of live performances, serves to illuminate the musical and dramatic presence of the mise-en-scène. Unlike most other roles Sills recorded, she had not staged *Bolena* prior to making the studio recording,[15] which predated the premiere of the NYCO production by a little over a year. On several occasions, Sills noted her regret in committing an interpretation to a recording before she had fully developed her characterization through staged performance.[16] For Sills, the mise-en-scène—which in the days when the NYCO was a repertory company took shape through something of a group creative process[17]—acted as a vital interpretive frame, and one that was useful to have in place before she entered the recording studio. Sills, therefore, entered the studio to record *Anna*

Bolena having not yet been through the rigors of developing and inhabiting the mise-en-scène. This creative process included the conceptualization of a broad dramatic arc, the subtleties of interpretation that formed through the dramatic and musical interaction with her fellow singing actors, and the physical assumption, which shaped all manner of movement and stance, of her Anna Bolena character.

The gulf between live and studio performance is wider with some singers than with others. For singers who place vocal perfection and beauty of sound above all—including acting with the body and voice—the gap can be relatively minor. Sills described herself as a singing actress with equal emphasis on each word; she was often cited as saying that she would happily sacrifice beauty of tone to make a dramatic point (e.g., Sills 1987, 219). In her *Time* cover story, Sills explained: "I'm a visual performer . . . I have to act, use facial expressions, get mood changes across. It's hard to share any of this with a microphone. I need an audience desperately" ("Beverly Sills: The Fastest Voice Alive" 1971, 76). Her statement points in several important directions. She references her delight in the sense of active engagement between herself and the audience, which was a vital part of her real-time performance, but obviously absent from, or severely limited in, the recording-studio setting. In live performance, she expressed the meaning of the text and her character's feelings through a seamless integration of voice and body, including facial expressions, hand gestures, whole-body movement, and the commanding presence of complete stillness. In-house recordings reveal Sills's statement regarding the impossibility of sharing any of this with a microphone to be only partially true. These recordings evidence that a great deal was, in fact, captured by a microphone, albeit typically a single microphone hidden from view by the bootlegging Tonmeister.

Hearing Intentionality

Attention is focused here on three segments from Sills's *Anna Bolena* premiere. The first is an excerpt from the first scene of act 2, "Dio, che mi vedi in core" (God, who seest into my heart). This solemn scene follows the fiery conclusion to act 1 in which King Henry VIII (played by Robert Hale) condemns Anne Boleyn to what amounts to a death sentence—trial by judge. Imprisoned in the Tower of London, the distraught Anne finds herself abandoned; even God has turned his back on her. Insight into how the scene was developed is found in a short "Talk of the Town" essay published in the October 8, 1973, issue of the *New Yorker.* The essay—reporting on the end of the musicians' strike that delayed the start of the NYCO season by nearly four weeks—takes us inside a rehearsal room as Tito Capobianco shared his conception with Sills: "'Up to this moment, you are tense and very strong. . . . Now, for the first time, you feel really alone. They have taken every thing away from you.'" Having spoken his interpretation, Capobianco then acted it out by first slumping in a chair and releasing his breath in a heavy sigh. He then "rose from the chair and hurtled around the room, beating futilely against invisible walls. Then he collapsed on the floor, and raised his head slowly to face the audience." He continued: "'Here is the prayer. . . . Then you are hysterical again.'" Capobianco collapsed to the floor once more, pounded it with his fists, and finally rolled over on his back. At first Sills complained that this might be too much given that she has to sing while performing these actions; after all, she still needed to reserve "something" for the more than twenty-minute-long mad scene at the opera's end. Next, he suggested that this could be the most dramatic moment in the opera: "'In the first three bars—when you sigh—you can really catch the emotion of the audience. What is important is timing.'" Sills then executed the move while singing "Dio, che mi vedi in core" in her "familiar silvery soprano." Capobianco rushed to her side on the floor and pulled her right arm up so that it pointed to the ceiling. "'This is not a prayer,'" he instructed. "'It's a demand. Like "Vissi d'arte." Boleyn is asking, "Why, God, after all I have done for You, do You do this to me?"'" ("Senza Rancor" 1973, 40).

FIGURE 1. Sills's Bolena points to heaven in act 2, "Dio, che mi vedi in core." New York City Opera, dress rehearsal, October 2, 1973. Copyright © Beth Bergman 2015, NYC.

Sills's personal score shows that she followed director Capobianco's interpretation very closely.[18] Above the start of the first stave, she penciled in "sit tense"; four measures later, "collapse audibly." She noted other specific movements, such as "stand," "head towards the stage-left wall," and then "collapse on the ground." Here we have a detailed description of stage action that allows us to follow Sills's movement through the scene. In the left margin before the phrase "Dio, che mi vedi in core," she wrote: "Demanding." In the margin before the iteration of "Dio," she wrote: "point finger to heaven." A photograph taken by Beth Bergman confirms that Sills employed the pointing-to-heaven gesture in her staged performance. In-house recordings capture the sound of Sills's audible collapse and pounding on the stage floor.[19]

As for the emotional and dramatic content Capobianco hoped to instill, a comparison of the studio recording and a bootleg recording of the premiere reveals notably different conceptions of the musical material. Julius Rudel conducted the studio recording and the live performance. Differences in interpretation can, therefore, be attributed in no small part to the framing of the mise-en-scène as devised by Tito Capobianco and to the intersubjectivity that formed and shaped creativity in the moment of performance. The most obvious difference between the two recordings—apart from the presence of the sounds of stage action in the bootleg—is that in the studio Sills sang this section as a solemn prayer. The tempo was slower, the mood melancholic. In the live performance, aggravation and anger overlay Bolena's victimhood; she demands to know why she is being punished. The flowing melody of the studio version is replaced with palpable angst.

Hearing Action and Reaction

In addition to preserving musical and dramatic realizations, bootleg recordings also allow for the recovery of reactions to a performance in the forms of verbal comments and "affect outbursts," which are "short, emotional non-speech expressions" (Schröder 2003, 103). Affect outbursts include "both clear non-speech sounds (e.g., laughter) and interjections with a phonemic structure (e.g., 'Wow!')," but exclude "'verbal' interjections that can occur as a different part of speech (like 'Heaven!,' 'No!' etc.)" (ibid.). Both types of reactions communicate a sense of how the performance was experienced in the moment. Only one bootleg of the *Anna Bolena* premiere has surfaced.[20] The recording is peppered with comments from those seated closest to the microphone. Some are intelligible while others are too muffled to decipher. The muffling may have resulted from the conversationalists trying to shield their speech from the microphone

FIGURES 2A & 2B. Annotated pages of the beginning of the first scene of act 2 from Sills's personal score. Used with permission of the Sills estate.

and from surrounding audience members. However, sound degradation, which resulted from generations of analog dubbing, has also contributed to their unintelligibility. Sound engineer Tom Erbe, who assisted in trying to recover these comments, found that the recording has reduced high frequencies, with levels dropping off by twelve to eighteen decibels above 2,000 Hz. While it is possible that the original tape had this low quality, it is more likely that this is generational loss from the tape being copied (and possibly filtered) many times. The recording also has a significant amount of broadband noise (hiss) that masks all but the loudest comments. The audience comments are more muffled than the sounds from the stage, which could be the result of the bootlegger employing a highly directional mic such as a shotgun microphone. With this type of mic, sounds that are off-axis have a much more limited high-frequency response due to phase cancellation. Finally, about half of the comments are made during applause, which effectively makes them unintelligible.

The first comments are heard at the end of the opening larghetto section of Bolena's first aria, "Come, innocente giovane." Two men engage in a brief exchange, but the applause makes their words unintelligible. At the aria's end, however, after Sills hits and holds her slightly under pitch high E-flat for about four seconds (or seven beats), the audience applauds and several people shout their approval. Sitting close to the mic, a man says: "She sounds fine," but another replies: "Nah, she's in trouble." The second listener was no doubt referring to her under-pitched singing of many of the notes above the staff, especially her flat high D in a cadenza near the aria's end, as well as a general sense of her being rushed and not well in control. As with her opening night of *Roberto Devereux*, Sills got off to a bit of a rocky start. Some, but not all, of the audience members were aware of her travails, as indicated in this brief conversation. Once Sills's voice warmed up, her singing flowed with greater ease and accuracy of intonation.

The dynamic interplay between Sills, Hale, and the others in the final scene of act 1, in which Enrico (King Henry VIII) condemns Anna to trial by judges, filled the auditorium with palpable excitement. Sills's final high E-flat at the end of act 1 is on pitch and is met with rousing applause and shouts of "Brava." One listener says: "She delivered." Of the other intelligible verbal comments, we hear general observations, such as "I like the music," heard at the end of the first-act duet between Giovanna (that is, Jane Seymour, played by Susanne Marsee) and Enrico. At the end of the fiery sextet near the close of act 1, the two conversationalists assess one of the male singers. There were three present: Enrico Di Giuseppe (Riccardo Percy), Samuel Ramey (Rochefort), and Robert Hale (Enrico). There is no verbal indication as to which of the three they are referring. But, as with the earlier dialogue, the first listener is positive: "He's good." The second replies:

"He's good, but he's not [unintelligible]." His last word is lost to the surging string melody. Keeping embodiment in mind, there is also the very personal "I gotta pee" following the rousing conclusion to the second scene of act 2, in which Sills slaps Hale. The last audible comments come from the conversationalists during Anna's mad scene at the conclusion of her plaintive "Al dolce guidami." Here, the dialogue begins with one of the pair making a loud, appreciative groan, "Mmm," to which his partner replies, "Beautiful"; the first commenter then adds, "Yeah." The final words from the audience are shouts of "Brava" as the curtain falls while the orchestra plays its last phrase.

Audience members' affect outbursts are, in fact, more useful than the verbal commentary because these nonverbal expressions not only aid in interpreting the stage action, but provide a sense of the emotional reaction to the performance as well. As for the accuracy of interpreting affect outbursts, Schröder found in his research on nonverbal expressions of emotion that listeners correctly interpret the emotion expressed by affect outbursts with more than 80 percent accuracy (2003, 107). In fact, other studies have reported: "Nonverbal vocal expressions of emotion tend to be better recognized than emotional speech stimuli reflecting the same emotion, especially for fear and disgust" (Sauter et al. 2010, 2252). The interpretation of these expressions as captured in the in-audience recording, therefore, represents a valuable portal into how Sills was experienced in the moment of performance.

A moment during the act 2 trio for Anna, Percy, and Enrico is illustrative of this point. The king informs Anna that Smeton, a young court musician, has admitted to having sexual relations with her. Smeton, of course, had been tricked and beaten into making his false confession. Writing for *Time,* William Bender observed that Capobianco gave Sills full rein when in "a triumph of histrionics over history," Sills's enraged Anna delivered a stinging slap to the king's cheek (Bender 1973, 55). The physical violence exhibited in this scene was just one of several instances of what Desmond Shawe-Taylor criticized in his *New Yorker* review as "amorous pawing and angry punching that would excite comment in a reasonably well-conducted pub and looked strange in a Tudor palace" (1973, 148). Members of the NYCO ensemble debated the validity of the slap, with some arguing that Anna would never have dared strike the king for fear of fatal retribution. Asserting that Anna did in fact lose her head, Sills won the right to slap Enrico. In her opinion, although it may not have been historically accurate, it was "certainly dramatically sound" (Sills 1976, 198). Initially, with only audio recordings as a guide, I guessed that an audience member's "Oh!" (uttered in shock and tinged with fear) as captured on the in-house recording from the premiere might mark the moment in which Sills delivered the blow. This was confirmed once I had a chance to see Sills's personal score. Penciled in her hand above the same measure in which we hear the "Oh!" affect outburst appears the word "slap." In this section of her score, Sills bracketed three staves and marked them "Important." Here, after exclaiming "Taci" (Stop) three times, Anna sings, "A questa iniqua accusa mia dignità riprendo, ed altamente di Smeton seduttor te, Sire, io grido" (At this evil accusation I resume my dignity, and loudly proclaim that the seducer of Smeton was you, Sire).[21] Under the first measure in this phrase, Sills scribed "PROUD" in blue pen. Insulted by the king's cruel accusation, pride emboldens Sills's Anna to slap Enrico in a stunning surge of self-righteous fury. As a final step in confirming the placement of the slap, I asked Robert Hale, who played Enrico to Sills's Anna in the premiere and in twelve of her sixteen performances of the role, about the slap.[22] Looking at his personal score, he recalled that he sang "audace" just after she slapped him. Enrico's "Audace donna!" (Audacious woman!) appears in the measure following the one over which Sills had written "slap."

The audience member's audible "Oh!" acted as a clear sonic marker that became the first clue in seeking the placement of the controversial slap. Even more important, however, this spontaneous exclamation continues to communicate over multiple decades a sense of how this charged moment was experienced in the moment of performance.

The third cluster of examples are drawn from the beginning of the opera's final scene (N. 16, scena and aria finale). As was characteristic of Sills, she sketched detailed annotations on her score throughout this section. Some record stage directions and others are dramatic and emotional cues; a few English translations of Italian words also appear. In addition, Sills notated the occasional melodic alteration, along with ornamentation, breath marks, and other interpretive musical signs.

In devising the mise-en-scène, Capobianco did not deviate from the details of the drama as depicted in Romani's libretto. However, the libretto alone, with its poetic sketch of Anna's delusions and madness, does not fully account for the dynamism of Sills's performance. It was her physical execution of dramatic gestures, and their translation into her voice and the music, that made her performance riveting. The dramatic arc that Sills builds from the first phrase of "Piangete voi?" through to the start of the cantabile introduction to the "Al dolce guidami" section is an illustration.

As the scene opens, Anna is delirious. Above her first phrase, Sills wrote "happy." In his article on Sills and her Anna Bolena, Garry Wills observed that she had "the smile of all these operas' pre-demented Ophelias at last gone around the bend" as she descends the stairs (1974, 190). Indeed, Anna has slipped back in time to the day that she married Enrico. Her tender joy carries her through the first several phrases. As Sills embodied Anna preparing for her wedding day long past, the bootleg of the premiere captured an audience member's empathetic sigh when, with a frenzied move, Sills mimed the presence of a veil on her head. Under the phrase "Datemi tosto il mio candido ammanto" (Give me quickly my white robe), Sills penciled in "quickly show veil on head" with an arrow running from "show" to the last syllable of "amman*to*." In the short two eighth-note rests between "ammanto" and Anna's next line, "il crin mornate del mio serto di rose" (adorn my hair with my crown of roses), we hear an audience member's "Oh" as a descending sigh. Even though Sills lightened her voice to sound young and happy, her actions were those of a madwoman. Her donning of an imaginary veil was especially heartrending, if not macabre, as it signaled Anna's complete break with reality. I hear the audience member's "Oh" as a spontaneous, visceral, and poignant recognition of Anna's tragic state.

Percy, whose presence in this scene only Anna perceives, increasingly haunts her. In her first mention of him, she sings that Percy knows nothing of the wedding. Above this phrase, "Che Percy non lo sappia" (That Percy knows nothing about it), Sills scribbled in and circled in blue ink "conspiratorialy" [*sic*]. Her clipped delivery of this line reveals cracks in her delusional happiness. The legato and pensive singing of "Il re l'impose" (The king has ordered it so) contrast noticeably with the clipped delivery of the previous line. This is the first of several rapid swings in sentiment; these swings become more violent as they work together to build to a frenetic climax.

Penciled in over several measures of the flute's melody, which enters at measure 39, Sills wrote: "voice speaking to her."[23] Although Romani's libretto registers Anna's auditory delusions from the start of the number, based on Sills's score markings, this was the first instance in which she acted out hearing them. Her singing of "Oh," with its descending portamento, echoes the grieving voice that she alone hears. Per her marking, Sills delivers the rest of the phrase "Oh! che si duole?" (Oh! who is grieving) slowly and somberly. In another abrupt mood change, she interjects "Chi parlò di Percy?" (Who spoke of Percy) with terrific urgency (she noted the word "urgent" above measure 50). In big, elongated letters that spread across three measures (measures 51–53), Sills scribed "frantic," which aptly describes her performance of "Ch'io non lo vegga; ch'io n'asconda a' suoi sguardi" (Let me not see him; let me hide myself from his gaze). At the end of m. 54, her stage direction was to "see Percy up steps." "E´ vano . . . Ei viene . . . ei máccusa (It's useless . . . He comes . . . he accuses me); with the panicked delivery of each of these lines, her terror becomes increasingly palpable.

Pressed nearly to the limit, Sills's Anna covers her ears (noted above measure 61) in a desperate effort to escape the sound. Still, Percy curses and accuses. With each of these phrases, the overall trajectory of Donizetti's line rises higher and higher. As Anna's hysteria reaches a breaking point, she screams "Ah!" Where Donizetti marked the scream to come on a G above the staff, Sills sings a high B-flat for two full measures. She releases the scream first through a quick descent to the G, and, finally, through a slightly more protracted descending portamento in a musical gesture of defeat. Exhausted, Sills's Anna draws her breath; sounding utterly overcome, she begs for forgiveness: "Mi perdona, mi perdona . . ."[24] Beneath the rests before her next phrase, Sills scribed "kneel & fall." It is not until the next measure (measure 71), however, just before the third syllable in "in-fe-li-ce son io" (I am unhappy), where, through the in-house recording, we hear her knees slam onto the stage floor. With the thud of her physical collapse, I feel the manic energy that has driven Sills through the previous fifty-one seconds rush from her body.[25] Broken, she sings the next plaintive line on her knees with her head down (per her penciled instruction above measure 73): "Toglimi a questa miseria estrema" (Take me away from this utter misery).

With Donizetti's allegro tempo change at measure 77, Sills's Anna rises as she sees Percy standing before her. Once again, we hear the clipped delivery of lines alternating with pensive legato passages. Sills wrote "up" before both clipped phrases of "Tu sorridi?" (Are you smiling?). While she did not write "head down" over the legato "non fia . . ." passage (the end of measure 79 through the beginning of measure 85), the "up" indication above measure 85's "Tu sorridi?" suggests her alternation between these stances. Finally, the schizophrenic struggle ends (temporarily) with her ecstatic octave leap to a high C on "Oh gio—!" (Oh joy—!). Only after five seconds does she begin her retreat from the high C to "—ja" (as in, "gio—ja") through a deliberate and sublime two-octave, chromatic descent. With the introduction to the cantabile "Al dolce guidami" section, Sills mimes an embrace (marked as "hug" above measure 90). She then turns to stage left and offers her hand to Percy. She begins her melancholy "Al dolce guidami" singing directly to Percy, whose image is still only a product of Anna's delirium.

A comparison of the studio recording with this brief section reveals a rather different interpretation. Interestingly, Sills's alterations to the melodic line are consistent between the two performances. A photocopied sheet in Roland Gagnon's hand, which was inside Sills's score, suggests that they began working on her musical interpretation of the role in the spring of 1970, more than two years prior to the studio recording. Not surprisingly, the major difference between the live and studio performances stems from the more intense and complicated dramatic interpretation heard in the theater. Overall, the mood of the studio recording in this section was one of melancholy. This was expressed in no small part through slower and more consistent tempi;[26] the rapid changes in tempi as Sills's Anna

FIGURE 3. Sills kneels during the mad scene.
New York City Opera, role debut, October 3, 1973.
Copyright © Beth Bergman 2015, NYC.

marked her schizophrenic shifts in mood during the live performance were less pronounced. A single note tells it all. Where in the stage production Anna had just been hearing voices, Sills infused "Oh" in measure 41 with fragility. She produced the sound of a woman whose mind was wavering between two realms. In the studio, Sills sang this note beautifully, perhaps a bit timidly; but it does not share the deeply tragic and troubled quality heard in the live performance.

FIGURES 4A–4E. Annotated pages of the opening of N. 16 from Sills's personal score. Used with permission of the Sills estate.

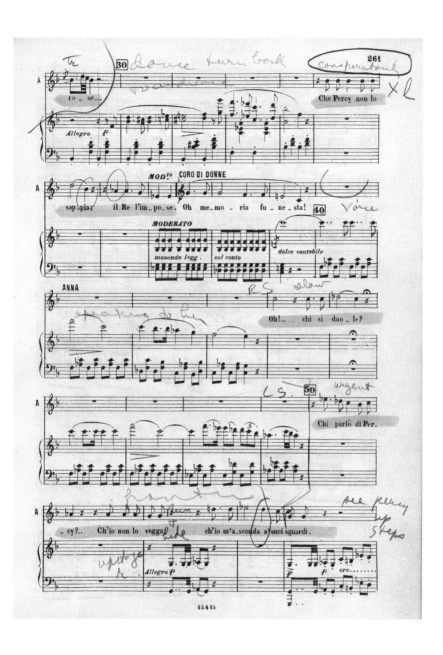

FIGURES 4A–4E. (continued)

FIGURES 4A–4E. (continued)

Listening for After-Vibrations

This exploration of Sills's artistry has drawn on the memories of both her performing colleagues and her fans in recalling specific aspects of her performance and of
their experiences of being in the moment with her. Some of these recollections
are of explicit details, confirmed through consultation with a variety of sources
(for example, others' memories, photos, recordings, score annotations, and so
on). Others are of purely personal reminiscences of how it felt to be in the house
as Sills entered deeply into the drama, concentrating her considerable energy in
the moment at hand. These insights contrast with the recorded "real-time" comments and nonverbal vocalizations, such as sighs and gasps, in that they have been
held in memories for decades.

Robert Nelson, discussed in chapter 7, situated his general impression of Sills's
Anna Bolena in the context of her portrayals of Donizetti's Tudor operas: "The
only Bolena memories I can pin down are really more about the whole Three
Queens phenomenon. Beverly, in all three of these operas, somehow displayed
just that little extra edge of concentration and involvement that comes with being
on an important mission. One impression that lingers is how, with such incredible
attention to detail, she was able to project the differences in age among the three
queens. More than just vocal coloration was involved in making Anne Boleyn
seem so young and thereby so vulnerable" (e-mail, August 5, 2011).

Days after receiving this message from Nelson—with whom I have been in
contact since first writing to him regarding his *Guestbook* entry—I came upon
the first page of N. 16, the scena and aria finale in Sills's score, where, at the top of
the page, she wrote, "Young, Young, Young." I immediately reported to Nelson
his accuracy in reading Sills's intention and included an image of the page. He
replied:

> To see that annotated page from Beverly's *Anna Bolena* score was to have a
> moment of real sadness about another place and another time, now long gone.
> Somehow I remember in particular an evening with Eddie, whom I had not
> yet known long, hearing Beverly in *Lucia*. We were both deeply moved, and it
> was such a joy to be sharing the experience. Now New York is far away, Beverly
> is gone and the world is darker. That Eddie and I still share so much helps a
> lot. And of course it is good to know that I was able to understand Beverly's
> intentions to whatever extent I did. (e-mail, August 21, 2011)

The most detailed account of Sills as Anna Bolena from the audience perspective has come from Thom Billadeau. I first contacted him after reading his
extended postings to several sites in the wake of Sills's passing.[27] He has possibly
one of the most extensive histories of seeing Sills live. His grandmother took him

to see her perform *Aida* in Paterson, New Jersey, in 1955, when he was a child. Billadeau followed her throughout her career, which spanned from his adolescence to his mid-thirties; he also became her friend. And, most important for this discussion, he witnessed her in *Anna Bolena* multiple times, including rehearsals and the premiere performance.

One memory Billadeau shared was of the act 1 finale, in which Anna's fate is sealed. Enrico has caught both Smeton and Percy in her chambers. The king orders them dragged to separate dungeons. He says that judges will hear the evidence of their crimes. Thus condemned, Anna delivers what is perhaps one of the most famous passages in the opera: "Giudici! . . . ad Anna! Guidici! . . . ad Anna . . . Ad Anna! . . . Giudici!" (Judges! . . . for Anne! . . . Judges! . . . for Anne! . . . For Anne . . . Judges!). Billadeau recalls: "Her interaction with Henry during that scene was incredible. The judges for Anna line was delivered staring right at him. Also an acute memory is how when the guards come to take her away after the singing was done, in addition to the ending high note, she delivered a pretty unkind slap across the face of the guard who tried to touch her, and then turned regally and walked off ahead of the guards. All these gestures in support of her disbelief that there will be judges for Anna" (e-mail, November 25, 2011).

As with Nelson's correct reading of Sills's intention to perform Anna as young, Billadeau accurately interpreted Sills's slapping of the guard and he correctly read her aim to exit regally. Evidence of her intent is found in her score on the last page of this number in the middle of the four measures of rests where, after her penciled-in high D, she wrote, "slaps guard exit slow like a queen." She underlined "queen" with four squiggly lines. As Billadeau elaborated: "That was the real purpose of the slap—you don't touch royalty. You might be arresting them, but you don't touch" (e-mail, December 29, 2011).

Back in July 2010, as I flipped through Tito and Gigi Capobianco's photo collection of productions with Beverly Sills, I was astonished by the sheer power of Sills's expression in a photo identified as a shot of her just after Enrico proclaims that Anna's case would be decided by a judge. Gigi explained that the image captured Sills as she delivered her first "Giudici! . . . ad Anna!" She noted that Anna said the line three times and that Sills was "almost spitting at him. Then she says it like she cannot believe [it], and then she collapses on the floor. That's the sequence" (Capobianco interview, July 28, 2010).

A close listening to the in-house recording of the premiere reveals the sound of Sills's body contacting the stage floor after she sings her final "Giudici." A similar sequence of flesh hitting the floor can be heard in all available bootlegs in the space of the quarter rest following "Giudici" and into her singing of "Ah!" that follows.[28] Interestingly, although the sound recordings of the premiere capture a comparable level of physical violence at this moment, Sills's singing of these three lines became increasingly violent during the three years in which she sang *Anna*

FIGURE 5. Sills sings her first "Giudici! . . . ad Anna!" in the finale to act 1. New York City Opera, dress rehearsal, October 2, 1973. Copyright © Beth Bergman 2015, NYC.

Bolena. In the recordings from 1974 and 1975, her third iteration of the sentiment is more shouted than sung.

Mike Moran's overall impression of Sills in the role of Anna Bolena complements Billadeau's and Gigi Capobianco's memories of specific moments in her performance. I found Moran through his comment on the opera blog parterre. com. In the context of a discussion of Anna Netrebko's performances of *Anna Bolena* at the Metropolitan Opera in fall 2011, Moran wrote: "Sills's performances as Anna Bolena were among the greatest live performances I have ever seen. The recording was only a pale shadow of the reality, as of course it must be. She was constantly astonishing in the role. Her movement, facial expressions and hand gestures were textbook examples of stage performance, but always seemed completely spontaneous."[29] With the help of parterre.com's blog mistress, La Cieca, I was able to contact Moran to ask him to elaborate. He replied:

> The Sills Bolena performances made extremely important impressions on me.
>
> I had seen her in several roles before that in *Giulio Cesare, Faust, Lucia, Devereux* and a few others. (Hard to believe it was forty years ago.) But for some reason, it was *Anna Bolena* that really thrilled me.
>
> I hardly knew the music at all. I was very young. And there were no such things as supertitles of any kind. But from the second she walked on the stage I was transfixed. I had a general idea of the outline of the plot. But even with me bringing so little to the performance, she conveyed a deep sense of Anna's character and conflicts.
>
> How did she do it? With the sound of her voice of course, and the great variety of shading she brought to each line. Her voice was not that large, but it carried well, even in the un-renovated New York State Theater. And it was a VERY expressive voice, and drew the audience into the essence of each scene.
>
> There was also the way she presented herself on stage. Her posture was carefully calibrated to express the emotions of each scene, of each line even. Her face, her gestures, her movements were always contributing to the drama and to the meaning of each moment. And it always seemed spontaneous, as if she were actually living it at that moment. (e-mail, December 20, 2011)

Although Sills's performance has long passed, residue of drastic experiences and actions lingers in many forms. Through extended contacts with Sills fans, I have learned that for some people, memories of performance events remain vivid and visceral after many years. Posting to the *Guestbook* several days after Sills's death, Nelson recalled: "I lived in New York City for fifteen years that coincided with the major triumphs Beverly Sills enjoyed at NYCO and elsewhere, and I was able to attend many of them. No memory of those years measures up to the memory of those beautiful events; in fact, few memories of my entire life do."

The experiential aspect of performance is generated in the moment, yet memories of the event, retained as feelings and thoughts (or, more aptly, as thoughts saturated by feelings) persist. As E. M. Forster penned, "after-vibrations" continue long after the performers leave the stage:

> [I]f the soul of an audience could be photographed it would resemble a flight of scattering dipping birds, who belong neither to the air nor the water nor the earth. In theory the audience is a solid slab, provided with a single pair of

enormous ears, which listen, and with a pair of hands, which clap. Actually it is that elusive scattering flight of winged creatures, darting around, and spending much of its time where it shouldn't, thinking now "how lovely!," now "my foot's gone to sleep," and passing in the beat of a bar from "there's Beethoven back in C minor again!" to "did I turn the gas off?" or "I do think he might have shaved." Meanwhile Beethoven persists, Beethoven does not flicker, Beethoven plays himself through. Applause. The piano is closed, the instruments re-enter their cases, the audience disperses more widely, the concert is over.

Over? But is the concert over? Here was the end, had anything an end, but experience proves that strange filaments cling to us after we have been with music, that the feet of the birds have, as it were become entangled in snares of heaven, that while we swooped hither and thither so aimlessly we were gathering something, and carrying it away for future use.... The concert is not over when the sweet voices die. It vibrates elsewhere....

These after-vibrations are not the whole truth about a concert, of course. There is, for instance, the immediate physical delight in sound, which can never be recaptured. There is the architectural emotion, when a composition extending through time is suddenly apprehended as a whole. There is scholarship. But the vibrations are part of the truth. The flittering inattentive birds, the audience which looks so reliable and is really all over the shop, the trailing filaments of beauty—they are part of the complex set up by any public performance. (Forster 1944, 6–7)

If we are resolved to speak of the ephemeral and, most important, to get at the experiential aspect of musical performance, we must embrace the notion that after-vibrations ring on long after the stage goes dark. The sounds of these fleeting events are preserved in recordings as well as in the memories of those who were copresent and in covibration as the performance unfolded. In addition to capturing singing voices and orchestral accompaniment, in-house recordings allow us to hear bodies in motion—flesh striking flesh, knees contacting the hard surface of a stage floor. We hear the repercussions of these actions as waves of shock and wonder are registered in breaths drawn, gasps, and sighs. For some audience members, aspects of the performance persist as vivid memories throughout their lives. Four decades after the event, after-vibrations continue to ring. Evidence of the continuing presence and power of a performance long ended can be found in the eyes of someone recalling a moment when, for them, Sills made time stand still. These memories, along with recordings, photographs, and annotated scores, continue to transmit the after-vibrations of performances, including that of Sills as Anna Bolena.

CHAPTER 9

Engaging with Sills's Artistry

Claudio Benzecry writes of "the moments in which cultural objects orient life, give meaning, and allow people to lose themselves" (2011, 184). I would amend his statement slightly to argue that we *find* ourselves by losing (or transcending) that which shackles us. Sills's recital was a key moment in my life. The kind of passion born in a flash of epiphany creates a "particular engagement with the world, both sensual and meaningful, that allows particular parts of the self to come to the fore, choosing particular lines of action and discarding others" (ibid.).

In listening carefully to Sills's development over the course of her career, I cannot help but wonder about the state of her voice in February 1977 when, as a young musician, I attended her recital. Did she push her voice that night? The Memorial Hall in Lima, Ohio, seated about one thousand, which was practically intimate when compared with the more than 2,700-seat New York State Theater or 3,800-seat Metropolitan Opera. She may have had no need to push her voice under such conditions. Regardless of whether her voice sounded weathered, I was astounded by her musicianship, florid technical display, touching pathos, and her presence, which beamed confidence and intelligence. I was fortunate to have lived in a hometown where I witnessed the performances of a number of internationally recognized artists, including Itzhak Perlman, Shirley Verrett, and Robert Merrill; however, no one struck me with the force of Sills. No doubt the palpable excitement that filled the auditorium even before she made her first appearance alerted me to the fact that something remarkable was about to happen. A month or so after her death, I returned home where I searched in the

museum of local history for documentation of Sills's visit. There I found a program from the 1984–85 season of the presenting organization, Friends of Music
of Northwest Ohio, which sponsored her visit. On the back page, it listed twelve
"Remembrances" of notable events. Last on the list, which included mention of
Victor Herbert's appearance with the Pittsburgh Symphony in 1909 and Duke
Ellington's performance (no date given), was the following remembrance: "Beverly Sills' magnificent personality, her glorious voice, and for those interested in
fashion, her stunning black gown and full length chinchilla coat. It was the only
concert in our time that the audience automatically stood when she entered as
well as when she left the stage."

As were countless others across the United States and the world, I was enraptured by Beverly Sills. Undoubtedly, we each were attracted to whatever we most
needed to see in her. For those who came to know her on late-night and afternoon
talk shows, it may have been her ebullient personality, down-to-earth quality, charity work, or her self-depreciating humor that struck a chord. All of this combined
with her musical performance made her an awe-inspiring figure. Her appearances
in the mainstream mass media won her widespread approbation. One measure
of this was her constant ranking from the mid-1970s to the early 1980s on lists of
most-admired public figures. For instance, she was chosen by the *Ladies' Home
Journal* as one of the top ten "Women of the Year" in 1976. One woman was
honored in each of ten categories; Sills topped the "Performing Arts" category.
Other honorees included Ella T. Grasso (the governor of Connecticut and the
first woman to hold a governorship in the United States) in "Political Life," Maya
Angelou in "Communications," Margaret Mead in "Science/Research," and Betty
Ford in "Inspirational Leadership." The awards were presented in a ninety-minute
prime-time special on NBC hosted by Barbara Walters. The *Good Housekeeping*
magazine published an annual list of its "Ten Most Admired Women." Unlike the
Ladies' Home Journal competition, the women were chosen and ranked without
regard to specific categories, such as performing arts. Sills first appeared on the
list in 1976 where she was ranked number ten. In 1977, she rose to sixth position
behind Pat Nixon, Betty Ford, Barbara Jordan, Mother Teresa of Calcutta, and
Princess Grace of Monaco, and ahead of Shirley Temple Black, Rose Kennedy,
Nancy Reagan, and Anne Morrow Lindbergh. In its January 1982 issue, the magazine reported that this was "Miss Sills's sixth appearance among the top 10 and
readers are always touched by her gallant handling of her private sorrow over her
handicapped children."

For those, like me, who were enchanted with her singing above all else, it was
her wholehearted expressivity that touched us most deeply. Through her singing,
Sills shared herself with honesty and intimacy. Through her acting, she allowed
herself to express the anguish in her personal life that she rarely acknowledged

publicly. Her mother's indoctrination in Christian Science philosophy and practice was in no small part responsible for Sills's resolve to be positive and cheerful. Performance provided a vital outlet where she permitted herself to feel that which was too painful in daily life. Garry Wills describes a poignant manifestation of this in her *Anna Bolena*:

> Her best lines come at times of near-despair, when she is not hurting but being hurt, as when it dawns on her that Jane Seymour is the one who has replaced her in Henry's bed. She wanders the stage, trying to pound that into her mind—*La* [*sic*] *mia rivale!* Over and over—unable to grasp the enormity of the betrayal; her head will finally break in the effort. She credibly prepares us for her later mad scene. . . . Beverly's strength is her weakness, her ability to take wounds on the stage. (Wills 1974, 82)

Sills was strong, resilient, and virtually unflappable in her public life. Fans saw her strength and were drawn to it; yet, in her singing, we also heard her vulnerability. Thus, we felt close to her, as though she had shared something deeply personal, as, of course, she had.

The question of how best to communicate emotion in operatic singing is a topic of constant debate for singers and vocal pedagogues. Generally, the aim is to express emotions rather than to fully experience them. A singer must suggest that she is crying rather than shed actual tears, because to do so would tighten the throat and make singing difficult. This is what we hear in the bootleg recording of Sills's one and only *Suor Angelica* performance. Her throat constricted as she was overcome by emotion; her struggle to quell her very real emotion is audible.[1] Outside of this performance, insofar as research makes me aware, she never again lost control of her emotions in performance;[2] however, Sills did permit herself to experience and express a good deal of feeling. The operatic version of acting in which emotions are indicated rather than felt was anathema to her. In an unpublished interview with Lee Polk from 1973, Sills spoke about singing with emotion and felt meaning: "I feel, since singing is really an art of communicating, not only the beauteous sound of whatever you can produce with those two vocal cords, but a kind of honesty of emotion, that if you believe in it, the audience will believe in it, too. . . . I think you have to give of yourself. I don't think you can hold back and say, 'Now, I have to be careful because six bars from now I have a high C to do.'"[3] Hence, we hear Sills scream and make other vocal expressions that were fitting dramatically but, some argue, stylistically inappropriate for bel canto performance practice.

Sills was drawn to the madness of Lucia, Elvira, Anne Boleyn, and Queen Elizabeth, and to the torment of her other tragic roles. These characters became surrogates through which she engaged with her own despair. As she said, her aim was to leave the theater at the end of a performance emotionally drained. The light "cream puff" roles, such as Norina, Rosina, or Marie, did not provide for the cathartic experience she craved. This need led her to perform roles that numerous critics charged were too heavy for her light, silvery voice. By her own admission, Queen Elizabeth took years off her singing career, but Elizabeth was not the only one. Parts of *Anna Bolena,* for instance, pushed her voice beyond its healthy limits. At times, to quote Gerald Martin Moore when commenting on the bootleg of the *Bolena* premiere, it was "almost like she is driving herself through it by sheer power of will, instead of taking time to shape it musically as she did on the commercial recording, and wisely revising her ornamentation to suit her more compromised vocal estate" (e-mail, September 14, 2013).

For Sills, the need to give a riveting dramatic performance trumped concerns for her vocal well-being. Shortly after her retirement from singing, she confessed that it was in bel canto roles where she started to employ her chest voice higher than ever before, as high as an F or F-sharp. She admitted this was "very dangerous for a voice like mine, and probably shortened its life, but it was a deliberate choice: I wanted to make a dramatic effect, and I made it, period!" (Hines 1982, 305). Near the end of her career, in March 1978, Sills canceled a performance of *Anna Bolena* in which she was scheduled to make her farewell appearance with the Tulsa Opera; she sang *I Puritani* instead. By necessity, Sills purged herself of her heavier roles. *I Puritani* and the comedic *Don Pasquale, Turco in Italia,* and *Il Barbiere di Siviglia* were all that remained of her bel canto repertoire by late 1977. In part, she returned to French opera, which suited her vocal gifts beautifully, with *Thaïs, Manon,* and *La Fille du Régiment* (although she sometimes sang this in English). To these, she also added *The Merry Widow* (in English).

Besides the intense emotional outlet that Lucia and other tragic bel canto heroines provided, Sills may also have initially moved in this direction because, as Peter Davis noted, the "only road to superstardom" during this period was "paved with bel canto revivals" (1973). Her bringing to life of Donizetti's three Tudor queens, for example, unquestionably drew widespread recognition, including a *Time* magazine cover.[4] Sills was an ambitious person; there is no denying an element of truth in Davis's observation. In a *New York Times* article in which Davis takes Sills's commercial recording of *Anna Bolena* as his focus, he writes: "[I]t seems pretty clear by now that certain aspects of these bel canto parts are not what nature intended for Sills' light lyric voice. One can hear this time and again—she simply does not possess sufficient vocal weight to project the forceful declamatory passages in the Act I finale, the Anna/Giovanna duet for the final cabaletta" (Davis 1973). He goes on to assert that Manon was "the role in which Sills realized her potential to perfection and it is a pity that she could not continue with other Massenet operas such as 'Sapho,' an equally juicy part and a gorgeous score that would suit her up and down" (ibid.).

Although her dramatically forceful performances of heavy roles took an undeniable toll on Sills's voice, it is important to consider that she began singing professionally in her mid-teens when she joined the Wagner and Shubert tours. She went on to sing with the New York City Opera for twenty-five years. Sills's singing career was not short by any measure. It was, however, only after she achieved stardom at the age of thirty-seven in 1966 that the world opened up to her. Suddenly, she had a plethora of singing opportunities. From 1967 onward, Sills kept up a frenetic schedule. Her appearances on the operatic stage represent only a portion of her time before the public once she hit the limelight. If she was not performing opera, she was giving concerts and recitals or making television appearances. If she was not singing, she was talking. While traveling, it was not uncommon for her to give a speech as a featured guest at a fund-raiser for the March of Dimes, or any number of other speaking engagements, in the afternoon before rehearsals and performances. Many singers refuse to speak, except for the basic essentials of human communication, on the day of a performance. Sills gave speeches, met with donors, or went shopping (one of her favorite pastimes). Furthermore, as the glittering star of the New York City Opera, she was in a position to request whatever repertoire she wanted to perform. This, ultimately, may have been to her voice's detriment. All of these factors, including others such as not retaining another voice teacher following Miss Liebling's passing in 1970, combined to affect the health of her voice.

To borrow a familiar metaphor, Sills's singing career was meteoric. Like a meteor that hurtles through space unnoticed, except by the keenest of observers, Sills sang for more than a decade with the New York City Opera, as well as other companies, without garnering a great deal of attention. Then, suddenly, with her breakthrough performance as Cleopatra, she began her radiant trajectory through the operatic skies. There, she shined brightly, as evidenced by the plethora of comments referring to the perception of her emitting light. As with Sills's fast and supple voice, what "meteoroids lack in mass they make up for in speed, and this is what causes the flash of light in the sky."[5]

Once fame allowed her the freedom to choose her repertoire, Sills opted for the dramatically intensive and for the recognition that reviving rarely performed roles would bring, knowing full well what the cost to her voice might be. In *Beverly,* she recalled her decision to move into the bel canto repertoire, even though Miss Liebling warned of the likely damage to her voice:

> She wanted me to stick pretty much to French repertoire like *Manon,* and told me that way I'd be able to save my voice. But what was I saving it for? Better to have ten glorious years than twenty safe and ultimately boring ones.

I wanted to live dangerously, I suppose. Even though my career had blossomed late, I didn't envision myself doing much singing past my fiftieth birthday. . . . To sing "safe" repertoire implied that *careful, noncontroversial,* and *easy* would take the place of *risky, provocative,* and *challenging,* which was the approach I'd always chosen in my career. I didn't feel as if I were in a marathon. It was never my ambition to sing longer than anyone else. (1987, 185)

Wondering if Sills perhaps constructed this argument after she had retired, as a retrospective smoke screen, I was able to confirm that as early as January 1973 (in an interview conducted by Lee Polk as part of an oral history project), she spoke of retiring around the age of fifty. The interview transcript was sealed until one year after Sills's death, per her signed release.[6] In response to Polk's question regarding the future possibility of performance being preserved and transmitted through video recordings, Sills replied, "I think by the time all of this comes to fruition I will have long since retired, I don't think we'll see this at least for ten years, and by then I don't plan to be singing anymore" (interview transcript, pp. 80–81).

When I told Gigi Capobianco that Anna Bolena was my favorite of Sills's characters, she responded that Bolena was the most difficult and visceral of all of Sills's roles: "She just spilled her guts there." She added that most singers will not engage with their characters to the degree that Sills did: "They're too concerned about singing perfectly." Echoing Sills's own words, she continued: "Beverly was not afraid to just speak. She could have sung it, and it would have been easier on her voice. But she said, 'I'm not going to save it, for what?' She started doing all these things when she was in her late thirties. Before that, she didn't commit herself so much to things. She had too many problems with her kids" (interview, July 28, 2010).

Perhaps that is what attracts me the most to her *Anna Bolena,* especially the premiere, even with its vocal imperfections. The unguarded manner in which Sills "spilled her guts," the directness and integrity with which she communicated leaps out from the recording. I commune with Sills through Anna's sorrow and her otherworldly madness. The honesty of a performer giving everything in communicating her joy and pain makes an indelible impression on those who are open to the experience. This was the hallmark of Sills's artistry. For the gift she shared, I, and countless others, will be "always and forever" grateful.

Discovering Sills's Influence

Returning to the question that launched this project: Why was I so affected by Beverly Sills's death? My quest for understanding has provided an incredible journey during which I discovered a great deal about Sills and the integral role that an art and a presence such as hers can play in shaping one's life. Much of this I learned through the relationships formed with her devotees, while some of my understanding has been enhanced by the theoretical work of scholars such as Jill Dolan and Claudio Benzecry.

My reaction to reading Sills's second autobiography for the first time shortly after her death is informative. I responded to her references to critics and their occasionally lukewarm or negative reviews of her performances with utter surprise. I wondered what fault they could possibly have found in Sills's singing. When I last engaged intensively with Sills and her music, I was in my early twenties. As a teenager, I listened over and over to her albums, which I either owned or borrowed from the local public library. My favorites were *Beverly Sills Sings Mozart and Strauss, Beverly Sills Concert, La Traviata* highlights, *Julius Caesar* highlights, and the *Thaïs* boxed set.[1] As I listened, I marveled at the speed and precision of Sills's coloratura. I remember the peculiar frustration of being unable to hum along with her. My inability to move my voice as she did hers only bolstered my sense that she was somehow superhuman. Never did it occur to me that her singing might be anything short of perfection. Even today when I listen to recordings I heard hundreds of times before I turned twenty, I feel just as I did when I listened to them all of those years ago: my body tenses and I hold my breath. I'm overcome with a wave of anticipation when she sings her soaring "Je sens une fraîcheur en mon âme ravie!" (I feel a freshness in my delighted soul!) from the first scene of act 2 of *Thaïs*. Sometimes the passage gives me chills exactly as it did three decades ago.

The first time I listened to the *Mozart and Strauss* album on a vinyl record purchased on eBay (I had donated all of my LPs to a thrift store the year before Sills died), the crackling yet warm analog sound seemed to cut through the years. During my binge purchasing in 2007 and 2008 of all commercially available Sills recordings, I heard for the first time her singing of Mahler's second symphony. As the solo soprano line emerged from the thick choral texture in the fifth movement, I had a peculiar sensation that felt akin to a child searching for her mother's voice in a crowd. Clearly, my connection to Sills and her voice reaches to my core. What was it within me that these sounds were tapping into? What were the long-dormant feelings they revived?

I initially looked to the experiences of other fans in hoping to gain insight into what Sills had meant to me. I gathered perspective not just from Sills admirers, but from a broad range of related anecdotal evidence. The recurring theme that resonated most strongly for me was the life-changing impact of encountering artistic greatness at an early age.

While finishing this study, two additional testimonies came to my attention, both of which bear a relationship to the liquidation of Sills's beloved New York City Opera. The first appeared in the September 9, 2013, issue of the *New Yorker* magazine in a "Talk of the Town" essay reporting on English-born librettist Richard Thomas. His *Anna Nicole* was the last opera staged by the NYCO before the company, under incompetent management, filed for bankruptcy in October 2013. Explaining his lifelong attraction to Americana, which has been deeply influential in his creative work, Thomas commented: "When I was eleven, I heard 'Kind of Blue,' by Miles Davis, and it changed my life" ("Madame Supersized," 30). The second such story appeared online on October 1, 2013, as the NYCO's demise was confirmed. The *New York Times* launched a page, "Remembering City Opera: 'We Will Miss It More than We Realize,'" on which people could share their memories of City Opera. I found the page sadly reminiscent of the "Remembering Beverly Sills" page created a little over six years prior. Writing from Hamburg, Germany, a former member of the company, Jonathan Guss, spoke of how a single performance he saw as a teenager changed his life in an instant:

> When I was in high school back in the 60s, I often shelled out a whopping buck-and-a-quarter for a 5th-ring seat. On one such occasion (Frank Corsaro's *Faust* production), my life changed when one of the cadavers in Faust's study answered his summoning of the devil with a cavernous "Me voici"—it was the

voice of Norman Treigle, and I was on the edge of my seat for the rest of the evening. I had decided then and there that if such a powerful mix of acting, singing, movement, and direction was really possible, then I wanted to be an opera singer. I wound up singing and acting with NYCO for 17 years. . . . Just as I had made lifelong friends at NYCO, I had always imagined NYCO and NY would also be friends for life.

In my case, Sills changed my life one evening less than two months after I turned sixteen. For me, Sills's recital was filled with what Dolan terms *utopian performatives*. During the course of her performance, I envisioned a bright future, one in which I would reach for greatness such as that I heard and saw blazing before me. That drive and inspiration, nourished by Sills's recordings, fueled me into my early twenties. Once in college, new inspirations claimed my attention. These ultimately took me to Taiwan.[2] Graduate school presented intellectual stimulation. But these experiences paled in comparison to the unbridled joy and depth of pathos I experienced with Sills, who was, by then, only a distant memory. Next came the hectic and sometimes trying years as an untenured professor. In summary, I had traveled light-years from my awe-inspiring Sills encounter.

Sills's passing somehow allowed me to reach back across the chasm that had formed between my former self and my present self. It was only through the odyssey of researching this book that I came to fully understand what I had left behind: the force of artistic greatness, talent, and ambition that could move me to a transcendent state. This was the magic generated by Sills in performance. Sills's magic enveloped those who fell under her spell and stayed with them, in one form or another, throughout their lives. The after-vibrations from my single experience of Sills in live performance ring audibly for me once more.

Notes

Introduction

1. Scholars of popular culture have been far quicker in taking up the study of iconic performers than scholars of high art forms. Even within the realm of cultural studies, however, anxiety over admitting to being a fan of the celebrity under study exists. For example, writing of her work on Madonna, Laurie Schulze admitted, "I also knew that being a Madonna fan in the context of the academy, especially since I was working on Madonna, would, for some, disqualify me as a member of the real academy—that 'real' academics would not think of me as one of their own or my work on Madonna as truly scholarly" (1999, 47).

2. Musicologist Gary Tomlinson holds fans partially responsible for the fact that opera is often not taken seriously. He writes that "we have all encountered the superficial allegiances of opera buffs, their cults of divas and heldentenors. . . . But difficulty in appreciating opera's serious drama is not the burden of sycophants and the naive alone" (1995, 7).

3. One of this book's anonymous reviewers suggested that I take up the question of Sills's Jewish identity. I refrained from elaborating on this aspect of her life because, as I state in the body of the text, the focus of this book is Sills's artistry and its impact on her audience. Although an analysis of her ethnic and religious identity may represent a subject worthy of study, it is beyond the intended scope of this book.

In her autobiographies and published interviews, Sills wrote freely of her early life being raised in Brooklyn, New York, in what was primarily a European and Jewish household. Growing up, her family moved multiple times, though always to Jewish neighborhoods. Throughout her career, she made no attempt to conceal her Jewish identity, often sprinkling her Brooklynese-accented speech with Yiddish words. In an interview (whose unpublished transcript is now held in the New York Public Library) for the William E. Wiener Oral

History Library, Sills said that "as Beverly Sills, the opera singer . . . it isn't that I try to stress it, but I am a Jewish woman and I'm very proud of it. I'm very proud of the fact that I have reached whatever heights I've reached. I haven't reached them because I'm Jewish, I'm not saying that, but I'm not saying that I will deny being Jewish, having reached these heights. I think it's all an integral part of whatever personality I have that allowed me to become what I've become" (October 13, 1972, interview transcript, p. 25).

In discussing this question with Katrine Ames (who is profiled in chapter 6), Ames said she felt that Sills's Jewish identity "didn't make one iota of difference to her performance" (phone call, September 27, 2014). Ames recalled that famed opera fan Lois Kirschenbaum once chided Sills for performing *Manon* on a high Jewish holiday. Sills replied that everyone worships in their own way. In *Beverly,* she wrote, "I consider myself religious, but I certainly don't need a temple to worship in. I'm not attached to ceremonies. I think one practices one's religion by how one behaves toward one's fellow creatures. The rest of it doesn't matter" (Sills 1987, 151). With my research I elected to respect Sills's privacy and did not strive to divulge further details regarding this aspect of her life.

4. Over his many years of meticulous research compiling Sills's performance annals, Roy C. Dicks has uncovered a number of these errors. I am indebted to Dicks for graciously sharing the fruits of his research with me.

5. Entry on the *New York Times*'s City Room blog posted on July 3, 2007, by Dr. Henry Hoffman; http://cityroom.blogs.nytimes.com/2007/07/03/remembering-beverly-sills/comment-page-3/#respond.

Chapter 1. The Beverly Sills Phenomenon

1. Release from Edgar Vincent–Cynthia Robbins Associates, public relations personal representation.

Chapter 2. From Early Life to Breakthrough

1. *Beverly: An Autobiography* (1987) was released in three different formats: hardcover, hardcover book-club edition, and paperback. The pagination is different across all three. For quotations, I refer to the hardcover edition.

2. Stanley Sills told this story during his speech at the Metropolitan Opera's "Tribute to Beverly Sills" held on September 16, 2007.

3. Edgar Vincent died just before the first anniversary of Sills's death on June 26, 2008.

4. Sills's birthday is given in some sources as May 25 and others as May 26. According to her brother Stanley Sills, she was born at home before midnight on the 25th. By the time the doctor arrived it was the 26th and this is the date that he entered into the official birth record. For further detail, please see http://www.beverlysillsonline.com/birthdate-controversy.htm (accessed July 28, 2012).

5. When I spoke with conductor Charles Wendelken-Wilson about her musicianship, he commented, "She was no Horowitz, but she could sit down at the piano and play her own accompaniments as long as they weren't super fast. Then she would just play kind of chords.

But, she could dissect a score and pretty much teach the role to herself" (Wendelken-Wilson interview, August 1, 2008).

6. Incidentally, famed operatic soprano Maria Callas appeared on the program in 1935 singing "Un bel dì" under the pseudonym "Nina Foresti" (Ardoin 1995, 1–2).

7. A recording of her performance is available on YouTube, http://www.youtube.com/watch?v=yVabQDMqj6s (accessed July 31, 2012).

8. According to the *New York Times,* at the time of J. J. Shubert's death in December 1963, the Shubert family still owned about half of all of the legitimate theaters in what constitutes Broadway (December 27, 1963). Outside of New York, they operated two theaters in Philadelphia, two in Chicago, two in Cincinnati, and one in Boston. Until 1956, when the Shuberts were hit with an antitrust lawsuit, they owned roughly half of the theaters in the country.

9. In numerous sources, including Winthrop Sargeant's extended Sills profile published in the *New Yorker* in 1971 and in Sills's 1987 autobiography, Sills is said to have made her professional operatic debut when Giuseppe Bamboschek hired her to play Frasquita in a Philadelphia Opera Company production of Bizet's *Carmen* in February 1947 (Sargeant 1971, 53; Sills 1987, 43). However, the *Philadelphia Performance Annals,* which were meticulously assembled by opera aficionado Frank Hamilton, does not list a performance of *Carmen* in Philadelphia in February 1947. The annals do show that Sills performed Frasquita with the Philadelphia Civic Grand Opera Company under Bamboschek's direction on February 14, 1951 (http://www.frankhamilton.org/ph/ph2.pdf, accessed September 17, 2012).

Furthermore, a three-page typewritten document, titled "Beverly Sills, American Soprano—Short Biography" (with corrections in Sills's hand), which I found inserted in Sills's *Carmen* score, narrates the highlights of Sills's career through 1953. This document, now housed in the New York City Public Library for the Performing Arts in Lincoln Center inside her *Carmen* score, does not include mention of the 1947 Philadelphia Frasquita. Therefore, it appears that the pushing back of her professional debut by several years is an inaccuracy that Sills perpetuated in interviews and in her own autobiography. This erroneous date was mentioned in many of her obituaries and now seems to be permanently embedded in a flawed public record of Sills's career.

10. In fact, when John Alexander made his New York City Opera debut on October 11, 1957, it was in the role of Alfredo with Beverly Sills as his Violetta.

11. DuMont featured artistic and educational programs. Its only significant competitor when it began broadcasting in the mid-1940s was NBC; DuMont ceased network operations in late 1955 (Weinstein 2004).

12. In her 1987 autobiography, Sills wrote that she did not feel that hers was a Puccini voice (1987, 63). Recognizing her need to gain performance experience, Miss Liebling practically forced her to sing Mimi and Musetta. With a tinge of resentment, she recalled: "I hated every minute of those performances and never sang those parts again" (ibid., 42).

13. Diana Price, John Price's daughter, said she remembered seeing Sills backstage in the hallway after the scene ended, mopping herself up and laughing herself silly along with the rest of the cast (e-mail, July 14, 2008).

14. A report on the divorce hearing published in the *Cleveland Plain Dealer* confirms that Greenough's eldest daughter feared that her mother would "steal" her a second time (March 21, 1956).

15. Sills sang three of the four performances of Baby Doe in the spring 1958 season. Jacquelynne Moody sang one (Sokol 1981, 304–6).

16. Longtime Sills fan Alison Ames, who would later hold the post of director of Deutsche Grammophon's operations in the United States for nine years, was working in public relations for the company in the mid-1970s. She convinced the powers that be to remaster and rerelease the recording in time for the American bicentennial in 1976, which also corresponded with the twentieth anniversary of the opera's premiere. Unfortunately, they discovered that the original master tapes had been lost. The DG recording, which is also the basis for the CD rerelease made in 1999 in time for Sills's seventieth birthday, was created from secondary or tertiary tapes (A. Ames interview, December 9, 2010). There are moments when the deterioration of the tapes is especially obvious.

17. One exception to this is a ten-inch LP recording, *Beverly Sills Sings Songs for Christmas*, released in 1955. The recording was commissioned by the Fordyce and Hamby architectural firm as a holiday gift for its clients and was not commercially available for general purchase.

18. From 1920 to 1972, the Cincinnati "Zoo" Opera presented its shows in an open-sided auditorium in the heart of the Cincinnati Zoo and Botanical Gardens. Sills's 1968 "magnificent rendering of the Lucia mad scene" was long remembered for its accompaniment of barking seals (John J. O'Conner, *Wall Street Journal*, October 14, 1968).

19. This letter, dated November 4, 1965, is in the Beverly Sills scrapbook no. 10 in the Library of Congress.

20. This phenomenon has given rise to concerns that the visual has taken precedence over voice and musicianship in opera performance. A dustup over critics' comments on mezzo-soprano Tara Erraught's appearance as Octavian in Richard Strauss's Der *Rosenkavalier* at Glyndebourne in May 2014 laid bare these tensions. Critics (all of whom were male) derided Erraught's appearance as being "dumpy of stature" (Rupert Christiansen of the *Telegraph*), "unsightly and unappealing" (Richard Morrison of the *Times*), and "stocky" (Andrew Clements of the *Guardian*). Although he commented that she sang "gloriously," Andrew Clark of the *Financial Times* added that Erraught appeared as a "chubby bundle of puppy-fat." Reactions to these reviews set off a firestorm, with outcries appearing in *Salon*, the *New Yorker* blog, and even *Time*, among other venues. In a letter published at slippedisc .com, mezzo-soprano Alice Coote argued passionately for the paramount position of the voice in opera:

> It is not about lights, it is not about costumes, it's not about sets, it's not even about sex or stature. . . . It is ALL about the human voice. This is the Olympics of the human larynx attached to a heart and mind that wants to communicate to other hearts and minds. It is something that is done without amplification and without barriers. . . . It is one human singing to another. LIVE.
>
> All the visual messages that a production and costume [bring] to an opera does not alter (even though they can try very hard) the fact that [its] true success in moving and making an audience love the Art form lies in the voice that sails across the pit

to the audience and into their ears. They are not moved by seeing a conventionally beautiful or attractive person walking around in a lovely or impressive costume or lights or environ. This they can get in the theatre . . . or in film or in daily life. Opera is NOT about that. . . . It is about and really ONLY about communication through great singing. (http://slippedisc.com/2014/05/alice-coote-an-open-letter-to-opera -critics/#sthash.90JQZYwN.dpuf, accessed July 17, 2014)

At the height of her career, Sills recognized the growing pressures to produce visually viable performances. In an interview in 1972 for the William E. Wiener Oral History Library, she said, "I think the era of the big fat opera singer walking to the center of the stage and singing is over. I think if we continue in that vein, opera will be dead in ten years because the present public has been exposed to too many visual arts now through television" (interview transcript, p. 63).

21. "Park and bark" is a derogatory slur denoting the type of operatic performance that primarily involved a singer moving to the center of the stage and delivering her or his aria with little acting or physical movement other than the occasional stilted gesture.

Chapter 3. From Breakthrough to Stardom

1. *Giulio Cesare* received its first performance in the United States by professional singers in 1965 in Kansas City (Dean 1969, 202).

2. Many years later, Curtin recalled the entire affair as the most painful episode in her entire forty-year singing career (Williams 1991, 33).

3. Gigi Capobianco (née Elena Denda) rarely received credit in programs or in the press for her work as a choreographer and dance/movement instructor. For example, Harold Schonberg mused that Tito "must have spent months with the cast, teaching them how to move and gesture" in his September 28, 1966, *New York Times* review of the opening of the *Giulio Cesare* production. Gigi was dedicated to her husband's success; they were an inseparable team.

4. Moore cited several other examples in which Sills employed her phenomenal *fil di voce,* including Strauss's "Breit' über mein Haupt," the "Willow Song" from *The Ballad of Baby Doe,* and the slow arias "Oh quante volte" and "Giusto ciel, in tal periglio" from *L'Assedio di Corinto.*

5. The first twentieth-century staging of *Giulio Cesare* with all of the voices at the pitch originally composed by Handel in 1724 did not take place until 1977 (Dean and Knapp 1987, 508).

6. In *Beverly,* Sills says that Bucky left home a few weeks before the *Suor Angelica* performance (1987, 169). However, in *Bubbles* she gives a more detailed account and writes that the performance and Bucky's departure were only separated by two days (1976, 117). Given the timing of events that she explains in *Bubbles,* including several concerts with Erich Leinsdorf and the Boston Symphony between February 23 and March 4, 1967, her earlier account seems more accurate (that is, Bucky's institutionalization and her *Suor Angelica* performance were separated by only two days).

7. Al Hirschfeld drew two caricatures of a toothy, smiling Sills. One appeared on the cover of the February 1979 issue of *Stereo Review* magazine. Another accompanied advertisements,

including those published in the *New Yorker* (May 12, 1980) and *Opera News* (May 1980), for the broadcast of Sills's performance at the Metropolitan Opera in *Don Pasquale* in 1979. Both sketches can be viewed at Hirschfeld's website: www.alhirschfeldfoundation.org/piece/beverly-sills-o and www.alhirschfeldfoundation.org/piece/don-pasquale (accessed July 24, 2014). An unsigned, and equally toothy, caricature appeared on the front cover the Cleveland *Press, Showtime* section, on August 6, 1976.

8. Readers are urged to find the recording and listen. At the time of writing, the complete performance is available at http://www.youtube.com/watch?v=oWVdgKtFx7o (accessed January 30, 2013).

Chapter 4. From Stardom to Retirement

1. *The Magic Flute* was the NYCO fall 1967 season opener. Unfortunately, Sills missed her high Fs in the Queen of the Night's second aria. Although her singing in the first act was better, Schonberg reports that she was generally not in the best voice opening night (*New York Times*, September 15, 1967). This would be her penultimate performance as the Queen of the Night, a role that she roundly detested. She was scheduled to sing it once again in the 1967 fall season, but Rita Shane replaced her. When the NYCO toured in Los Angeles at the end of the year, Sills was forced to substitute for an ailing singer and had to sing the Queen of the Night one last time. She missed her high note at the end of the first act and was booed. She then refused to sing the second-act aria, although she did join in the ensemble at the end of the opera, according to Martin Bernheimer of the *Los Angeles Times* (December 7, 1967). Anthea de Forest recalls that the LA *Magic Flute* was the only time she ever heard Beverly booed. De Forest continued: "The strength and courage she used to pull herself together for the following night's performance of *Julius Caesar* were a testament to her strength of character" (e-mail, January 29, 2013).

2. Dominic Cossa compared the two stage directors' working methods during our interview. "Tito would have this phenomenal picture in mind that worked. He wanted you to see that, to absorb it, and to begin living within his picture. And his picture really worked. His *Manon* was a masterpiece. His *Mefistofeles* was a masterpiece, his concept of it. The *Pagliacci*s I did with Tito were great. I did my first *Pagliacci* with Tito. They worked so well, because there was nothing one could question about the validity of his vision. Frank, however, came in with ideas; but if the idea wasn't working, some of them were kind of offbeat, he had ten other ideas. His attitude was, 'Try this'" (interview, December 3, 2010).

3. Rudel had no interest in conducting what he felt was an inferior opera and ceded the job to Charles Wendelken-Wilson, who wrote cadenzas for all of the cast members except for Beverly (Wendelken-Wilson interview, August 1, 2008).

4. Cut from this extended quotation is Sargeant's mentioning that Sills gave this opening performance while quite ill. He wrote: "Once or twice during this scene I detected signs of fatigue. The final high note was cut a bit short, and there were a couple of chromatic scales in which Miss Sills slid instead of articulating each note clearly. Next day, I learned that she had been singing with a hundred-and-three-degree temperature, having caught a bug of some sort. Nevertheless, hers is the most satisfactory Lucia I have ever heard. . . . A ten-minute standing ovation greeted the end of the mad scene, and though the diva made her

curtain calls looking a bit pallid and worn, she appeared again and again in response to the audience's cheers. This was one of the big events of the season; it will be even bigger when Miss Sills' temperature returns to normal" (Sargeant 1969b, 170). Of the same evening, Gigi Capobianco recalled that Tito followed Sills up the backstage stairs to the platform from which Sills would make her mad-scene entrance to ensure that in her feverish state she made it onto the stage safely (Capobianco interview, July 28, 2010).

5. The lack of synergy between Sills and her performing colleagues evidenced on the bootleg of the December 28 Covent Garden performance was exacerbated by the fact that Ermanno Mauro, who played Edgardo on opening night, was replaced by Giacomo Aragall with whom she had had no rehearsal.

6. The NYCO staged the three queens in the opposite order of their composition: *Roberto Devereux* (premiered 1837), *Maria Stuarda* (premiered 1835), and *Anna Bolena* (premiered 1830).

7. The *Fach* system categorizes voices according to tessitura, timbre (on a spectrum from light to dark), and agility (with coloratura being the most agile and, therefore, capable of executing fast-moving runs, trills, and ornaments). On the basis of range or tessitura, female voices are categorized from low to high as contralto, mezzo-soprano, or soprano. Sopranos are further categorized as dramatic, lyric, or coloratura according to their timbre, size of voice (that is, the ability to be heard over thick orchestrations), and agility. Further subcategories include dramatic coloratura (a big, dark, yet flexible voice) and lyric coloratura (not as dark or powerful as the dramatic coloratura, but more so than the pure coloratura). For more on *Fach* and how the categorization of specific roles has shifted over time, see Cotton (2012).

8. Maria Callas, whose astounding versatility was sometimes compared to that of Giuditta Pasta's, once commented: "I'm just doing what once upon a time was done. Once upon a time, sopranos were considered sopranos—not light or heavy or medium or whatever you call it. A soprano was supposed to do every kind of opera. It's like a violinist, a pianist has to perform any kind of music" (quoted in Lawson 1988, 158).

9. Montserrat Caballé possessed a beautiful voice and was widely acclaimed in the bel canto repertoire, but was also infamous for her lackluster acting.

10. According to her daughter, performing the role of Queen Elizabeth took a significant physical toll on Sills. Wearing the queen's costumes, which each weighed over fifty pounds, caused her back pain that only increased in severity as she aged (conversation with Meredith Greenough, January 18, 2015, New York City).

11. Montserrat Caballé sang the role of Queen Elizabeth in a concert setting of *Roberto Devereux* in Carnegie Hall in 1965.

12. When Marissa Galvany took over the role from Pauline Tinsley for the show's third performance on March 16, 1972, the explosive energy between the two queens erupted into a real-life conflict. As conductor Charles Wendelken-Wilson said in our interview, he never specifically told Galvany that she and Sills needed to release their unison high D together. Galvany "grabbed a good one" and held it longer than Sills. As soon as the curtain came down, all hell broke loose. He had to address the squabble immediately, assuring the two sopranos that in the future they would cut off together. Wendelken-Wilson mused: "It was a moment that she [Sills] needed to step back a little bit after it got organized and realize

that it was making for *damn* good theater." Her explosion was simply a gut reaction to being upstaged. As he noted, "it was part of what made her so great. I mean, without that gut reaction, it would have been any ordinary soprano that everybody else in the world could have walked over" (Wendelken-Wilson interview, August 1, 2008). Energies were always high by the end of this scene. For example, during the August 30, 1972, performance, Sills ripped Elizabeth's riding crop from Pauline Tinsley's hand (as she always did at end of the scene) with such force that it ended up flying into the orchestra pit (*New York Times*, August 31, 1972).

13. Numerous sources have commented that Sills performed all three Tudor queens within one week; however, I have uncovered no data to support this claim. The closest she came was when she performed the three within a span of twenty-four days in September 1974 and within twenty-two days in November and December 1973 during the NYCO's annual tour to Los Angeles.

14. In telling this story, which Gigi Capobianco also confirmed in my interview with her and Tito, Susanne Marsee said, "I think that she went right to the hospital that night or the next morning. She was so ill, so ill." When asked how Sills could have performed in this state, Marsee replied, "If your vocal chords are not affected—and she was a natural breather—and the muscles weren't affected, because she was internally ill, you can just shut your eyes and let it come out" (Marsee interview, January 25, 2008).

15. Bain's memory of working with Sills can be viewed at http://classicjazzguitar.com/articles/article.jsp?article=63 (accessed March 17, 2013). He misremembers a few details. For example, he says that she had just arrived from Dallas, when in fact she had sung in Los Angeles the previous evening.

16. At the time of writing, there is a clip of the Sills-Bain *Tonight Show* performance on YouTube: www.youtube.com/watch?feature=endscreen&v=T49s9mOAreM&NR=1.

17. Joan Sutherland finally sang her first *I Puritani* at the Metropolitan Opera in a new production on February 25, 1976.

18. *Danny Kaye's Look-In at the Metropolitan Opera* was filmed before an audience of children and young adults for nationwide broadcast on CBS as part of the network's "Festival of Lively Arts for Young People."

19. Charles Wendelken-Wilson mentioned in our interview that there were nights when he conducted Sills when she could not speak, but "she sang up a storm." I asked him how Sills could sing when her speaking voice was gone. He explained: "The trick was that she had to put less and less pressure on the cords so the fast things were even faster; and yet, you heard every sixteenth note. The woman had an incredible technique. It was not done with mirrors or smoke screens. She was one of those instinctive singers that either had *exceedingly* great training early on or [was] just so instinctive" (interview, August 1, 2008).

20. It is important to note that singers' intonation problems are not always linked to poor musicianship. The reasons for even great singers singing slightly off pitch are complicated and must be addressed individually. Some singers, particularly tenors, have a tendency to sing a bit sharp. Plácido Domingo, even in his prime, tended to worry about hitting notes above high A. As a result, he sometimes over-supported and veered sharp as a result. Vocal pedagogue Gerald Martin Moore points out that "singing flat, on the other hand, is often

due to under-supporting, or reliance on the wrong set of muscles to support the breath flow, together with tongue tension, and is usually less forgiven among critics or pedagogues than sharpening." In speculating on the reason for Sills's tendency to sing flat later in her career, he suggests that the root of the problem can be traced to her fundamental vocal training and her shifting to heavier bel canto roles without correct technical guidance. As Moore explained:

> Beverly's technique was that of a pure head-voiced coloratura—that is how she was trained by Liebling in the Marchesi school. Marchesi was indeed a famous teacher of sopranos, but she was controversial, not everyone loved her method. She was often accused by rival voice teachers of teaching a particularly bright, sometimes shallow way of singing with the focus completely on the head voice. Furthermore, her breathing technique has been criticized for a lack of emphasis on lower body connection, or use of the back muscles. Therefore, I felt that when Beverly wanted to sing the bigger repertoire (which Liebling advised against) she did not seek technical guidance, but instead told me that she had to find a "new, more open-throated" way of singing (see Moore 2006 for more).

> The open-throat concept can be a tricky one to grasp correctly, and I felt that Beverly approached it by trying to open her throat more to make bigger sounds, but did not address her breathing technique. A true open throat has to be supported with a real lower body connection to the breath—something she had never been taught. I feel her effort to achieve a wider range of colours was centered too much on her throat and less on her body. So, she was trying to make these bigger fatter sounds with the same breathing technique she used to produce her beautiful floated covered head tones. That, together with her ridiculously punishing schedule, plus her fund-raising and travel activities, took a toll on her lovely light coloratura voice. Without the technique of opening the body and engaging muscles from lower down (pelvic floor, lumbar muscles, etc.), she had to force too much breath pressure at her cords to create the sounds she was looking for. This tired her voice and pressed it unduly, leading to the flatness and wide vibrato which started to creep in from as early as 1972, but had become really problematic in '74 and onwards. (e-mail, March 22, 2013)

21. Sills first witnessed supertitles as part of Peking opera performances she attended in China in 1981. Under her leadership, the NYCO was the first company in the United States to employ them. Lotfi Mansouri gets credit for being the first impresario in North America to use supertitles when the Canadian Opera Company under his direction introduced them in January 1983.

22. Sills died of cancer. By the time she was diagnosed in May 2007, the disease had spread throughout her body. She had previously had a melanoma removed and had battled ovarian and breast cancers.

Chapter 5. Loving Sills

1. In a tragic example of life-imitating-art-imitating-life, Nell Theobald, a delusional fan of soprano Birgit Nilsson, modeled her affections for Nilsson on the actions of the

fan, Elsie deHaven, in Davenport's novel. The first time Theobald sent roses to Nilsson in 1968 at Bayreuth, her card included a line from the novel *Of Lena Geyer*. Like the fictional deHaven, Theobald always sat in the first row dressed in black when she came to Nilsson's performances; she sent roses to the diva's dressing room whether or not she was able to attend. Unfortunately for Theobald, Nilsson did not return her affection as had her fictional counterpart. Things escalated over nine years with Theobald booking herself onto the same flights and into the same hotels as Nilsson. Eventually, she became so bold as to break into Nilsson's hotel rooms and steal her personal items, including underwear. The whole affair was terrifying for the singer. In an act of high drama, Theobald sent Nilsson a farewell letter in which she quoted Isolde's death lament and asked that her ashes be spread over Nilsson's grave. Nilsson alerted the hotel staff, where both she and Theobald were staying, and they found the young woman unconscious from an overdose of tranquilizers. Not long after this failed attempt, the obsessed Theobald succeeded in committing suicide (*New York Times*, May 21, 2006).

2. Shortly after Sills's Met debut, Garry Wills penned an essay in which he wove together his musings on McCourt's novel and Sills, her Met event, and her fandom. Wills writes: "Beverly is Mawrdew of the novel—she has her own Secret Seven, her prior incarnations, her shrines, and the keepers of her shrines"; yet, he makes clear that *Mawrdew Czgowchwz* is not a roman à clef written for Sills. Instead, he explains that every diva is "Every-Diva." "They all began as Cinderellas and turned pumpkins into carriages to get to the party. Beverly's party was just bigger than anybody else's" (Wills 1975, 36).

3. Claudio Benzecry's book won the 2012 Mary Douglas Best Book Award conferred by the Sociology of Culture section of the American Sociological Association.

4. Media studies scholar Mark Duffett argues convincingly that evidence from his own ethnographic work with Elvis devotees shows that notions of fandom as consumerism—theories typically constructed by scholars who have little or no meaningful contact with actual fans—must be reassessed (2000, 76).

5. The *Don Pasquale* performance was taped January 11, 1979, for broadcast on PBS on Saturday evening, May 17, 1980.

6. I have chosen to retain the names of the *Guestbook* contributors for three reasons: First, the *Guestbook* is—at the time of writing—still available online. Site owners Roy Dicks and Larry Strachan have no plans to take it down; therefore, the contributors' identities are easily available. Second, I feel the epitaph writers should be recognized for their thoughtful contributions. Third, the contributors posted their epitaphs in a public forum. As Joseph Walther argued in his essay "Research Ethics in Internet-Enabled Research," "it is important to recognize that *any person who uses publicly-available* [*sic*] *communication systems on the Internet must be aware that these systems are, at their foundation and by definition, mechanisms for the storage, transmission, and retrieval of comments* (emphasis in the original, 2002, 207). Therefore, retrieving epitaphs from the *Guestbook* is no different from using "newspapers stories, broadcasts, the Congressional Record, or other archival data, for research" (ibid.).

7. Tidyman posted epitaphs to both the *Guestbook* and to the *New York Times* "City Room" blog. I cite his "City Room" entry.

8. Media studies scholar Mark Duffett notes that because "Freud's fascination with disorders like hysteria might pathologize fandom, fan studies researchers have usually chosen *not* to focus on his work, or that of his famous disciple, Jacques Lacan" (2013, 114). Duffett also notes that Henry Jenkins, the leading scholar in the field, "carefully avoids a psychological approach to fandom in his work" (ibid., 120).

9. An unfortunate example of an interpretation of fandom that contradicts practitioners' views is found in Erika Doss's *Elvis Culture: Fans, Faith, and Image* (1999). Despite the fact that most Elvis fans, even those she interviewed, reject the idea that their Elvis adoration (in particular the activities surrounding visits to Graceland) comprises a religious practice, Doss is unrelenting in forwarding her interpretation. At her book's outset, she states unequivocally that she is not an Elvis fan (1999, 26). In fact, she writes with a tone of class condescension that makes her distance from those under her study very clear. For a concise overview of the problems with Doss's approach, see Reece 2006, 15–16; for an extended and meticulous critique, see Duffett 2003.

10. In his essay on his Beverly Sills fandom published in *Opera Quarterly,* Roy C. Dicks also comments that listening to Sills keeps him balanced: "Outsiders may think opera lovers are crazy, but we know such relationships keep us sane" (2004, 689).

11. The *New York Times*'s City Room blog garnered just under two hundred epitaphs (http://cityroom.blogs.nytimes.com/2007/07/03/remembering-beverly-sills, accessed July 27, 2007). Sills admirers posted similar memorializing statements on many other sites, such as in the comments sections for articles reporting her death. For example, fifty-one comments followed the MSNBC story titled "Opera Legend Beverly Sills Has Died at 78: Brooklyn-Born Diva was Global Icon of Can-Do American Culture" (http://boards.msn .com/MSNBCboards/thread.aspx?boardid=78, accessed July 12, 2009).

12. "The Scores of Beverly Sills Come to the Music Division," blogged by Bob Kosovsky, curator, Rare Books and Manuscripts Music Division, the New York Public Library for the Performing Arts (http://www.nypl.org/blog/2009/10/27/scores-beverly-sills-come-music -division, accessed October 27, 2009).

13. Davis's disparagement of fans is not reserved for Sills fans. In reviewing Renée Fleming's CD *Homage: The Age of the Diva,* he writes: "Sometimes Fleming does have a fresh idea, but too often it simply misfires—the almost comically extended climax of Tosca's prayer, for instance, or her mannered dissection of Leonora's first aria from *Il Trovatore*—though the voice is mostly gorgeous and the breath control astonishing, and that will be enough for the fans" (Davis 2006).

14. See, for example, comment #32 posted on July 25, 2009: "On the other hand if you do not even know the italian [*sic*] words you are critcizing [*sic*], then you really deserve oprobium [*sic*] for your pretentions [*sic*] above your station. . . . . . Who gives a shit about an exclamation point!!!! Typical SillsBilly!!!!!!! (http://parterre.com/2009/07/24/norma -is-that-you/#). An earlier appearance of the term, which the author of comment #32 credits as his inspiration, came in a thread titled "Island Magic." In comment #128 posted on July 22, 2009, a participant wrote: "I think the rather strong and passionate opinions here were triggered by a gaggle of Beverly Sillsbillies, some of whom very likely never heard her in her

prime, making elevated and ludicrous comparisons" (http://parterre.com/2009/07/19/island-magic/#comments).

15. For a vivid description of the ways in which opera was woven into the lives of a broad segment of the population in early and mid-nineteenth-century America, see Levine 1988, esp. pp. 85–146.

16. Katherine Preston, in her important work on opera in late nineteenth-century America, finds that itinerant troupes performing opera in English translation attracted large audiences in much of the country (especially beyond the East Coast where the shadow of "aristocratic" institutions such as the Metropolitan Opera loomed large). Through their touring, opera continued to have a place on the American popular stage well after foreign-language opera ascended to elite status in the 1870s and 1880s (Preston 2003, 350).

17. As discussed in chapter 4, these comedic roles comprised a larger and larger portion of her repertoire as she neared the end of her singing career. The most important factor in turning her to lighter roles was the declining state of her vocal equipment. After several years of singing Elisabetta and other taxing roles, coupled with her cancer surgery, she was not able to continue with the more physically demanding tragic heroines.

Chapter 6. Sills in the Lives of Her Fans

1. In lieu of warming up, Sills would often "try out" her voice backstage during a loud orchestral passage just prior to her first stage entrance (G. Capobianco interview, July 28, 2010). Her practices changed somewhat near the end of her career when she found that she needed to exercise her voice more extensively before taking the stage.

2. The Ames sisters' forming of lifelong friendships through their experiences as fans at the opera house contradicts Benzecry's findings. He reports in his study of opera fans in Buenos Aires that they separated their social lives from "that part that involved the opera" (2011, 142). Furthermore, the Sills fan friendships that have formed through social-networking sites, which then resulted in embodied get-togethers and sustained contact, also contradicts the data from the Argentinian study. It is difficult to determine if these dissimilarities are the result of cultural differences between the various fan groups or of contrasting research methods employed in this and Benzecry's study.

3. Incidentally, Alison Ames is frequently cited in both popular-press articles and scholarly works on Leonard Bernstein.

4. It was only within the context of his devotional or tribute performances to Sills that David donned women's clothing and makeup. He never wore a dress if he wasn't singing as Beverly Trills or Davina Pons. In his experience, this set him apart from other drag performers he came to know. He approached drag as an actor who could sing. While other "girls" usually arrived for shows in full makeup and women's attire, he would show up in his signature baseball cap and a flannel shirt, and with his makeup in a toolbox (e-mail, October 7, 2013).

5. Ponder earned a BA in piano performance at the University of Northern Iowa, a MA in piano performance from the University of Iowa, and an MM in harp performance from the Peabody Conservatory (e-mail, December 8, 2013).

6. Book historian Kirsten MacLeod opines that fan discourse often employs "hyperbolic irrational mystico-religious language" (2004, 128). My study leads me to believe that this

value judgment imposed on fan expression should be suspended. Rather, we should consider that fan discourse might signal a sincere connection—one that scientific method has no means of measuring and that social conventions cast as abject—between the fan and performing artist. Music at its best is a form of ineffable communication. When the message is received, a connection is formed. The expressions of such feelings of connection are often not significantly different from those articulated in the context of religio-spiritual experience, though I am in no way suggesting that Sills fans take Beverly as a god (though as a *diva,* she certainly was a "goddess"), nor are their actions akin to religious or cultish practice. For discussions on fandom and religiosity, see Reece (2006) and Duffett (2003).

7. Resonating well with the meaning of his Sills collection in Ed Specht's life, historian and journalist Philipp Blom writes: "Every collection is a theatre of memories, a dramatization and a *mise-en-scène* of personal and collective pasts, of a remembered childhood and of remembrance after death. It guarantees the presence of these memories through the objects evoking them. It is more even than a symbolic presence: a transubstantiation. The world beyond what we can touch is with us in and through them, and through communion with them it is possible to commune with it and become part of it" (2002, 191).

8. In October 2009, Sills's daughter, Meredith Greenough, sold many of her mother's personal and career-related items at auction. With so many of her material possessions now strewn across the country and world, Stamper (who attended the auction) may fairly claim the largest number of Sills-related materials in the world.

9. At the age of seventy-four, Sills became the target of a deranged, thirty-nine-year-old woman from Detroit. The unemployed truck driver contacted the Metropolitan Opera on a regular basis for several months saying that she needed to marry Beverly Sills. Finally, she was taken into police custody after she appeared at the Met's stage door in May 2004 saying, "I am Jesus Emmanuel. I want to see Beverly Sills. I came here to marry her" (UPI, May 21, 2004). She was later declared mentally unfit to stand trial and was placed in the custody of the New York state mental health system. Sills had also contended with several death threats during the course of her singing career.

10. Sills discussed her unfortunate experience with the helmet during her one and only performance as a Valkyrie in both of her autobiographies (see Sills 1976, 54; or Sills 1987, 72–73). Stamper purchased it at the Sills estate auction in 2009. He was pleased to outbid a representative from the New York Wagner Society when the price topped $1,200.

11. Buchanan can be seen making his New Year's 2013 greeting to the members of the "The Beverly Sills Crazies!"—which he first posted on his YouTube channel and then linked to Facebook—here: http://www.youtube.com/watch?v=DCnxxOyYZ1k, accessed June 17, 2013.

12. According to Facebook, a "closed group" means: "Anyone can see the group and who's in it. Only members see posts" (https://www.facebook.com/about/groups, accessed June 17, 2013).

Chapter 7. Experiencing Magic

1. Writing in his first autobiography about his performance with Sills in *Roberto Devereux,* Domingo commented: "It was always a pure joy to sing with her. Apart from being the

greatest vocal actress with whom I have worked, she is also a delightful, straightforward person" (1983, 86).

2. Greenstein's exuberant declaration that Sills "was the stage" harkens back to an early nineteenth-century ideal as articulated by Johann Wolfgang von Goethe in his "The 'Rules for Actors'": "An actor standing alone on the stage should remember that he is called to fill out the stage with his presence, and this is so much the more when the attention is focused solely upon him" (Goethe 1952, 432).

3. Theodor Adorno, for example, writes that it would be appropriate to consider opera, in a world "bereft of magic," as the genre that "endeavors to preserve the magical element of art" (1994, 29).

4. The handwritten letter on Salk Institute letterhead is dated October 8, 1980, and belongs to the Beverly Sills scrapbook no. 23 held in the Library of Congress.

5. This quote is taken from the documentary film *Beverly Sills: Made in America.* The voice-over is heard during a scene of Sills singing Cleopatra's aria "Da Tempeste"; the scene's original source is a CBS *Camera Three* program about Sills.

6. A charming anecdote from Sills's guest performance with the Palm Beach Opera illustrates this well. In the middle of a performance of Donizetti's *La Fille du Régiment,* Sills came offstage to find three games of bridge going. Chorus member Tom Carlisle reported that she joined in one of the games, did a small slam, and made it. "Then she said, 'Oh, I've got to go on stage,' and she did" (*Palm Beach Post,* December 11, 2011).

7. One time she dropped character, though imperceptible to the audience, when, as Queen Elizabeth, she realized that her dresser had forgotten to take off her rings, including a huge diamond solitaire. With just a few moments to spare before she was going to deliver Devereux a resounding slap, she tossed her rings into the wings (K. Ames interview, December 27, 2010).

8. Interestingly, Goodall finds that one of the "staples of mesmeric practices is the power of eye contact. . . . The eyes are the means by which the mesmerist generates a contagious interiority, drawing others into an imagined scene he or she has conjured" (2008, 106). As Robert Hale reports, it was partially through eye contact with Sills that he became deeply engaged in the world in which Sills as her character existed in the heat of the performative moment.

9. Edith Turner tells of similar experiences in her discussion of communitas and the "strange characteristics of music" (2012, 47). She writes that performers "sometimes seem to talk as if they have proof of God or a god. They have become aware that the music is playing itself. They sense a mysterious control from outside" and speak of time standing still (ibid).

10. Text taken from a fax Tito Capobianco sent in advance of our interview at his and Gigi's home in late July 2010. The English-language text is a translation of a eulogy they published in an Italian magazine, *Opera,* shortly after Sills's death in July 2007. They were unable to supply more specific publication information such as an exact date or issue number.

11. Charles Wadsworth was the founding director of the Chamber Music Society of Lincoln Center and led the organization for twenty years. As an accompanist, he played for some of the world's greatest singers, including Montserrat Caballé, Shirley Verrett, and Dietrich Fischer-Dieskau, among others.

12. Sills also used her considerable time spent on airplanes keeping up with her correspondence, including fan mail.

13. Cynthia Edwards, a stage director and former member of the NYCO, mentioned that she saw Sills perform *I Puritani* numerous times. I asked Edwards to read Cornish's description to verify its accuracy. In her reply, she touched on several of this chapter's main themes: "I do indeed remember her entering from above and walking slowly down toward the audience with her arms raised. I don't remember clearly the timing of when she reached the deck or when she lowered her arms, though. She simply owned the music and the character so completely that no one (onstage or off) could fail to pay attention to every word and gesture. What I remember most is how she conveyed the aching, hurting heart of Elvira. It made me cry every time I saw her do it. No histrionics; she just absolutely inhabited the character" (e-mail, July 6, 2014).

14. Seeking to verbalize the quality that attracted people to Beverly through her appearance in the popular media, Julius Rudel rejected the word *charisma,* saying it is overused. Instead, he preferred to call it *energy* (interview, October 6, 2009).

15. Shigo's personal blog, *Voice Talk: Perspectives on Singing,* http://www.voice-talk.net/2010/02/remembering-beverly-sills.html, accessed February 9, 2010.

16. An exception is Barba and Savarese's *Dictionary of Theatre Anthropology,* whose entry on *energy* surveys the presence of this force in Western and Eastern theatrical practices. Barba, in his entry on *dilation,* asserts that there are "certain performers who attract the spectator with an elementary energy which 'seduces' without mediation" (Barba and Savarese 2006, 52).

17. As she approached retirement, Sills's loss of the easy and reliable control of her instrument became a source of terrific frustration and sadness, as she confided in several colleagues (who wish to remain anonymous) with whom I spoke.

18. A decade or so before her death, Sills confided in one of my interviewees (who wishes to remain anonymous) on this subject—that she questioned whether her son even recognized her.

19. Sills was criticized publicly for her "desire to be loved by everyone" during her tenure as the chairman of Lincoln Center (Volpe 2006, 233). Reporting on the turmoil surrounding a redevelopment plan Sills launched, one top official at Lincoln Center was cited anonymously in the *New York Times* as saying, "She's a diva, you know. . . . She wants everybody to love her and everything that's said about her to be positive. . . . Not being loved . . . does more harm to a diva than anything else." Reporter Frank Bruni concluded that competing interests made it impossible for everyone to be satisfied with Sills and "there are times when she seems beaten down by it" (January 6, 2002).

Chapter 8. Listening for After-Vibrations

1. Moore named several other operatic voices that are said to have not recorded particularly well, including Birgit Nilsson, Renata Scotto, Alfredo Kraus, Ruth Welting, and Jon Vickers.

2. According to Osborne, some recordings were made at the behest of opera singers. He noted that generally the artists were pleased their performances generated interest, enjoyed

having the recordings themselves, and sometimes even gave signed permission to bootleggers to put their recordings into production (1966, 47).

3. I take this count from Roy C. Dicks, who notes that these three hundred recordings include complete operas, concerts, recitals, television and radio programs, and special events (www.beverlysillsonline.com/liveopera.htm, accessed September 10, 2013).

4. I am grateful to Mark Schubin for supplying the details regarding video camera technology and the history of its employment in opera broadcasting through both personal communication and his website (www.schubincafe.com/2013/03/19/media-technology -and-opera-history, accessed May 23, 2013). Schubin is a multiple Emmy-award-winning motion picture and television engineer whose clients have included the Metropolitan Opera, *Sesame Street,* Court TV, and the *PBS NewsHour.*

5. The private recording from Carnegie Hall was made by one of Sills's fans who became her close personal friend and confidant. It documents Sills in her prime with her shimmering pure tone, impeccably clean coloratura, and effortless high notes. In his 1971 essay "Piracy on the High C," Alan Rich comments that this recording "is far ahead of Sutherland's London album in sound and performance" (1971, 72).

6. In a cross-cultural aside, in watching hundreds of hours of Peking opera live over many years, I became highly sensitized to the beauty of a performance in which a trained actor seamlessly and precisely synchronizes his or her movements with the music. The organic integration of sound and movement is one of the cornerstones of Peking opera performance. I have witnessed no other music-theater tradition in the world in which the integration is more finely tuned and gracefully executed. Virtually every physical movement—from an elegant hand gesture, to the stunned expression of widening eyes, to a magnificent somersault—is accompanied by musical sound, most often that of a drum, gong, or cymbal, or all of these, in combination. Literatus Qi Rushan once summed up this aesthetic: "There's no sound that isn't song and no movement that isn't dance." This impeccable synchronization is trained through hard work and discipline into the actors' bodies and minds from a very early age. In the West, there is no systematic training for opera singers' bodies (beyond their voices and the most rudimentary of physical movements); therefore, Sills's organic integration of her movements, gestures, and facial expression with the music is quite rare. I find that I watch her videos with the same close attention to detail as that demanded by Peking opera performance.

7. Roland Gagnon was a vocal coach, not a voice teacher. As such, physical matters of technique and vocal production were largely beyond his expertise.

8. Leontyne Price's "O patria mia" from Verdi's *Aida* from her last performance at the Met on January 3, 1985, won first place.

9. This scene was recorded in London, England, in May 1971 for a BBC *Profile in Music* special. Other segments include: "Una voce poco fa" from *Il Barbiere di Siviglia,* "Willow Song" from *The Ballad of Baby Doe,* "Da tempeste" from *Giulio Cesare,* "Vivi, ingrato" from *Roberto Devereux,* and the "Gavotte" from *Manon.* The program aired in the United Kingdom in 1972, but did not air in the United States until 1975, when it won Sills an Emmy award.

10. I leave issues surrounding the work and its texts, such as manuscripts, scores, and librettos, to those who have spent years dedicated to their study. Of direct importance here

are the scholarly achievements of Philip Gossett, including his book *Anna Bolena and the Artistic Maturity of Gaetano Donizetti* (1985), and his contribution to Ricordi's *Anna Bolena* vocal score.

11. A bootleg video of a 1980 revival of the production provides useful glimpses of the costumes and setting in which Sills acted out her Bolena. Olivia Stapp is in the title role with Samuel Ramey as Enrico. According to Donal Henahan, the revival appeared basically the same as the original (*New York Times*, September 13, 1980). Director Jay Lesenger made only minor changes to Capobiano's original staging. However, conductor Charles Wendelken-Wilson employed a new performing score that included several cuts and dispensed with the overture. Stapp's acting and stage movements are markedly different from Sills's, however. For instance, she does not slap Enrico. Samuel Ramey shared the story of how the bootleg video came to be. A friend of his, known in New York circles at the time as "Mr. Tape," boldly carried the large video camera into the hall, saying that he was on official business. He simply walked up to one of the theater's upper rings and set up his equipment (Ramey interview, June 18, 2012).

12. A bootleg of Sills's *Anna Bolena* carrying the date of March 3, 1974, is also in circulation. However, this is, in fact, a recording from the opera's premiere. Furthermore, it originates from the same original recording as the correctly dated bootleg as is clearly heard in the audience's comments.

13. Sills's personal copy of her *Anna Bolena* score was acquired by the New York Public Library for the Performing Arts, along with more than forty of her other scores, at an auction of Sills's personal belongings held in October 2009. I am grateful to the music division's curator Robert Kosovsky, who was instrumental in bringing these volumes into the collection and who has been of terrific assistance during my visits to work with them.

14. Beth Bergman captured better than any other photographer Sills's extraordinary ability to express emotion through her organic integration of musical flow and physical gesture. Unknown to most is that Bergman holds advanced degrees in music. Her sensitivity to the music guided her as she sought to capture on film the moments when music, emotion, and physicality converged with poignant intensity.

15. Sills made each of her studio recordings of the three Donizetti queen operas, *Roberto Devereux, Maria Stuarda,* and *Anna Bolena,* prior to their NYCO productions. Although unable to confirm this, I believe that the motivation in reversing Sills's preferred order of events was one of marketing. The albums were on store shelves when each of the productions opened. Her other full-length opera recordings were made after she had performed the roles in a complete production.

16. During my interview with Tito and Gigi Capobianco, Gigi recalled Sills's attitude toward staging an opera after the studio recording was already made. She said that when they would begin rehearsing a new production, Sills would jokingly say: "'Well, what do you have in store for me this time? . . . I know that you're going to ruin my recording.'" In other words, in working through the mise-en-scène as devised by Tito, Sills's interpretation would come to differ significantly from the one preserved in the studio recording (interview, July 28, 2010).

17. Published a few days after the NYCO premiere of *Anna Bolena,* an article in the *New Yorker* described the company's strong points as "ensemble work and an adventurous

repertoire" with "chumminess (nearly everybody, from singer to stagehand, is on a first-name basis with the director, Julius Rudel)" being a defining trademark (*New Yorker,* October 8, 1973, 38).

18. Sills's score annotations are detailed when compared with those that I have had a chance to see of her colleagues. Typically, she noted stage directions, such as "head towards SL [stage left] wall," or "kneel & fall," but she also marked clues to her character's psychological, emotional, or physical state, such as "nervously," "happy," "kooky," or "frightened." Handwritten musical notation, such as ornamentation and octave displacements, is also penciled in sporadically.

19. Her pounding on the stage floor is audible in all of the in-house recordings I have heard. The audible collapse Capobianco devised is only captured clearly in the recording from March 10, 1974.

20. Unfortunately, it appears that the tape used to make the recording of the *Anna Bolena* premiere was not new and not properly erased. As a result, the ghostly sounds of a previous recording are still audible. Furthermore, the pitch was too high and tempi too fast at various points, indicating that the bootlegger's batteries were running low when he made the recording. Recording engineers at the University of California, San Diego, kindly corrected the pitch and tempi for my purposes.

21. Throughout, I borrow William Ashbrook's translation of the *Anna Bolena* libretto (Romani 1973).

22. I asked Hale to confirm that Sills had indeed slapped him. He said, "Oh yeah, definitely. But she was a pro. She knew how to do it without killing you" (interview, August 17, 2010).

23. I cannot help but wonder if Capobianco chose to play on the association of the flute with madness and hallucination, which has become part of *Lucia di Lammermoor's* performance tradition, in making this Bolena's first visible indication of hearing voices.

24. "Presto" appears in the score above the second half of the first iteration of "do-na" and the "mi" in measure 69. A rallentando is marked for the second half of measure 69. However, Sills sang this entire phrase slowly per her penciled-in marking above "mi per" on the last beat of measure 68.

25. I experience this particular arc extending from "Chi parlò di Percy?" (measure 50) through to the crash in measure 71.

26. For example, N. 16 begins with a tempo of approximately 72 beats per minute in the studio recording; it is performed at roughly 77 in the live recording. The measures in which the demented Anna danced on stage (beginning at measure 30) are at a lively 111 beats per minute; this section is played at a much slower 84 beats per minute on the studio recording. I suggest that prior to the staging of the mise-en-scène, Rudel had not yet imagined this section as a dance.

27. The day after Sills's death, Billadeau posted two epitaphs to the *Guestbook* and one to the *New York Times* Cityroom blog (http://www.beverlysillsonline.com/text/farewellbook03 .htm and http://cityroom.blogs.nytimes.com/2007/07/03/remembering-beverly-sills/ ?apage=3#comments).

28. The recording of the October 10, 1973, performance captures the unmistakable sound of hands smacking the stage floor as Sills lands.

29. Moran posted his comment using his parterre.com username, mandryka, on December 10, 2011 (http://parterre.com/2011/12/08/anna-squared/comment-page-1/#comments, accessed December 11, 2011).

Chapter 9. Engaging with Sills's Artistry

1. Sills frankly discussed her struggle to sing as she wept in an interview conducted on January 22, 1973, by Lee Polk for the William E. Wiener Oral History Library: "I once did a performance of *Suor Angelica* at a very emotional time of my life and on stage I just wept and wept and wept and I couldn't go on singing, you know, that defeats the whole purpose" (interview transcript, p. 72). The interview transcript is now held by the New York City Library for the Performing Arts.

2. Sills said she shed real tears every night when Horace Tabor died in her arms when she played his faithful wife Baby Doe, and that she found singing her final aria difficult as a result (Sills 1999, 9). However, she did not lose control as she did the night that she sang Suor Angelica.

3. Ibid., 73.

4. It should be noted that Turkish soprano Leyla Gencer had performed all three roles previously, although they were not presented as a trilogy by a single opera company as they were for Sills by the New York City Opera. Gencer premiered *Anna Bolena* in 1958, *Roberto Devereux* in 1964, and *Maria Stuarda* in 1967.

5. "How Stuff Works" website (http://science.howstuffworks.com/question486.htm, accessed October 1, 2013).

6. See note 1 for more on this interview and the location of its transcript.

Afterword

1. I was entirely unaware of the *Bellini and Donizetti Heroines* and the *Scenes and Arias from French Opera* albums, and most of her complete opera sets. I had never heard *The Ballad of Baby Doe* or any of Donizetti's three queens.

2. I fell in love with Taiwan, continue to find it fascinating, and formed friendships there that remain strong. I also fell in love with Peking opera. As discussed in my first book, the tradition, as I witnessed it in Taiwan, was not first-rate. When Peking opera actors accompanied the Nationalist government to Taiwan in the late 1940s, the best actors and musicians stayed behind in the Chinese mainland. So although I saw many wonderful performances in Taiwan, and certainly had my favorite artists, rarely was the highest level of artistry achieved. This point became especially clear to me in 2001 when I was invited to give a paper at a small conference at Hong Kong University on Peking opera. As part of the proceedings, graduates of the earliest classes of one of China's top training schools, the National Academy of Chinese Theatrical Arts (Zhongguo Xiqu Xueyuan) performed. Some of them had not performed together since they were classmates in the 1950s. These artists were trained by some of the finest performers the Peking opera tradition had ever seen. Even though they were of retirement age, their performances were astounding. They served, however, to clarify for me the general performance standard that I had witnessed for many years in Taiwan.

References

Abbate, Carolyn. 2001. *In Search of Opera*. Princeton, NJ: Princeton University Press.
———. 2004. "Music—Drastic or Gnostic?" *Critical Inquiry* 30:505–36.
Abel, Sam. 1996. *Opera in the Flesh: Sexuality in Operatic Performance*. Boulder, CO: Westview Press.
Adorno, Theodor W. 1994. "Bourgeois Opera." In *Opera through Other Eyes*, edited by David J. Levin, 25–43. Stanford, CA: Stanford University Press.
Ames, Katrine. 2007. "Reaching the High Notes." *Newsweek*, July 16, 12.
Ardoin, John. 1995. *The Callas Legacy: The Complete Guide to Her Recordings on Compact Disc*, 4th ed. Portland, OR: Amadeus Press.
Ashley, Tim. 1999. "Review of *French Opera at the Fin-de-Siècle: Wagnerism, Nationalism, and Style* by Steven Huebner." *Musical Times* 140 (1869): 72–73.
Barba, Eugenio, and Nicola Savarese. 2006. *A Dictionary of Theatre Anthropology: The Secret Arts of the Performer*, translated by Richard Fowler, 2nd ed. New York: Routledge.
Barker, Frank Granville. 1971. "Reports: Foreign." *Opera News*, February, 30.
Barthel, Joan. 1975. "Bel Canto Beverly." *New York Times Magazine*, April 6, 16–17, 63–68.
———. 1978. "Beverly Sills: The Woman Who Has Everything—Almost." *Good Housekeeping*, June, 170–74.
Barthes, Roland. 1977. *Image, Music, Text: Essays Selected and Translated by Stephen Heath*. New York: Hill and Wang.
Becker, Judith. 2004. *Deep Listeners: Music, Emotion, and Trancing*. Bloomington: Indiana University Press.
Bender, William. 1970. "Making Love to the Public." *Time*, October 26, 86.
———. 1973. "Boldly Back in Business." *Time*, October 15, 55.

———. 1974a. "Besting Bellini." *Time,* March 4. 55.

———. 1974b. "Sills Takes to the Tube." *Time,* October 14. 83.

———. 1975. "Sills Meets the Met: The Long Road Up." *Time,* April 7. 56.

Benzecry, Claudio E. 2011. *The Opera Fanatic: Ethnography of an Obsession.* Chicago: University of Chicago Press.

"Beverly Sills: The Fastest Voice Alive." 1971. *Time,* November 22, 74–82.

Bing, Rudolf. 1972. *5000 Nights at the Opera: The Memoirs of Sir Rudolf Bing.* Garden City, NY: Doubleday.

Bjarkman, Kim. 2004. "To Have and to Hold: The Video Collector's Relationship with an Ethereal Medium." *Television and New Media* 5:217–46.

Blom, Philipp. 2002. *To Have and to Hold: An Intimate History of Collectors and Collecting.* New York: Overlook Press.

Bok, Sissela. 2010. *Exploring Happiness: From Aristotle to Brain Science.* New Haven, CT: Yale University Press.

Boulet, Monique J., and Björn J. Oddens. 1996. "Female Voice Changes around and after the Menopause: An Initial Investigation. *Maturitas* 23:15–21.

Bourdieu, Pierre. 1984. *Distinction: A Social Critique of the Judgement of Taste.* Translated by Richard Nice. Cambridge, MA: Harvard University Press.

Bowers, Faubion. 1970. "Bubbles." *Opera News,* September, 18–21.

Capobiano, Tito, and Gigi Capobianco. 2007. "America Has Lost Her 'Queen of Opera'" [original published in Italian]. *Opera,* n.p.

Castle, Terry. 1995. "In Praise of Brigitte Fassbaender: Reflections on Diva Worship." In *En Travesti: Women, Gender Subversion, Opera,* edited by Corinne E. Blackmer and Patricia Juliana Smith, 20–58. New York: Columbia University Press.

Cavicchi, Daniel. 1998. *Tramps Like Us: Music and Meaning among Springsteen Fans.* New York: Oxford University Press.

Chapin, Schuyler. 1977. *Musical Chairs: A Life in the Arts.* New York: Putnam.

Chase, Chris. 1976. "Sills and Burnett." *Good Housekeeping,* August, 68–78.

Cotton, Sandra. 2012. "Fach vs. Voice Type: A Call for Critical Discussion." *Journal of Singing* 69 (2): 153–66.

Corsaro, Frank. 1978. *Maverick: A Director's Personal Experience in Opera and Theater.* New York: Vanguard Press.

Csikszentmihalyi, Mihaly. 1990. *Flow: The Psychology of Optimal Experience.* New York: Harperperennial.

Davis, Peter G. 1973. "Beverly Sills' Royal Trills." *New York Times,* April 8.

———. 1975. "Beverly Sills: Media Heroine or Genuine Superstar?" *New York Times,* October 12.

———. 1976. "Recordings Review." *New York Times,* June 20.

———. 1985. "Prime Time." *New York Magazine,* April 1, 79–80.

———. 1987. "Settling Old Scores." *New York Magazine,* June 1, 93–94.

———. 1997. *The American Opera Singer.* New York: Bantam Doubleday.

———. 2000. "Drama Queen." *New York Magazine,* September 25.

———. 2006. "Diva Emergency." *New York Magazine,* November 6.

———. 2007 "Obituaries: Beverly Sills." *Opera*, September, 1064–66.

Dean, Winton. 1969. *Handel and the Opera Seria.* Berkeley: University of California Press.

———. 1988. "How to Learn to Live with the Convention of the Opera Seria Form." *New York Times*, September 25.

Dean, Winton, and John Merrill Knapp. 1987. *Handel's Operas 1704–1726.* Oxford: Clarendon Press.

"Il Destino di Bubbles: The Libretto of a Success Story." 1968. *Time*, June 7. http://www.time.com/time/magazine/article/0,9171,838438,00.html.

Dicks, Roy C. 2004. "Beverly Sills." *Opera Quarterly* 20 (4): 687–89.

Dolan, Jill. 2005. *Utopia in Performance: Finding Hope at the Theater.* Ann Arbor: University of Michigan Press.

Domingo, Plácido. 1983. *My First Forty Years.* New York: Knopf.

Domínguez, Virginia R. 2000. "For a Politics of Love and Rescue." *Cultural Anthropology* 15 (3): 361–93.

Doss, Erika. 1999. *Elvis Culture: Fans, Faith, and Image.* Lawrence: University of Kansas Press.

———, ed. 2001. *Looking at* Life *Magazine.* Washington, DC: Smithsonian Institution Press.

Duffett, Mark. 2000. "Transcending Audience Generalizations: Consumerism Reconsidered in the Case of Elvis Presley Fans." *Popular Music and Society* 24 (2): 75–92.

———. 2001. "Caught in a Trap? Beyond Pop Theory's 'Butch' Construction of Male Elvis Fans." *Popular Music* 20 (3): 395–408.

———. 2003. "False Faith or False Comparison? A Critique of the Religious Interpretation of Elvis Fan Culture." *Popular Music and Society* 26 (4): 513–22.

———. 2013. *Understanding Fandom: An Introduction to the Study of Media Fan Culture.* New York: Bloomsbury.

Dunn, Betty. 1969. "Unpretentious Prima Donna." *Life*, January 17, 37–38.

Dunning, John. 1998. *On the Air: The Encyclopedia of Old-Time Radio.* New York: Oxford University Press.

Feldman, Martha. 1995. "Magic Mirrors and the Seria Stage: Thoughts toward a Ritual View." *Journal of the American Musicological Society* 48 (3): 423–84.

Fischer-Lichte, Erika. 2008. *The Transformative Power of Performance: A New Aesthetics.* Translated by Saskya Iris Jain. New York: Routledge.

Forster, E. M. 1944. "From the Audience." In *National Gallery Concerts: In Aid of the Musicians' Benevolent Fund, 10th October 1939–10th October 1944, 6–7.* London: Trustees.

Fowler, Alandra Dean. 1994. "Estelle Liebling: An Exploration of Her Pedagogical Principles as an Extension and Elaboration of the Marchesi Method, Including a Survey of Her Music and Editing for Coloratura Soprano and Other Voices." DMA diss., University of Arizona.

"Gala." 1980. *New Yorker*, November 10, 47–48.

Gelatt, Roland. 1969. "But Julius, I've Always Sung This Way: A Look at the 'New' Beverly Sills." *High Fidelity*, February, 24, 27.

Goehr, Lydia. 1995–96. "The Perfect Performance of Music and the Perfect Musical Performance." *Performance Matters* 27:1–22.

Goethe, Johann Wolfgang von. 1952. "The 'Rules for Actors.'" In *Sources of Theatrical History*, edited by A. M. Nagler, 428–33. New York: Theatre Annual.

Goodall, Jane. 2008. *Stage Presence.* New York: Routledge.

Gossett, Philip. 1985. *Anna Bolena and the Artistic Maturity of Gaetano Donizetti.* Oxford: Clarendon Press.

———. 2006. *Divas and Scholars: Performing Italian Opera.* Chicago: University of Chicago Press.

Green, London. 1997. "Il Barbiere di Siviglia." In *The Metropolitan Opera Guide to Opera on Video,* edited by Paul Gruber, 284. New York: Metropolitan Opera Guild/W. W. Norton.

Grotowski, Jerzy. 2002. *Towards a Poor Theatre.* Edited by Eugenio Barba. New York: Routledge.

Gurewitsch, Matthew. 2000. "Sills's Queens at Last Reclaim Their Thrones." *New York Times,* December 10.

Guy, Nancy. 2000. "Performing Taiwan: Music, Dance, and Spectacle in the Celebration of President Chen Shui-bian's Inauguration." *ACMR Reports* 13:21–50.

———. 2002. "'Republic of China National Anthem' on Taiwan: One Anthem, One Performance, Multiple Realities." *Ethnomusicology* 46 (1): 96–119.

———. 2005. *Peking Opera and Politics in Taiwan.* Urbana: University of Illinois Press.

———. 2007. "Claiming a Righteous Past through Song: Music and Taiwan's 2006 'Anti-Corruption' Protest." Paper presented at the 39th World Conference of the International Council for Traditional Music, July 4–11, Vienna, Austria.

———. 2008. "Feeling a Shared History through Song: 'A Flower in the Rainy Night' as a Key Cultural Symbol in Taiwan." *TDR: The Drama Review* 52 (4): 64–81.

Hall-Witt, Jennifer. 2007. *Fashionable Acts: Opera and Elite Culture in London, 1780–1880.* Durham: University of New Hampshire Press.

Harris, Eleanor. 1956. "The Happy Genius." *Saturday Evening Post,* June 16, 40–56.

Hart, Beth. 2004. "What Becomes a Legend Most? A Tribute to Beverly Sills." *Opera Quarterly* 20 (4): 624–56.

Hines, Jerome. 1982. *Great Singers on Great Singing.* Garden City, NY: Doubleday.

Hoffer, Peter. 1969. "Reports: Milan." *Opera News,* June 14, 28.

Jackson, Greg. 2007. *ABC News Classics: Beverly Sills.* Season l. ABC News Productions.

Jackson, Susan A. 1992. "Athletes in Flow: A Qualitative Investigation of Flow States in Elite Figure Skaters." *Journal of Applied Sport Psychology* 4 (2): 161–80.

Jacobs, Arthur. 1971. "Lucia di Lammermoor." *Opera,* February, 165–67.

Jacobson, Robert. 1980. "Miss American Superstar." *Opera News,* October, 8–14.

Jenkins, Henry. 2007. "Afterword: The Future of Fandom." In *Fandom: Identities and Communities in a Mediated World,* edited by Jonathan Gray, Cornel Sandvoss, and C. Lee Harrington, 357–64. New York: New York University Press.

Jensen, Joli. 1992. "Fandom as Pathology." In *The Adoring Audience,* edited by Lisa Lewis, 9–29. New York: Routledge.

Kershaw, Baz. 2007. *Theatre Ecology: Environments and Performance Events.* Cambridge: Cambridge University Press.

Koestenbaum, Wayne. 1990. "Ode to Anna Moffo." In *Ode to Anna Moffo and Other Poems,* 37–51. New York: Persea Press.

———. 1993. *The Queen's Throat: Opera, Homosexuality, and the Mystery of Desire.* New York: Poseidon Press.

Kolodin, Irving. 1970. "Music to My Ears: Sills as Queen Bess." *Saturday Review,* October 31, 41, 63.

"*Ladies' Home Journal*: Women of the Year 1976." 1976. *Ladies' Home Journal,* May, 73–75.

Lawton, David. 1988. "Callas: In Her Own Words." *Opera Quarterly* 6 (2): 156–60.

Levin, David J. 2007. *Unsettling Opera: Staging Mozart, Verdi, Wagner, and Zemlinsky.* Chicago: University of Chicago Press.

Levine, Lawrence W. 1988. *Highbrow/Lowbrow: The Emergence of Cultural Hierarchy in America.* Cambridge, MA: Harvard University Press.

Livingstone, William. 1979. "Beverly Sills: 'Everything I Set Out to Do in My Career, I Have Done.'" *Stereo Review,* February, 88–96.

MacLeod, Kirsten. 2004. "Romps with Ransom's King: Fans, Collectors, Academics, and the M. P. Shiel Archives." *ESC: English Studies in Canada* 30 (1): 117–36.

"Madame Supersized: Verismo." 2013. *New Yorker,* September 9, 30–32.

McClary, Susan. 2002. *Feminine Endings: Music, Gender, and Sexuality.* Minneapolis: University of Minnesota Press.

McNamara, Brooks. 1990. *The Shuberts of Broadway: A History Drawn from the Collection of the Shubert Archive.* New York: Oxford University Press.

Melnick, Ross. 2011. "Reality Radio: Remediating the Radio Contest Genre in Major Bowes' Amateur Hour Films." *Film History* 23 (3): 331–47.

Moist, Kevin. 2008. "'To Renew the Old World': Record Collecting as Cultural Production." *Studies in Popular Culture* 31 (1): 99–122.

Moore, Gerald Martin. 2006. "Tough Kid from Brooklyn: Beverly Sills Looks Back on Her Learning Processes in Conversation with Gerald Martin Moore." *Opera* 57 (2): 1418–22.

Moore, Sally. 1975. "'Bubbles' Sills Finally Makes It to the Met." *People,* April 7, 14–18.

Morrison, Carey-Ann, Lynda Johnston, and Robyn Longhurst. 2013. "Critical Geographies of Love as Spatial, Relational and Political." *Progress in Human Geography,* 37 (4): 505–21.

Murray, William. 1970. "The Year's Most Important Theatrical Event." *Los Angeles Magazine,* January, 48–51.

Osborne, Conrad L. 1966. "The Tape Underground." *High Fidelity Magazine,* August, 42–48.

———. 1997. "Manon." In *The Metropolitan Opera Guide to Opera on Video,* edited by Paul Gruber, 129. New York: Metropolitan Opera Guild/W. W. Norton.

Panos, Mark. 2005. "The Extraordinary Gift of an Enigmatic Diva." *QVegas Magazine,* March, 55–56.

Penman, Joshua, and Judith Becker. 2009. "Religious Ecstatics, 'Deep Listeners,' and Musical Emotion." *Empirical Musicology Review* 4 (2): 49–70.

Pennino, John. 1989. "Mary Garden and the American Press." *Opera Quarterly* 6 (4): 61–75.

Penrod, Diane. 2010. "Writing and Rhetoric for a Ludic Democracy: YouTube, Fandom, and Participatory Pleasure." In *Writing and the Digital Generation,* edited by Heather Urbanski, 141–51. Jefferson, NC: McFarland.

Poizat, Michel. 1992. *The Angel's Cry: Beyond the Pleasure Principle in Opera.* Translated by Arthur Denner. Ithaca, NY: Cornell University Press.

Porter, Andrew. 1976. "Musical Events: Verdi and Violettas." *New Yorker,* January 26, 86–91.

———. 1980. "Musical Events: Beverly!" *New Yorker,* November 10, 177–85.

"Portrait." 1957. *Musical America.* 77:10.

Preston, Katherine K. 2003. "Between the Cracks: The Performance of English-Language Opera in the Late Nineteenth-Century America." *American Music* 21 (3): 349–74.

Reece, Gregory L. 2006. *Elvis Religion: The Cult of the King.* New York: I. B. Tauris.

Rich, Alan. 1971. "Piracy on the High C." *New York Magazine,* April 26, 72.

Risi, Clemens. 2011a. "The Diva's Fans: Opera and Bodily Participation." *Performance Research* 16 (3): 49–54.

———. 2011b. "Opera in Performance—In Search of New Analytical Approaches." *Opera Quarterly* 27 (2–3): 283–95.

Robinson, Paul. 1994. "The Opera Queen: A Voice from the Closet." *Cambridge Opera Journal* 6 (3): 283–91.

Rokem, Freddie. 2003. "Theatrical and Transgressive Energies." In *Performance: Critical Concepts in Literary and Cultural Studies,* vol. 1, edited by Philip Auslander. London: Routledge.

Román, David. 2002. "Comment—Theatre Journals." *Theatre Journal* 54 (3): vii–xix.

Romani, Felice. 1973. *Anna Bolena: Italian-English Libretto.* Translated by William Ashbrook. New York: Program.

Rosenwald, Peter J. 1997. "Contented Coloratura: An Interview with Beverly Sills." *Records and Recording,* January, 16–18.

Saal, Hubert. 1966. "Going for Baroque." *Newsweek,* October 10, 100.

———. 1967a. "The True Story of Beverly Sills." *New York Times Magazine,* September 17, 34–35, 58, 60, 62–72, 74, 78.

———. 1967b. "Two for the C-Note." *Newsweek,* October 2, 86.

———. 1968. "Opera's New Superstar." *Newsweek,* April 8, 108.

———. 1969. "La Sills at the Summit." *Newsweek,* April 21, 69–70, 72, 75.

———. 1975. "New Girl at the Met." *Newsweek,* April 21, 86.

Sanderson, Jimmy, and Pauline Hope Cheong. 2010. "Tweeting Prayers and Communicating Grief over Michael Jackson Online." *Bulletin of Science, Technology, and Society* 30:328.

Sandvoss, Cornel. 2005. *Fans: The Mirror of Consumption.* Malden, MA: Polity.

Sargeant, Winthrop. 1965a. "Musical Events: Crowded Week." *New Yorker,* October 16, 199–202.

———. 1965b. "Musical Events: International Week." *New Yorker,* October 23, 149–52.

———. 1966a. "Musical Events: Triumph." *New Yorker,* October 8, 119–20.

———. 1966b. "Musical Events: Hertz and Avis." *New Yorker,* October 22, 236–41.

———. 1968a. "Musical Events: If You Can Get a Ticket, Go!" *New Yorker,* March 30, 120–24.

———. 1968b. "Musical Events: Well-Tempered Faust." *New Yorker,* October 26, 200–202.

———. 1969a. "Musical Events: Civic Wonder." *New Yorker,* March 1, 105–8.

———. 1969b. "Musical Events: Prima Lucia." *New Yorker,* October 18, 169–72.

———. 1970. "Musical Events: Good Queen Bess." *New Yorker,* October 24, 161–63.

———. 1971. "Profiles: Superstar." *New Yorker,* March 6, 42–64.

———. 1973. *Divas: Impressions of Six Opera Superstars.* New York: Coward, McCann, and Geoghegan.

Sauter, Disa A., Frank Eisner, Andrew J. Calder, and Sophie K. Scott. 2010. "Perceptual Cues in Nonverbal Vocal Expressions of Emotion." *Quarterly Journal of Experimental Psychology* 63 (11): 2251–72.

Scheader, Catherine. 1985. *Contributions of Women: Music.* Minneapolis, MN: Dillon Press.

Schneider, Rebecca. 2011. *Performing Remains: Art and War in Times of Theatrical Reenactment.* New York: Routledge.

Schröder, Marc. 2003. "Experimental Study of Affect Bursts." *Speech Communication* 40:99–116.

Schulze, Laurie. 1999. "Not an Immaculate Reception: Ideology, *The Madonna Connection,* and Academic Wannabes." *Velvet Light Trap* 43 (Spring): 37–50.

Scovell, Jane. 2009. *Samuel Ramey: American Bass.* Fort Worth, TX: Baskerville.

"Senza Rancor." 1973. *New Yorker,* October 8, 38–40.

Sharp, Joanne P. 2000. *Condensing the Cold War:* Reader's Digest *and American Identity.* Minneapolis: University of Minnesota Press.

Shawe-Taylor, Desmond. 1973. "Musical Events: Justice Long Delayed." *New Yorker,* November 5, 143–48.

Siefert, Marsha. 2004. "The Metropolitan Opera in the American Century: Opera Singers, Europe, and Cultural Politics." *Journal of Arts Management, Law, and Society* 33 (4): 298–315.

Siff, Ira. 2007. "Pentimento." *Opera News,* October, 30–33.

"Sills at the Met: The Long Road Up." 1975. *Time,* April 7. http://www.time.com/time/magazine/article/0,9171,917250,00.html.

Sills, Beverly. 1976. *Bubbles: A Self Portrait.* Indianapolis, IN/New York: Bobbs-Merrill.

———. 1981. *Bubbles: An Encore.* New York: Grosset and Dunlap.

———, with Lawrence Linderman. 1987. *Beverly: An Autobiography.* New York: Bantam Books.

———. 1999. "Introduction." Liner notes, *The Ballad of Baby Doe.* Deutsche Grammophon 289 465 148–2, compact disc.

———. 2007. "Beverly Sills on the Opera Singer as Pop Star." *Playbill Arts,* July 30.

"Singer to Watch." 1956. *Time,* February 13, 39.

Sokol, Martin L. 1981. *The New York City Opera: An American Adventure.* New York: Macmillan.

Smith, Patrick J. 1967. "The New York City Opera." *High Fidelity,* December, MA 10–11, 31.

Staples, Mike. 1998. "A Cause and a Heart." *SquareUp!* 14 (February/March/April): 3–5.

Stevenson, Florence. 1970. "*Stereo Review* Talks to Beverly Sills." *Stereo Review,* October, 84.

Sweeney, Louise. 1985. "Former Diva, Now Director, Aims for New Dreams." *Christian Science Monitor,* December 2. http://www.csmonitor.com/1985/1202/lsills.html, accessed May 20, 2013.

Taruskin, Richard. 1984. "The Authenticity Movement Can Become a Positivistic Purgatory, Literalistic and Dehumanizing." *Early Music* 12 (1): 3–12.

Time. 1971. "Beverly Sills: The Fastest Voice Alive." November 22, 74–76, 81–82.

Tolansky, Jon. "Garden, Mary." 2012. In *The Oxford Companion to Music.* Oxford Music Online, accessed August 17, 2012.

Tomlinson, Gary. 1995. "Pastoral and Musical Magic in the Birth of Opera." In *Opera and the Enlightenment,* edited by Thomas Bauman and Marita Petzoldt McClymonds, 7–22. Cambridge: Cambridge University Press.

Tommasini, Anthony. 2005. "Wanted: A New Cheerleader for Opera." *New York Times,* March 20.

———. 2007a. "Beverly Sills, Acclaimed Soprano, Dies at 78." *New York Times,* July 2.

———. 2007b. "Taking Opera to the Heights and Down to Earth." *New York Times,* July 4.

Turner, Edith. 2012. *Communitas: The Anthropology of Collective Joy.* New York: Palgrave Macmillan.

Turner, Victor. 1969. *The Ritual Process: Structure and Anti-Structure.* New York: Aldine de Gruyter.

———. 1974. *Dramas, Fields, and Metaphors: Symbolic Action in Human Society.* Ithaca, NY: Cornell University Press.

———. 1982. *From Ritual to Theatre: The Human Seriousness of Play.* New York: PAJ.

———. 1985. "Are There Universals of Performance in Myth, Ritual, and Drama?" In *On the Edge of the Bush: Anthropology as Experience,* edited by Edith Turner, 291–301. Tucson: University of Arizona Press.

Vacha, John. 2004. *The Music Went 'Round and Around: The Story of Musicarnival.* Kent, OH: Kent State University Press.

Volpe, Joseph. 2006. *The Toughest Show on Earth.* New York: Alfred A. Knopf.

Walker, John, writer and producer. 2006. *Beverly Sills: Made in America.* New York: Deutsche Grammophon. DVD, 84 min.

Walther, Joseph B. 2002. "Research Ethics in Internet-Enabled Research: Human Subjects Issues and Methodological Myopia." *Ethics and Information Technology* 4:205–16.

Weinstein, David. 2004. *The Forgotten Network: DuMont and the Birth of American Television.* Philadelphia: Temple University Press.

Williams, Jeannie. 1991. "Julius Rudel." *Opera Monthly,* March, 31–37.

Williams, Jack A., and Laven Sowell. 1992. *Tulsa Opera Chronicles,* s.l.: s.n.

Wills, Garry. 1974. "Here's Beverly Sills, Singing in the Reign." *Esquire,* September, 80–84, 188–90.

———. 1975. "Gorgeous Sills." *New York Review of Books,* May 1, 36–37.

Yang, Sunny. 2013. "Emotion, Experiential Memory and Selfhood." *Organon* 20 (1): 18–36.

Young, Allen. 1993. *Opera in Central City.* Denver: Spectographics.

Formal Interviews

Aghssa, Pirooz: December 30, 2010, New York, NY

Ames, Alison: December 9, 2010, New York, NY

Ames, Katrine: December 27, 2010; March 17, 2011; May 11, 2013, New York, NY

Beeson, Richard: May 9, 2013, New York, NY

Brennan, Jay: April 18, 2010, New York, NY

Capobianco, Tito and Gigi: July 28, 2010, Lutz, FL

Citarella, Joseph: September 16, 2011, Briarcliff, NY

Converse, Tony: October 9, 2009, New York, NY

Cornish, Taylor: September 7, 2012, Hayward, CA

Corsaro, Frank: May 13, 2013, New York, NY

Cossa, Dominic: December 3, 2010, College Park, MD

Davis, Anthony, and Cynthia Aaronson: July 24, 2008, San Diego, CA

de Forest, Anthea: May 10, 2013, New York, NY

Ellison, Cori: March 18, 2011, New York, NY

Evans, Joseph: April 27, 2012, Houston, TX

Hale, Robert: August 17, 2010, Paradise Valley, AZ

Hill, Barbara: March 29, 2012, New York, NY

Levine, Rhoda: June 25, 2010, New York, NY

Malas, Marlena Kleinman: October 9, 2009, New York, NY

Malas, Spiro: October 9, 2009, New York, NY

Malloy, Joseph: September 15, 2011, New York, NY

Mansouri, Lotfi: February 15, 2010, San Diego, CA

Marsee, Susanne: January 25, 2008, Pittsburgh, PA; June 23, 2010, Washington, DC

Mastroianni, Jack: March 19, 2011, New York, NY

Moore, Gerald Martin: March 25 and 26, 2012, New York, NY

Ponder, David: June 22, 2010, Washington, DC

Ramey, Samuel: June 18, 2012, San Francisco, CA

Rudel, Julius: October 6, 2009, New York, NY

Rolandi, Gianna: June 26, 2011, Chicago, IL

Shirley, George: August 23, 2013, Ann Arbor, MI

Tidyman, David: August 15–16, 2013, Cleveland, OH

Wadsworth, Charles: April 19 and 20, 2010, New York, NY

Wendelken-Wilson, Charles: August 1, 2008, Dayton, OH

Wylie, David: April 19, 2011, New York, NY

NOTE: I define *formal interviews* as those encounters for which I prepared a list of questions and made a digital sound recording. In the case of more than two-thirds of the interviewees listed here, I enjoyed further communications following the initial interview either through e-mail, phone calls, Facebook messaging, or additional personal meetings. I also had substantial contact with other consultants, including Pete Buchanan, Roy C. Dicks, Meredith Greenough, Kenny Morse, and Charles Freeman Stamper, to name a few, that never took the form of formal interviews.

Index

NANCY GUY is an associate professor of music at the University of California, San Diego. She is the author of *Peking Opera and Politics in Taiwan*.

Only a Miner: Studies in Recorded Coal-Mining Songs   *Archie Green*
Great Day Coming: Folk Music and the American Left   *R. Serge Denisoff*
John Philip Sousa: A Descriptive Catalog of His Works   *Paul E. Bierley*
The Hell-Bound Train: A Cowboy Songbook   *Glenn Ohrlin*
Oh, Didn't He Ramble: The Life Story of Lee Collins, as Told to Mary Collins
    Edited by Frank J. Gillis and John W. Miner
American Labor Songs of the Nineteenth Century   *Philip S. Foner*
Stars of Country Music: Uncle Dave Macon to Johnny Rodriguez
    Edited by Bill C. Malone and Judith McCulloh
Git Along, Little Dogies: Songs and Songmakers of the American West   *John I. White*
A Texas-Mexican *Cancionero*: Folksongs of the Lower Border   *Américo Paredes*
San Antonio Rose: The Life and Music of Bob Wills   *Charles R. Townsend*
Early Downhome Blues: A Musical and Cultural Analysis   *Jeff Todd Titon*
An Ives Celebration: Papers and Panels of the Charles Ives Centennial Festival-Conference
    Edited by H. Wiley Hitchcock and Vivian Perlis
Sinful Tunes and Spirituals: Black Folk Music to the Civil War   *Dena J. Epstein*
Joe Scott, the Woodsman-Songmaker   *Edward D. Ives*
Jimmie Rodgers: The Life and Times of America's Blue Yodeler   *Nolan Porterfield*
Early American Music Engraving and Printing: A History of Music Publishing in America
    from 1787 to 1825, with Commentary on Earlier and Later Practices   *Richard J. Wolfe*
Sing a Sad Song: The Life of Hank Williams   *Roger M. Williams*
Long Steel Rail: The Railroad in American Folksong   *Norm Cohen*
Resources of American Music History: A Directory of Source Materials from Colonial Times
    to World War II   *D. W. Krummel, Jean Geil, Doris J. Dyen, and Deane L. Root*
Tenement Songs: The Popular Music of the Jewish Immigrants   *Mark Slobin*
Ozark Folksongs   *Vance Randolph; edited and abridged by Norm Cohen*
Oscar Sonneck and American Music   *Edited by William Lichtenwanger*
Bluegrass Breakdown: The Making of the Old Southern Sound   *Robert Cantwell*
Bluegrass: A History   *Neil V. Rosenberg*
Music at the White House: A History of the American Spirit   *Elise K. Kirk*
Red River Blues: The Blues Tradition in the Southeast   *Bruce Bastin*
Good Friends and Bad Enemies: Robert Winslow Gordon and the Study
    of American Folksong   *Debora Kodish*
Fiddlin' Georgia Crazy: Fiddlin' John Carson, His Real World, and the World of His Songs
    Gene Wiggins
America's Music: From the Pilgrims to the Present (rev. 3d ed.)   *Gilbert Chase*
Secular Music in Colonial Annapolis: The Tuesday Club, 1745–56   *John Barry Talley*
Bibliographical Handbook of American Music   *D. W. Krummel*
Goin' to Kansas City   *Nathan W. Pearson, Jr.*
"Susanna," "Jeanie," and "The Old Folks at Home": The Songs of Stephen C. Foster
    from His Time to Ours (2d ed.)   *William W. Austin*
Songprints: The Musical Experience of Five Shoshone Women   *Judith Vander*

The University of Illinois Press
is a founding member of the
Association of American University Presses.

Composed in 10.75/13 Arno Pro
by Kirsten Dennison
at the University of Illinois Press
Manufactured by Sheridan Books, Inc.

University of Illinois Press
1325 South Oak Street
Champaign, IL 61820-6903
www.press.uillinois.edu